When Unions Merge

When Unions Merge

Gary N. Chaison
Clark University

Lexington Books
D.C. Heath and Company/Lexington, Massachusetts/Toronto

Library of Congress Cataloging-in-Publication Data

Chaison, Gary N.
 When Unions Merge.

 Includes bibliographies and index.
 1. Trade-unions—United States—Consolidation. 2. Trade-
unions—Canada—Consolidation. 3. Trade-unions—Great Britain—Consolidation. I. Title
HD6490.C622U63 1986   331′87   85-40455
ISBN 0-669-11081-7 (alk. paper)

Published simultaneously in Canada
Printed in the United States of America
Casebound International Standard Book Number: 0-669-11081-7
Library of Congress Catalog Card Number: 85-40455

The paper used in this publication meets the minimum requirements of American National
Standard for Information Sciences—Permanence of Paper for Printed Library Materials,
ANSI Z39.48-1984.

The last numbers on the right below indicate the number and date of printing.

10 9 8 7 6 5 4 3 2 1

95 94 93 92 91 90 89 88 87 86

To
Ada and Alfred Chaison

Contents

List of Figures

List of Tables

Acknowledgments

This book attempts to unify and extend the research that I have conducted on union mergers over the past fifteen years. It would be impossible to name all of those who have assisted and encouraged me over those years. I am indebted to numerous colleagues, journal editors and reviewers, and librarians in the United States and Canada, as well as to the union officers who agreed to be interviewed or who returned questionnaires in my earlier studies. My research has been supported by grants from the University of New Brunswick and Clark University.

I was assisted by several individuals in the preparation of this book. Special thanks to Joe Rose at McMaster University for reviewing and commenting on drafts of several chapters. Larry Adams of the U.S. Department of Labor and Louise Walsh of the *Washington Post* are two insightful observers of contemporary union mergers and I benefited from their writings and our discussions. Laura Carchia at the MIT Industrial Relations Library provided invaluable assistance and access to a fine collection of research materials. Jessica Jenner and Madeleine Lemieux at Clark University made helpful editorial suggestions in the revisions of some chapters and Julie Parent typed numerous drafts of the manuscript with great care. Bruce Sylvester did an outstanding job as copyeditor for Lexington Books and I am grateful for his thoughtful and meticulous work on the manuscript.

I would be remiss if I didn't thank Scooter for his patience and I appreciate his understanding on those days when I was too busy for longer and more interesting walks. Finally, I thank my wife Joanne for assisting on the index and manuscript revisions, and for much more.

When Unions Merge

1

Introduction

Union mergers are commonly treated as events rather than processes. Observers seem to be concerned mostly with whether or not a merger occurred, which unions were disbanded, or which officers were re-elected or replaced. They often overlook the actual merger process, with its intricate negotiations and the transition of the union during the postmerger period. This narrow and rather simplistic view of mergers is ironic in light of the high expectations we have for mergers in the restructuring and the revitalization of the labor movement.

A recurring vision (some would say dream) of many labor scholars and leaders is the development through union mergers of a rationalized, streamlined union structure. Massive conglomerate unions would be formed in those industries such as printing, transportation, and construction that were previously organized by many small unions. The more than two hundred national unions that exist now in the United States would be reduced to twenty or thirty large organizations.[1] Bargaining power would be increased and the elimination of interunion competition would stabilize labor relations and free resources for massive organizing campaigns.[2] Large unions, one for each major industry, would attract weak unions seeking a safe haven from organizing and financial adversity. The new conglomerate unions, many with over one million members, would emerge as militant organizers and efficient representatives, countering the power of the expanding conglomerate employers.[3]

To a large degree, our expectations about mergers may stem from a recognition of their important historical role. Mergers brought about the demise of such once influential unions as the Sleeping Car Porters, the Cigar Makers, and the Mine, Mill and Smelter Workers. We are also aware of the major new unions recently formed by mergers, notably the United Food and Commercial Workers, the United Transportation Union, and the Amalgamated Clothing and Textile Workers Union. Moreover, there is clear evidence that some of the largest unions (for example the Teamsters, the Steelworkers, and the American Federation of State, County and Municipal Employees) are using mergers as a growth strategy, seemingly recruiting unions as well as workers.

Despite the recognition of the past and future importance of union mergers, there is still no unifying or comprehensive theory of the union merger process.[4] For example, in the introduction to his 1975 case studies, Chitayat remarked that there is no theory of union mergers comparable to theories developed in such other areas of industrial relations as wages and collective bargaining. He emphasized that this absence is made even more noticeable in light of the many books and articles written on corporate mergers.[5]

In this book I will attempt to fill the gap in the research by drawing together what is known about mergers and by developing a model of the national union merger process, along with its antecedents and outcomes. Mergers will be seen as an exceptionally complex institutional phenomenon. At times they involve partners of fairly equal size and strength in combinations of mutual benefit. In other instances mergers bring together the weakest and strongest of unions—the dying union seeking an honorable way to disband and the aggrandizing union actively absorbing unions as well as workers. The union merger must be viewed as more than just a quick, convenient, and straightforward structural rearrangement. Mergers involve internal union politics, local–national union relations, representational effectiveness, union rivalries, and a host of other contentious issues.

Weber has stated that merger trends provide an early warning of "prospective upheavals and subsidence" in the American labor movement.[6] To decipher these trends we will have to develop an understanding of why mergers occur and, probably just as important, why they do not occur.

Defining National Union Mergers

I begin with a fairly broad definition of the union merger; in later chapters several variations will be introduced. One recent case study defined a union merger as the combination of two or more unions under common control.[7] An alternative definition is that a merger is the fusion of two or more trade unions to form a single organization in the process of which one or more of the unions loses its separate identity.[8]

Table 1–1 shows some characteristics of the two basic forms of union mergers. An *amalgamation* is the joining together of two or more unions, usually of roughly equal size, to form a new organization. An *absorption* is the merging of one union into a considerably larger one. In an absorption a smaller union is often "saved" by a stronger one expanding into new areas.[9] Earlier studies of union mergers have used a variety of definitions and categories resembling those proposed here. For example, Janus identified three types of mergers: (1) the uniting of two or more organizations to form a new entity; (2) the absorption of one union by another; and (3) the affiliation of two organizations, with each retaining its own identity.[10] The first two forms

Table 1–1
Basic Types of Union Mergers

	Amalgamations	*Absorptions*
Method of merger	The merging together of two or more unions to form a new union	The merging of one union into another
Relative size of merger partners	Amalgamating unions are often similar in size	Absorbing union is much larger than the absorbed union
Number of unions involved in each merger	Usually two unions, but some amalgamations have combined three, four, or five unions	Two unions
Examples	The merger of the Textile Workers International Union and the Amalgamated Clothing Workers International Union to form the Amalgamated Clothing and Textile Workers International Union (1976)	The merger of the Brotherhood of Sleeping Car Porters into the Brotherhood of Railway and Airline Clerks (1977)
	The merger of the Retail Clerks International Union and the Amalgamated Meat Cutters and Butcher Workmen to form the United Food and Commercial Workers (1979)	The merger of the International Jewelry Workers Union into the Service Employees International Union (1980)

are the amalgamation and the absorption. The last is just a form of organizational integration that is possible in both types of mergers and will be described in detail in later chapters.

This book deals with mergers among the national unions: organizations that have collective agreements with different employers in more than one state, are affiliates of the AFL–CIO, or represent federal or state employees. Included among these are the internationals—American unions which have also organized Canadian workers.[11] In later chapters I will discuss some mergers among local unions (the branches of national unions), but this will be done in relation to the activities of parent national unions.

Union absorptions on the national level involve two unions—the absorbed union and the absorbing union. While there are a few cases where one union absorbed several other unions within a short period of time, each absorption is a separate event with its own negotiations, merger agreement, postmerger governing structure, and so on. Amalgamations commonly involve two unions but there have been instances where three, four, and even five unions simultaneously amalgamated. These are sometimes referred to as "composite mergers."[12]

At this point there is no need to go into all of the distinctions between amalgamations and absorptions. In later chapters it will be seen that there can be substantial variations within each and that the line between the two is not always clear.[13]

The Study of Union Mergers: Case Studies, Data Analyses, and Chronologies

At the onset to our study we should review the three most common ways to look at union mergers: the case study, the data analysis, and the chronology. Each has its strengths and weaknesses, and each can contribute to the development of a model of the merger process.

The Case Study

In the case study approach, one or a few instances of mergers are investigated in an attempt to reveal the intricate details of the historical background, merger outcomes, and bargaining and representational implications. Investigators delve into convention proceedings, union reports, memos, and officers' correspondence, along with such secondary sources as books, magazine articles, and newspaper accounts. Quite often interviews are conducted in the field with close observers and participants in the merger.

The most comprehensive set of merger case studies, "The Causes and Effects of Union Mergers with Special Reference to Selected Cases in the '60s and '70s," was completed by Brooks and Gamm in 1976.[14] In a report funded by the U.S. Department of Labor, the authors examined mergers among unions in the pulp and paper, printing, and railroad industries as well as several absorptions of the Steelworkers. Considerable attention was devoted to the external and internal forces leading to the mergers and their impact on bargaining and internal union governance. Another series of case studies on mergers is found in a 1975 doctoral dissertation and 1979 book by Gideon Chitayat.[15] He selected for examination "mergers of large unions with small unions" (the absorptions of the Steelworkers, Teamsters, and Laborers International Union) and "mergers of two or more unions to form a new one" (the amalgamations forming the Bakery and Confectionery Workers, the United Paper Workers, and the United Transportation Union). Conclusions were reached in regard to the motivation to merge and the impact of mergers on union growth, financial stability, and bargaining power.

Probably the most detailed case study of an individual merger attempt was completed by Walsh in 1985.[16] Walsh carried out numerous interviews and examined union memorandums and a variety of secondary sources in order to trace the unsuccessful merger negotiations between the International

Typographical Union and the Newspaper Guild. Case studies were also used by DeCenzo to analyze the merger negotiation process of two unidentified unions operating in the foundry and metal fabricating industries, and by Graham to describe the merger barriers faced by pulp and paper unions.[17]

In the case study approach, a basic strategy is to present some model or typography of mergers (or a part of the merger process) and illustrate or test this with an in-depth investigation of a limited number of representative cases. The rationale for the use of this approach is the need to recognize the exceptional complexity of the merger process and the critical role of union politics, including officers' aspirations and members' expectations.

Case studies of union mergers have provided some massive depositories of information. At their best, case studies such as those by Walsh and by Brooks and Gamm represent exceptional investigatory efforts, with remarkable attention to detail and a keen appreciation of the complexity of the phenomena under examination. Case studies enable the investigator to sift through original data and discover facts which lead to the development of theory.[18] Brooks and Gamm used the case study approach because they believed that mergers were best viewed through a "traditional and institutional" approach. They stated: "It is our belief that studies of institutions like unions must rest upon a clear and intimate understanding of their internal political life."[19]

While the case study approach does provide us with a wealth of details about the intricacies of the merger process, it is not without some major limitations. One drawback is its questionable generalizability. Can we generalize from the specific cases under investigation to all mergers? Can we say that the causal relationships uncovered in a case study will also be found in all or at least many other union mergers? Generalizing from case studies would be hazardous if the mergers selected for study were closely tied to the speical needs of the unions involved and did not reflect general conditions.[20] Each case study would then develop a complex but unique model of the merger process.

There is another major difficulty with case studies. Based primarily on union records and interviews, case studies may place too great a reliance on the truthfulness and objectivity of the sources. As we will see later, mergers are often politically charged events, planned and negotiated in secret at their earliest stages. Vital information may not be found in such standard sources as convention proceedings or reports, while correspondence and interviews with close participants may be biased. For example, in their statements national officers may be building a case for merger in order to win the support of local officers and the membership. They may tend to gloss over the major structural changes required by the merger.[21] Their interviews and correspondence may also be self-serving, particularly if the merger results in the officers' receiving higher salaries or greater power under the new union's constitution. This is not to say that these sources should be ignored. Rather, their veracity should be evaluated in light of whether there could be an overriding intent to create a favorable impression.

In sum, case studies may provide a wealth of information about a few mergers but lack the methodological rigor to build and test a model of the union merger process. Can this purpose be better served by data analyses?

Data Analyses

In empirical studies of union mergers, the unit of analysis is the merger itself. Generally, these studies attempt to uncover statistically significant relationships between frequency of mergers or types of mergers as well as measures of economic and union conditions.

Data analyses require some degree of abstraction—a belief that there are a sufficient number of common elements in all mergers for the cases to form a fairly homogeneous population. This approach, in direct contrast to the assumptions of the case studies, was justified by Freeman:

> One must perforce oversimplify reality. There will always be the case where the purpose is a search for generalizations. The issue is not whether they hold up in every instance, but whether they capture commonalities in the general experience under study.[22]

The 1977 Freeman and Brittain study provides a good illustration of the empirical approach.[23] The authors examined the frequency of mergers in relation to environmental conditions considered either favorable or threatening for union growth and development. They also investigated the jurisdiction and size relationships among the merging unions. The analysis was based on a typography of mergers derived from studies of the ecology of organizations. The central theme was that unions manage their dependencies through the merger process. The data analysis covered eighty-five mergers from 1935 to 1973.

Freeman and Brittain have been criticized because of their degree of abstraction and the assumptions underlying their data analysis. Chaison claimed that they falied to consider the diverse motives for union mergers as well as the political nature of the merger barriers.[24] Their approach also led to the following problems:

> The analysis used aggregate measures of union growth, strikes, and economic conditions. These may not reflect the specific conditions faced by those unions deciding to merge. For example, during a period of rapid overall union growth, the merging unions may have been losing members.
>
> In their regression model, Freeman and Brittain used a one-year time lag for the time series. This was assumed to represent the time between the

emergence of the factors that motivated the unions to merge and the actual implementation of the merger. Case studies have shown that this period is probably too short and that it may vary widely from merger to merger. For example, prior to their merger in 1979, the Retail Clerks International Union and the Amalgamated Meat Cutters and Butcher Workmen had been engaged in fourteen years of sporadic merger discussions and six years of final negotiations.[25] The United Shoe Workers had been searching for a merger partner for eighteen years before it was absorbed by the Amalgamated Clothing and Textile Workers Union.[26]

An empirical analysis of mergers cannot deal with those mergers which were proposed but for which negotiations broke down. Many merger negotiations are initially kept secret, so if they fail, the fact that they took place may never be publicly known.[27] By using readily available data (mergers actually entered into rather than those proposed), the authors were confusing the ability to merge with the desire to merge.[28] As we will see in later chapters, a sufficient number of unsuccessful merger attempts can be identified and studied, and this reveals an important dimension of the merger process.

Some British studies have also used merger data to relate merger frequency to generalized economic conditions and corporate mergers.[29] In these works, though to a lesser degree than in the Freeman and Brittain study, there seems to be a tendency to view mergers in an abstract sense, linking aggregate merger measures (Was there a merger? How many mergers occurred?) to overall conditions of the labor movement or the economy. Data analyses may seem to uncover major trends but this is done by forcing the merger process into the confines of the statistical procedures. Mergers are stripped of their political content, merger negotiations are ignored, unsuccessful mergers are not counted, and the outcomes of mergers are not examined.

Chronologies

A third way of looking at mergers has been through what we may call "chronologies." Prepared periodically by the research staff of the Bureau of Labor Statistics, these studies describe the merger activity during fairly brief time spans. Dewey covered the period 1956 to 1971, Janus reviewed the years 1971 to 1978, and Adams examined mergers from 1978 to 1984.[30] Attempts were made to categorize mergers; these were followed by reviews of merger activity in specific industries. The authors briefly described the reasons for merger and there were occasional details on postmerger arrangements. Overall merger trends during the period were evaluated and this was usually followed by some comments on possible mergers in the near future.

These three chronologies are frequently used sources of factual information on which unions merged and why. However, their descriptions of mergers are limited, merger negotiations are seldom mentioned, and unsuccessful merger attempts are usually not discussed unless they involved unions which eventually merged. The reports provide the fundamental details of all mergers during a short period, but no attempt is made to build any comprehensive theory that explains and links together these and earlier mergers.

It would appear, then, that both case studies and data analyses have some serious limitations and that chronologies do not go far enough. My task in this book is to find a middle ground between the first two and expand upon the last.[31] On the one hand, I will remain aware of the complexity of mergers, a lesson taught by the case studies. When I develop and test my model, illustrations will be presented of a variety of merger forms and consequences over a long time period. I will examine experiences in premerger and postmerger periods, as well as unsuccessful merger attempts. This will be accomplished with brief examples to emphasize major points rather than going into a few overly detailed case studies. The results of data analyses will also be discussed when the factors under investigation appear amenable to quantification. In other words, the presentation of survey results and aggregate merger data will be tempered with a recognition of the rich historical, political, and structural diversity of mergers. Hopefully, I can steer a path between the idiosyncratic nature of case studies and the rather sterile view of mergers found in data analyses. In doing so, I will be expanding on some of the relationships suggested but not elaborated upon in the chronologies.

A Model of the Union Merger Process

A great deal has been written about union mergers from a variety of perspectives. What I am attempting to accomplish in this book is to integrate these divergent studies into a general model that tells us why and how unions merge as well as the outcomes of this process. The model is presented in figure 1–1 and will serve as the basis for the organization of this book. I will view mergers from the perspective of systems theory, an approach finding increasing use in

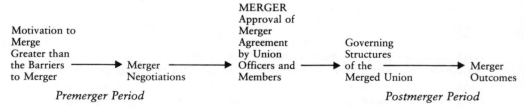

Figure 1–1. A Model of the Union Merger Process

industrial relations research. As Kochan described this approach in his pioneering study of collective bargaining, the major premise is that "a complex social or economic system can only be understood by first standing back and conceptualizing its major components and then examining in detail each component and its interconnections with other parts of the system."[32] This is precisely what I will be doing as I examine and link together the components and stages of the merger process.

Union mergers can be divided into the premerger and postmerger periods indicated in figure 1–1. The boundary between the two periods is marked by the formal signing of the merger agreement or the membership's approval of that agreement, whichever occurs last. Postmerger union governing structures are determined in the merger negotiations, which are in turn shaped by both the motivation and the barriers toward merging.

In all merger attempts the participants face some barriers, usually in the forms of membership and leadership opposition or difficulties in resolving institutional differences. The ability to overcome these barriers is a function of the relative strengths of both the motivation to merge and the barriers to merger.[33] Stated another way, one union with a strong need to merge may fail if the barriers are too high. Another may face minimal barriers but may still not merge because there is insufficient motivation. And a third union may encounter substantial barriers and will not merge after several years of intermittent negotiations until finally the motivation to merge is overwhelming. A merger will be consummated when the barriers are overcome by both unions in the negotiations. If neither or only one union can overcome the barriers, the negotiations will prove unsuccessful. Accordingly, the development of the model must extend to unions that merge fairly easily, those that fail to merge, and those that somehow succeed after years or even decades of repeated attempts.

In the section on the definition of union mergers, I discussed the basic merger forms—the amalgamation and the absorption. We will see in later chapters that there are differing motivations and barriers in the cases of amalgamating, absorbing, and absorbed unions. Furthermore, the postmerger conditions may vary for the three types of merger participants. This will be shown for both the degree to which unions integrate governing structures after merger and for merger outcomes in such areas as union administration and governance, collective bargaining, and organizing.

The format of this book is based on the components and sequence of model. In the following chapter there will be a brief introduction to the historical development of union mergers. The next two chapters describe the motivations and barriers to mergers. This is followed by a discussion of the integration of union governing structures, a function of the relative strengths of the motivating factors and barriers. I then examine the various merger outcomes and the manner in which they are affected directly or indirectly by the premerger conditions. Finally, I consider mergers from an international perspective, determining the degree to which my model is relevant to the mergers in the comparable labor movements of Great Britain and Canada. In a concluding chapter I summarize the findings and try to reach some conclusions about the role of mergers in union attempts to overcome their present difficulties.

It was suggested earlier that a limitation of most studies of union mergers is that their perspective is shaped by the narrow confines of their methodology. In this study the issues being investigated will dictate the research approach taken. Throughout the book I will be integrating the evidence and conclusions from previous case studies, data analyses, and chronologies. In the chapters on motivation, barriers, and outcomes, I will also draw on a wide variety of primary and secondary sources, including general-circulation and union periodicals, union and federation convention proceedings, and articles from academic journals and reporting services such as the Bureau of National Affairs' *Daily Labor Report, Labor Relations Reporter,* and the *Government Employee Relations Report.* Similar sources from Canada and Great Britain will be used in the comparative application of the model. In the chapter on the historical background to mergers, I will draw on both the details culled from labor histories and union and federation proceedings, and the data from a time series of merger form and frequency. The investigation of the integration of union governing structures will focus primarily on information from union constitutions and merger agreements. Questionnaire responses will be analyzed in sections of chapters dealing with the historical background and postmerger integration. In short, the methodological approach will vary according to the component of the model under scrutiny.

Union and Business Mergers: A Brief Digression

In light of the recent flurry of well-publicized business mergers, one is tempted to compare these and union mergers. Before developing my model further, it might be best to explain why I have not borrowed from the extensive research and popular literature on business mergers.

While the terms *merger* and *consolidation* tend to be used interchangeably in the business context, in a strict sense a merger is the combination of two companies in which one survives, while a consolidation involves the combining of two or more companies to form a new company. The former can also be called an acquisition or takeover.[34] For example, in the food industry, Nestle SA acquired Carnation Co., and Beatrice Foods acquired Esmark, Inc., but Nabisco consolidated with Standard Brands to form Nabisco Brands Inc. At first glance, these business mergers would seem to be counterparts to union absorptions and amalgamations in both form and purpose. An argument could be made that both companies and unions merge as an adjustment to a challenging environment, changing the boundaries of the organization in an attempt to manage risk and uncertainty. However, beyond this sweeping statement we find important reasons for business mergers that are not shared by merging unions. These include the desire to take advantage of a situation where a company's assets are undervalued, the attempt through merger to satisfy market demand for additional products and services, the need to increase earnings per share, and the avoidance of the risks associated with the start-up of new products.[35]

The merger tactics may also differ. Business mergers may involve complex legal and financial strategies which are often aimed at purchasing a company's assets or stocks. They are controlled by accounting guidelines and must satisfy the Antitrust Division of the Department of Justice or the Federal Trade Commission. In contrast, there are few legal restrictions on union mergers other than the requirement that unions follow their constitutions, particularly those sections on the amending of the constitution and the disbanding of the organization. Moreover, while union mergers do require legal assistance and the payment of legal fees, such fees do not even come close to the exceptionally high fees paid by corporations to the lawyers and investment bankers who engineer mergers.[36]

It is also important to recognize that because unions are representative and political organizations, approval for mergers must come from the officer hierarchy and the membership. Their intransigence can form a type of barrier not often found in business mergers. Finally, as we will see in the next chapter, federations may play an important role in encouraging or discouraging union mergers; merging businesses face no organizations comparable to federations.

In the final analysis, corporate mergers differ significantly from union mergers in motivation, form, and process. Perhaps most important, financial advantage or gain is not considered a high priority in union mergers.[37] Larger unions cannot buy smaller unions; unions do not have stock or ownership comparable to business.

It is interesting that union leaders often disparage any comparison between business and union mergers, claiming that union mergers are carried out in a more scrupulous manner and for loftier reasons. Typical are the comments of Lane Kirkland, President of the AFL–CIO:

> Business mergers . . . bear little resemblance to union mergers. In the business world, mergers are seldom a matter of mutual accommodation or democratic agreement. Normally, they start in the dark of night, they are cold and predatory, designed to concentrate economic power in few hands.[38]

While there may be more differences than meaningful similarities between business and union mergers, this is not to say that the latter are not relevant to this study. We will have to deal with the causal links between union and business mergers—the common view that "bigger companies require bigger unions."[39] Some union leaders have argued that union mergers are necessary to adjust bargaining structure and organizing strategies to the expanding operations of conglomerate employers.[40] In later sections we will see that company mergers and diversification, may provide an important motivation and justification for union mergers.

We will also come across some unions that seem to mimic corporations when they pursue merger partners. Just as a company might merge to diversify or enter into a new product market, some absorbing unions use mergers to make instant inroads into new organizing fields.

The evidence indicates that corporate and union mergers are distinct phenomena, though there may be some causal relationships between the two. The model of the union merger process will have to be developed from an understanding of the institutional nature of labor unions rather than borrowed from the extensive and quite sophisticated studies of business mergers. The unique institutional character of union mergers should become apparent in a brief historical review.

Notes

1. Jerry Wurf, "Labor's Battle With Itself," *Washington Post*, October 14, 1973, p. C3; William M. Chernish, *Coalition Bargaining* (Philadelphia: University of Pennsylvania Press, 1969), p. 4.

2. Arnold R. Weber, "Mergers: Union Style," *Wall Street Journal*, May 14, 1979, p. 20.

3. Harry Graham, "Union Mergers," *Relations Industrielles—Industrial Relations* 25 (1970):566. For the case against the formation of large unions through mergers, see George W. Brooks and Sara Gamm, "The Causes and Effects of Union Mergers with Special Reference to Selected Cases in the '60s and '70s." (Washington, D.C.: U.S. Department of Labor, Labor–Management Services Administration, September 1976), p. a57.

4. For example, Freeman and Brittain claim "there is virtually no scientific work on the frequency or nature of union mergers." John Freeman and Jack Brittain, "Union Merger Process and Indusrial Environment," *Industrial Relations* 16 (May 1977):173.

5. Gideon Chitayat, *Trade Union Mergers and Labor Conglomerates* (New York: Praeger, 1979), p. 9.

6. Weber, *op. cit.*, p. 20.

7. Chitayat, *op cit.*, pp. 2–3.

8. Michael A. Coady, "Trade Union Mergers and Their Significance in the Canadian Union Movement" (Toronto: unpublished LL.M. dissertation, Osgood Hall Law School, 1976), p. 1, fn. 1.

9. Gary N. Chaison, "Union Growth and Union Mergers," *Industrial Relations* 20 (Winter 1981):98.

10. Charles J. Janus, "Union Mergers in the 1970's: A Look at the Reasons and Results," *Monthly Labor Review* 101 (October 1978):13.

11. This seems to be a widely accepted definition of the national union. For example, see Leonard Sayles, *The Unions: Structure, Development and Management,* 2d ed. (New York: Harcourt Brace Jovanovich, 1976), p. 41. This definition is used for determining which unions are included in the U.S. Department of Labor's *Directory of National Unions and Employee Associations,* published periodically until 1978.

12. Robert T. Buchanan, "Merger Waves in British Unionism," *Industrial Relations Journal* 5 (1974):37.

13. John P. Windmuller, "Concentration Trends in Union Structures: An International Comparison," *Industrial and Labor Relations Review* 35 (October 1981):53; Louise D. Walsh, "A Study of the Proposed Merger of the International Typographical Union and the Newspaper Guild: 1974–1983" (Ithaca, N.Y.: unpublished M.S. thesis, Cornell University, January 1985), pp. 10–13.

14. Brooks and Gamm, *op cit.*

15. Gideon Chitayat, "Mergers of Trade Unions" (Philadelphia: unpublished Ph.D. dissertation, University of Pennsylvania, 1975); Chitayat, *Trade Union Mergers and Labor Conglomerates.*

16. Louise D. Walsh, *op cit.*

17. David DeCenzo, "Union Merger Negotiations" (Morgantown: unpublished Ph.D. dissertation, University of West Virginia, 1981); Graham, *op. cit.*

18. Tamara Gilman, "Union Administration: Strategy, Structures and Organizing Behavior" (Boston: unpublished D.B.A. dissertation, Harvard University, 1981), pp. 142–48. This dissertation presents an excellent defense of the case study approach.

19. Brooks and Gamm, *op. cit.,* p. ii.

20. Coady, *op. cit.,* p. 10.

21. For example, see Brooks's criticism of the veracity of some of the interviews used to develop Chitayat's case studies. George W. Brooks, "Review of *Trade Union Mergers and Labor Conglomerates,*" *Industrial and Labor Relations Review* 35 (January 1982):277.

22. John Freeman, "Competitive Process and Patterns of Selection in Union Mergers" in *Proceedings of the Thirty-third Annual Meeting of the Industrial Relations Research Association* (Madison, Wis.: IRRA, 1980), p. 210.

23. Freeman and Brittain, *op. cit.*

24. Gary N. Chaison, "Comment: Union Merger Process and Industrial Environment," *Industrial Relations* 17 (February 1978):119–23.

25. Larry T. Adams, "Labor Organization Mergers, 1979–1984: Adapting to Change," *Monthly Labor Review* 107 (September 1984):22.

26. "Merger is Voted: Special Convention Nearly Unanimous," *The United Shoe Worker* (January–February 1979):3.

27. Adams, *op. cit.,* p. 26.

28. Gary N. Chaison, "Comment: Union Merger Process and Industrial Environment," pp. 119–23. For additional criticism of the study and Freeman and Brittain's response, see George Seltzer, "Comment: Union Merger Process and Industrial Environment," *Industrial Relations* 17 (February 1978):124–26; John Freeman and Jack Brittain, "Reply to Professor Chaison and Seltzer," *Industrial Relations* 17 (February 1978):127–29.

29. Buchanan, *op. cit.*; Robert T. Buchanan, "Mergers in British Trade Unions: 1949–1979," *Industrial Relations Journal* 12 (1981):40–49.

30. Lucretia M. Dewey, "Union Merger Pace Quickens," *Monthly Labor Review* 94 (June 1971):63–69; Janus, *op. cit.*; Adams, *op. cit.*

31. The need for this approach is emphasized by Gary N. Chaison in "A Note on the Critical Dimensions of the Union Merger Process," *Relations Industrielles—Industrial Relations* 37 (1982):200.

32. Thomas A. Kochan, *Collective Bargaining and Industrial Relations* (Homewood, Ill.: Richard D. Irwin, 1980), p. 35.

33. Such a relationship is suggested in Adams's merger chronology: "They [mergers] usually occur when the economic and institutional problems that create the need to merge outweigh the problems of satisfying that need." Adams, *op. cit.*, p. 21.

34. For a brief overview of business mergers, see James C. VanHorne, *Financial Management and Policy*, 6th ed. (Englewood Cliffs, N.J.: Prentice-Hall, 1983), pp. 603–27.

35. Discussions of the reasons for business mergers are found in Kenneth M. Davidson, "Looking at the Strategic Impact of Mergers," *The Journal of Business Strategy* 2 (Summer 1981):13–22; and Walter H. Goldberg, *Mergers: Motives, Modes, Methods* (New York: Nichols Publishing, 1983). The theory of mergers is reviewed and extended in Craig S. Galbraith and Curt H. Stiles, "Merger Strategies as a Response to Bilateral Market Power," *Academy of Management Journal* 27 (September 1984):511–24. A review of recent corporate merger activity is found in Daniel F. Cuff, "The Rising Tide of Mergers," *New York Times*, June 28, 1985, p. D1.

36. Fred R. Bleakley, "The Merger Makers' Spiraling Fees," *New York Times*, September 30, 1984, pp. F1, F24.

37. Chitayat, "Mergers of Trade Unions," p. 223.

38. *Proceedings of the Thirtieth Constitutional Convention of the Bakery and Confectionery Workers International Union (1978)*, p. 485.

39. "Bigger Unions Will Pack a Bigger Wallop," *Nations Business* (May 1973):51.

40. Chitayat, "Mergers of Trade Unions," pp. 5–7, 50–51.

2
A Historical Overview of National Union Mergers

Mergers have occurred since the emergence of the first unions. Indeed, as one observer remarked: "Even among the first workers' guilds . . . which marked the advent of trade unionism, mergers have provided a means to decrease friction among unions with overlapping or similar jurisdictions."[1] Mergers also became a basic building mechanism of many of the earliest unions as citywide locals banded together at conventions to form regional or national organizations. As a result many unions carried in their titles the term *amalgamated*, referring to their formation by the combining of local or regional bodies.

In this chapter I will examine the historical dimensions of the national union mergers. Major trends in merger activity will be reviewed along with the impact of federation policies and movements for merger over the past one hundred years. This chapter is not intended to serve as a comprehensive labor history but rather as an introduction to and appreciation of the history of national union mergers.

The Early Mergers

In the first half of the nineteenth century, labor organizations emerged on a local level with only sporadic attempts to form citywide or regional bodies.[2] The emergence of broader-based unions started in the 1850s, and intensified after the Civil War, as nationalization of markets prompted unions to claim wider organizing jurisdictions. This period was marked by the growth of unions which joined together the locals in a particular trade.[3] In 1852, the National Typographical Union (our oldest surviving national union) was formed. Five other national unions were chartered later in that decade.[4]

The national unions of the early period bore little resemblance to their present namesakes. As labor historian Norman Ware observed:

> The national unions of the fifties and sixties were national only in name. They were loose federations of craft locals having little authority and less

money. The locals made their own agreements with employers with no reference to the national organization and the slightest depression wiped them out. The depression of the seventies left only a handful of national unions, none of which had as many as 5,000 members and a few as many as 1,000.[5]

The early national unions participated in several merger variations. Sometimes a national merged with a regional body, as in 1860, when city-wide shoemakers unions were absorbed by the national Knights of St. Crispin.[6] In other instances, national unions amalgamated with each other, as seen in the mergers between the Machinists and Blacksmiths in 1859, or between conductors' unions in that year.[7]

In the 1870s, one union was formed by merger while four unions were disbanded by being absorbed.[8] The merger of the iron and steel unions was typical of the complex mergers of highly specialized unions during that time. Union organization in this industry began in 1859, with the formation in Pittsburg of the Sons of Vulcan. This organization was soon disbanded, but reemerged three years later as the National Forge of the Sons of Vulcan, with a membership comprised mostly of puddlers and boilers. Another union, taking in heaters and later roughers and rollers, was formed in 1872, under the name of the Associated Brotherhood of Iron and Steel Heaters. In 1873, a third union was formed among the rollers, roughers, catchers, and hookers, calling itself the Iron and Steel Roll Hands Union.

Declining membership soon forced these unions to retreat from their policies of craft exclusiveness, (the practice of limiting membership to a narrowly defined craft) and overtures were made for amalgamation. In August 1875, the Heaters and Roll Hands held a joint convention in Philadelphia at the same time that the Sons of Vulcan were meeting in the city. A few months later, the three unions formed a merger committee and, upon reaching an agreement, held a convention for the founding of a new union—the Amalgamated Association of Iron and Steel Workers. They were joined by a local organization, the United Nailers, which withdrew in 1885, but returned in 1886.[9] This amalgamation appears to be representative of those of the period, as craft unions joined with others in related trades to offset membership declines.

The 1880s and 1890s saw a variety of amalgamations and absorptions. Some of these involved secessionist unions rejoining their original organizations. For example, in 1888, locals favoring more aggressive policies withdrew from the Order of Railway Conductors and started the Brotherhood of Railway Conductors. Four years later, the two unions resolved their differences and merged. In other cases, regional bodies of the Knights of Labor joined with national unions; in 1890, the Knights' District Assembly No. 135 combined with the National Progressive Union of Miners and Mine Laborers to form the United Mine Workers of America. In 1895, the Knights' District Assembly No. 25 merged with the United Brotherhood of Brass Workers to form the United Brotherhood of Brass and Composition Metal Workers, Polishers and Buffers.[10]

Toward the end of the nineteenth century, the labor movement was ripe for mergers. It was marked by an abundance of small unions with narrowly defined jurisdictions, limited potential for growth, and a high likelihood for jurisdictional conflict with neighboring uinons. The merger of unions in related trades became a leading method of rationalizing union structure.

Amalgamations of Related Trades

Many early amalgamations involved related trades.[11] As differences in skill levels lessened and the division of labor became greater, it was increasingly difficult for craft unions to justify their practice of only organizing workers in very narrow jurisdictions. Workers engaged at the same enterprise but in different parts of the production process were finding it to their advantage to combine or form some kind of cooperative alliance.[12]

One key reason for combining related trades was the need to effectively strike a common employer. For example:

> A strike of the unions of iron boilers and puddlers in Pittsburg in 1875 failed because the struck employers were able to keep the heaters and rollers at work on muck iron produced by non-union boilers and puddlers in other localities. Convinced that their strike would have been successful had the heaters and rollers supported them, the highly skilled puddlers and boilers abandoned their policy of craft exclusiveness and entered into an "Amalgamated Association" with other trades in the industry the following year.[13]

It was also found that when an enterprise was organized by several unions, the strike of a union of skilled and difficult to replace craftspeople could result in layoffs of the members of the nonstriking unions. Accordingly, the strike was seen as fairer (at least to the workers) and more effective when carried out by amalgamated trades.

Amalgamations were also promoted on the grounds that workers move from one related trade to another both during a strike and at normal times, and that the members in one craft are frequently recruited from another.

> A railroad brakeman may later become a railroad conductor. The pressman's assistant rises to the position of printing-pressman. The cigar maker of ability learns enough concerning the varieties of tobacco and the making of the cigar to do the work of the cigar packer. Many carpenters and cabinet-makers enter the craft of pattern-makers.[14]

Amalgamations of related trades were used to control the supply of labor in an industry while preventing competition for employment among the members of different unions. They also reduced jurisdictional disputes over the assignment of work. After a merger, such disputes would occur among groups within the union rather than between unions, and consequently the lines of demarcation around crafts would not be as rigid.[15]

An alternative to amalgamation was the federation of related trades. Here, distinct craft groups would retain their own identities and there would be less difficulty in reconciling competing interests. In an amalgamation, the smaller unions might not feel that they are adequately represented in union government, a problem that could be overcome within the structure of an alliance. While most alliances were temporary and loosely organized, some did evolve into ongoing federations.[16] Later chapters will examine the use of alliances as merger alternatives as well as those amalgamations that adopt the structure of a federation.

The Federations and Mergers

AFL Policies and the Scranton Declaration

Throughout its history the American Federation of Labor had to contend with the problems arising from the different structures of its member unions. At the time of its founding in 1886, the AFL blocked out the work force into jurisdictions for its present and future affiliates. When new affiliates were chartered they were given an organizing sector not already reserved for a present affiliate. Within a short time, several new unions were created to fill out the available jurisdictions: the number of affiliated national unions increased from 67 in 1898 to 120 in 1904.[17]

The large number of affiliates resulted in a conflict in the AFL's exercise of its two fundamental policies. Under the doctrine of exclusive jurisdiction, only one affiliate would be authorized to recruit workers in a given craft.[18] The doctrine provided that "each affiliate union shall have a clear and specified job territory and boundary ordinarily defined in terms of work operations, crafts, trades, occupations or industrial groupings or jobs, and occasionally defined in terms of geography."[19]

But the federation had an equally important doctrine of affiliate autonomy requiring that it refrain from interfering with the internal affairs of affiliates. Consequently, it had to restrain itself from too strongly or openly acting against the shifting jurisdictions of affiliates.[20] The result was a rather ambiguous and vacillating policy toward union mergers which centered around the question of whether the federation should require the mergers of affiliates to uphold the concept of exclusive jurisdiction.

The inevitable dilemma arose early in the life of the federation. The 1888 convention declared that it was unwise for there to be two or more unions in any one trade and that the AFL should "advise" the amalgamations of trades in such cases. At the following convention, the federation was again encouraged to make some effort to bring about the amalgamations of "dual" unions.[21]

The federation soon saw the inappropriateness of the narrow craft structures and the potential for continued structural conflict among affiliates. Samuel Gompers, the AFL's president and the prime developer of its structural orientation, recognized the need for the recruitment of unskilled workers. This was often done through local bodies, called federal labor unions, that were directly chartered by the AFL. Unskilled workers first joined the mixed federal unions and were later drawn into the appropriate national or local affiliates. At the same time that this form of organizing was being carried out, the AFL also began to charter some unions (for example, the Tin Plate Workers) for unskilled and semiskilled workers in particular industries. However, the federation's preference seems to have been for the less skilled workers to join already existing unions covering occupations specific to the industry.[22] Unions were urged to amalgamate or broaden jurisdiction, and the resulting organizations enveloped numerous occupations—skilled and unskilled—within industries. Conflicts soon arose between these emerging industrial unions and the craft unions.

In 1899, the craft unions supported a resolution of James O'Connell, president of the Machinists, "guaranteeing to each craft absolute self government and complete jurisdiction over its members, wherever employed."[23] However, jurisdictional disputes continued, and in 1900, the AFL urged that narrow concepts of jurisdiction be abandoned and disputes settled through amalgamations. That year the convention instructed the AFL Executive Council not to grant charters in the future without a careful examination and definition of jurisdiction.[24]

A dispute soon arose between the United Mine Workers and the craft unions that organized workers in and around mines. The International Blacksmiths' Union claimed that members of its craft had been recruited by the Mine Workers. The latter justified its activities on the grounds that organization on a strictly craft basis would mean that a strike by a few could affect the employment of a much larger group. At its 1901 convention the AFL was compelled by its affiliates to investigate the dispute. The resulting proposal, called the Scranton Declaration, reaffirmed that organizing should be along craft lines. At the same time it declared that workers should be enrolled in the "paramount organization" (not necessarily the union of their craft) in isolated industries and "when few workers are engaged over whom separate organizations claim jurisdiction."[25] The committee proposing the declaration also examined the question of amalgamations but had to admit to the federation's inherent weakness; it could only suggest that affiliates consider amalgamations.

We hold that the trade union movement will be promoted by closely allying the subdivided crafts, *giving consideration to amalgamation* and to the organization of district and national trade councils to which should be referred questions in dispute, and which should be adjusted within allied craft lines.[26] (Emphasis added.)

In adjusting jurisdictional encroachments, it was widely believed that the AFL should only encourage and assist affiliates. ("The AFL, being a voluntary association, cannot and should not adopt methods antagonistic to or in conflict with established trade union laws."[27]) As one observer noted, the Scranton Declaration "exposed the lack of power of the ALF to enforce any rule with respect to jurisdiction upon a powerful affiliate."[28]

The AFL policy was best summarized in Gompers' 1905 report on mergers of affiliates: "Not by force, which usually arouses repulsion, but by intelligent persuasion and helpfulness, we bring about unity and amalgamation among kindred trade organizations under the banner of one international union, for the common good of all."[29]

Forced Mergers

Despite the apparent merger policy pronounced in the Scranton Declaration, the AFL did occasionally find a need to force mergers of affiliates and even apply its strongest sanction, expulsion, against unions which refused to merge. Typical are the forced mergers of the Railway Carmen and the Carpenters.

In the case of the Railway Carmen, a weaker affiliate was forced to merge with a stronger unaffiliated union. The unaffiliated Brotherhood of Railway Carmen was formed in 1888, while the International Association of Car Workers was chartered by the AFL in 1901. Jurisdictional rivalry flared up soon after the formation of the Car Workers and there began a movement for the amalgamation of the two rivals. The Brotherhood, not strongly disposed toward merger, suggested that any merger should require a referendum vote of the two unions' membership but should be restricted to those who would qualify to join the Brotherhood. The Car Workers rejected this approach because the process would disenfranchise some of its members. Despite the failure of negotiations, there remained some desire to merge and in 1904, the Brotherhood responded to an invitation and sent a delegation to the Car Workers convention. A joint convention was arranged but a merger agreement could still not be reached.[30]

Two years later, after it had absorbed some citywide locals, the Brotherhood had grown from 15,000 to 35,000 members and became attractive to the AFL. The legitimacy of the smaller affiliated Car Workers was called to question.

Very circumspectly . . . [the AFL] started the delicate process of correcting its error without public admission. For evidently, it had been misled in 1901, and had adopted the wrong twin. The [Car Workers] failed to grow, while the Brotherhood was growing apace.[31]

The Car Workers, sensing their less favorable position, rejected amalgamation and attempted to block the affiliation of the Brotherhood. The AFL was faced with an affiliate that was "obstructing a valuable acquisition to the Federation family."[32] In 1910, the Car Workers' charter was cancelled and the Brotherhood was made the union in the jurisdiction. Five years later, the Car Workers changed its name to the American Federation of Railroad Workers, attempting unsuccessfully to be a general rival to all railroad unions.

Another example of federation pressure for merger is found in the case of the carpentry and woodworking unions. In 1895, the International Furniture Workers and the Machine Wood Workers merged to form the Amalgamated Woodworkers International Union. Jurisdictional disputes soon arose between this union and the affiliated United Brotherhood of Carpenters in the organization of planing mill workers and sash and door makers. A jurisdictional agreement between the two was reached in 1897, but this was abrogated by the Carpenters in the following year. The Amalgamated Woodworkers complained to the AFL convention that the Brotherhood of Carpenters was organizing woodworkers. In 1902, the Carpenters demanded the revocation of the charter of both the Amalgamated Woodworkers and an earlier rival, the Amalgamated Society of Carpenters. The AFL appointed an impartial umpire to the dispute and an award was issued dividing the contested work categories between the Carpenters and the Woodworkers. The umpire also decreed that the Carpenters and the Amalgamated Society should merge. The Carpenters rejected the jurisdictional award and the Amalgamated Society refused merger.

By 1906, the officers of the Amalgamated Woodworkers finally decided that the best option available was to merge with the Carpenters, but this was rejected by Amalgamated's membership. Gompers, as the AFL president, went to the next convention of the Amalgamated Woodworkers to try to elicit support for a merger but was not successful. In 1911, after there was still no action, the federation ordered the mergers of both the Amalgamated Woodworkers and the Amalgamated Society into the Carpenters. Unable to hold out any longer under intense pressure, the Amalgamated Woodworkers was absorbed by the Carpenters. The Amalgamated Society resisted merger and had its charter revoked by the federation. In 1924 it was finally absorbed by the Carpenters.[33]

The AFL often used the threat of expulsion to "encourage" mergers and sometimes, as in the woodworking case, it had to carry out this punishment. There were other expulsions because of refusals to merge.

In 1912 the International Association of Steam and Hot Water Fitters was suspended by the AFL for refusing to merge with the United Association of Plumbers and Steam Fitters.

In 1919 the Brotherhood of Steamshovel and Dredgemen was expelled for refusing to merge with the Union of Steam and Operating Engineers. (The two unions eventually merged in 1927.)

In 1919 the Amalgamated Lace Operatives and the International Mule Spinners were expelled for refusing to merge with the United Textile Workers.[34]

In resolving jurisdictional disputes the AFL applied pressure primarily on the smaller unions to merge into the larger ones. As Philip Taft, a leading observer of union government, remarked:

> The federation, in all the cases involving a 'forced' merger . . . in the end favored the stronger organization. . . . [It] yielded to the pressures of the more powerful union, although it tried for a time to find a solution which would enable the weaker union to exist. . . . The existence of more than one union in a craft would have, at the time, stimulated jurisdictional disputes, which the A.F. of L. was anxious to prevent. The A.F. of L. sided with the more powerful unions; it could find no alternative to such decisions.[35]

The federation found itself in a predicament. The policy of exclusive jurisdiction, combined with the potential for widespread jurisdictional disputes because of the changing craft boundaries, forced AFL involvement in affiliate mergers. This was an apparent violation of affiliate autonomy. The federation was supported by the per capita dues payments of its members, while its officers were elected by convention delegates; not surprisingly the occasional intrusions into affiliate autonomy were usually to the benefit of the larger affiliates.

The Amalgamationists

The early mergers within the AFL involved only minimal expansion of jurisdictions. In the 1920s the federation encountered a short-lived amalgamation movement aimed at widespread structural changes.

On the surface, the amalgamation movement within the AFL was based on the premise that the industrial union (representing all workers in an industry, regardless of their crafts) was the most effective and desirable means of union organization. Amalgamationists believed that all existing unions should be merged into a few industrial unions and the economy should be divided into a few broad jurisdictions.[36] In the pursuit of this program, the amalgamationists became a center of organized opposition to the conservative trade unionism espoused by the AFL leadership.

The amalgamation movement was spearheaded by the Chicago Federation of Labor, a major progressive force within the AFL. In March 1922, the

Chicago Federation of Labor proposed a motion to the AFL Executive Council that a conference be called to merge craft and amalgamated unions into industrial unions. The resolution was sponsored by William Z. Foster, then a rising union leader and later to become a major communist labor activist. The council rejected the proposal and stated that no such conference would be held. Gompers was sent to Chicago to urge the reconsideration of the motion. When the motion was not rescinded, the AFL ended its contribution of half the expenses of the Chicago Federation of Labor.

At the next AFL convention in Portland, Oregon, three resolutions endorsing amalgamation were rejected. However, the principle of amalgamation was endorsed by fifteen state federations as well as unions of the retail clerks, meat cutters, bakers, lithographers, textile workers, maintenance of way employees, molders, typographers, brewery workers, machinists and bookbinders.[37] Despite this support, there appears to have been little chance of the amalgamationists' success. As Taft notes, the adoption of an AFL resolution could never have forced such widespread changes in union structure and jurisdiction: "[T]he first phase of the amalgamation movement can be regarded largely as a manifestation of protest and dissatisfaction with the old leadership of the A.F. of L."[38]

Foster and his communist followers used the amalgamation movement as a vehicle for challenging the power structure of the AFL and promoting a movement toward independent political action for labor unions. In 1922, Foster called a meeting of so-called "progressive groups" interested in engaging in political action through organizations independent of the established political parties. The Chicago Federation attended but found itself outvoted on every issue by the communists and their supporters. Disillusioned, it withdrew from the movement for independent political action as well as the drive for amalgamations.

The amalgamationists and their supporters were vehemently denounced in the proceedings of the 1923 AFL convention:

> Demonstrable proof is overwhelming that those who are constantly at work dividing the organized workers on abstract discussions of forms of organization and spreading the poison of suspicion against the officers of trade unions have never been loyal trade unionists and have always antagonized the trade union movement. In addition, the self proclaimed 'amalgamationists' are not bent on amalgamation, but upon the disruption and destruction of organized labor in America.[39]

Rejected by the AFL and finding itself out of the mainstream of American labor, the amalgamationists amounted to little. At that period the AFL was already reducing its role in affiliate mergers. New structural arrangements would occur through organizing rather than changes in union charters or the regrouping of existing unions. At the 1929 AFL convention, a resolution was introduced to appoint a committee to devise a plan for reducing the number of national unions through mergers. The resolution was voted down.[40]

Mergers Among the Expelled Unions

We have seen that the federation forced affiliate mergers under the threat of expulsions. In several cases, unions expelled for other reasons have found themselves in a climate conducive to mergers.[41]

Since 1949, eighteen unions have faced expulsion; eleven from the CIO from 1949 to 1950, one from the AFL in 1953, and six from the AFL–CIO between 1957 and 1973. The causes for expulsion have been communist domination, corruption, and dual unionism (simultaneous membership in two federations or in a federation and an unaffiliated organization). Among the expelled unions there has been an exceptionally high rate of mergers, often as absorptions into other expelled unions or affiliates. The following sections review this merger trend.

Causes for Expulsion.
Communist domination. Not long after its establishment the CIO had attracted some communist-led labor unions as well as members of the Communist Party. The communists gained influence during the prewar period and, though well entrenched, they soon found themselves under attack within the federation because of their views on American foreign and domestic policy. Communists and their followers were purged from positions of influence in the United Auto Workers, the Transportation Workers Union, and the National Maritime Union. In late 1949, the CIO moved against its communist-dominated affiliates, bitterly denouncing the United Electrical, Radio and Machine Workers (UE) and the United Farm Equipment and Metal Workers (FE). Both faced severe raiding campaigns from the CIO affiliates. Under such threatening conditions, the UE absorbed the FE and announced its independence of the federation. Despite this, the two unions were formally and separately expelled in November 1949. At that time, the CIO Executive Board was given the authority to expel any other affiliate with communist-dominated leadership. Charges were brought against other unions, and after several months of hearings it was recommended that nine affiliates be expelled. This was approved by the CIO Executive Board, and at the 1950 convention the federation severed relationships with nine unions having more than half a million members.

Expulsion for corruption. In 1951, a New York State crime commission had revealed extensive corruption within the governing structure of the International Longshoremens' Association (ILA), an AFL affiliate. A federation sub-

committee investigated and demanded several reforms from the
ing the removal of officers with criminal records and a modifi
methods used to hire longshoremen. When sufficient changes we
by 1953 the AFL revoked the ILA's charter. At the time the unio
seventy-five thousand members.

Soon after the formation of the AFL-CIO, allegations began
about the corruption of some affiliates' officers. In 1957, the AFL–CIO Ethical
Practices Committee considered bringing charges of improper activities against
several affiliates: the International Brotherhood of Teamsters, the Textile
Workers Union, the Laundry Workers International Union, the International
Union of Cleaning and Dye House Workers (CDHW), the Bakery and Con-
fectionery Workers International Union (BC), and the Allied Industrial
Workers. Some of these unions met the terms for retaining affiliation set by the
AFL–CIO. However, the continuation of the alleged corruption resulted in
the expulsion of the Teamsters, BC, and the two laundry unions.

Dual Unionism. In 1968, the expelled Teamsters and the United Auto
Workers (which had withdrawn from the AFL–CIO) joined in an organizing
alliance called the Alliance for Labor Action (ALA). Although the ALA attempted to enter into a no-raiding agreement with the AFL–CIO, affiliates of
the latter were warned that ALA membership would be considered dual
unionism and would constitute grounds for federation expulsion. In 1969,
the International Chemical Workers Union, seeking organizing allies, formally
joined the ALA but claimed that it would refrain from raiding affiliates.
Nonetheless, the AFL–CIO branded this act as dual unionism and expelled
the ICWU at its 1959 convention. When expelled, the ICWU claimed
104,000 members.

In 1973, the Brewery Workers were expelled by the AFL–CIO convention
for a form of dual unionism—an absorption into an expelled union, the
Teamsters. It was claimed that the Brewery Workers had violated the AFL–
CIO Constitution (or at least would soon violate it) by providing an indirect
means for the AFL–CIO representation of an expelled union. The revocation
of the Brewery Workers' charter was also justified on the basis that it would
no longer be an international union once the absorption took place and therefore it would not qualify for federation membership.[42]

Merger Activity. The status of the eighteen expelled unions is summarized in
table 2–1. Only three of the unions still survive and remain unaffiliated: the
UE, the ILWU, and the Teamsters. Two unions have disbanded: the National Union of Marine Cooks and Stewards and the United Public Workers
of America. In both cases, there was substantial membership decline and economic difficulties before and after expulsion. The Chemical Workers
reentered the federation after severing its ties with the ALA in 1971. The

Table 2–1
Unions Expelled from the Federations (AFL, CIO, AFL–CIO) Since 1949

Date of Expulsion	Federation	Expelled Union	Present Status
1949	CIO	United Electrical Radio and Machine Workers (UE)	Unaffiliated
1949	CIO	United Farm Equipment and Metal Workers	Merged into UE in 1949
1950	CIO	International Longshoremens' and Warehousemens' Union (ILWU)	Unaffiliated
1950	CIO	American Communications Association	Merged into Teamsters in 1966
1950	CIO	International Union of Mine, Mill and Smelter Workers	Merged into United Steelworkers of America in 1967
1950	CIO	National Union of Marine Cooks and Stewards	Disbanded in 1954
1950	CIO	International Union of Fishermen and Allied Workers	Merged into ILWU in 1949
1950	CIO	International Union of Fur and Leather Workers	Merged into the Amalgamated Meat Cutters and Butcher Workmen in 1955
1950	CIO	Food, Tobacco, Agricultural, and Allied Workers Union[a]	Merged into Retail, Wholesale, Department Store Union (RWDSU) in 1954
1950	CIO	United Office and Professional Workers of America[a]	Merged into RWDSU in 1954
1950	CIO	United Public Workers of America	Disbanded in 1953
1953	AFL	International Longshoremens' Association	Merged with the International Brotherhood of Longshoremen in 1959
1957	AFL–CIO	International Brotherhood of Teamsters, Chauffeurs, Warehousemen and Helpers (Teamsters)	Unaffiliated
1957	AFL–CIO	Bakery and Confectionery Workers International Union	Merged into the American Bakery and Confectionery Workers International Union in 1969

Table 2–1 continued

Date of Expulsion	Federation	Expelled Union	Present Status
1957	AFL–CIO	Laundry Workers International Union[b]	Merged into Teamsters in 1962
1957	AFL–CIO	International Association of Dry Cleaning and Dye House Workers[b]	Merged into Teamsters in 1962
1969	AFL–CIO	International Chemical Workers Union	Reaffiliated with AFL–CIO in 1971
1973	AFL–CIO	United Brewery, Flour, Cereal, Soft Drink and Distillery Workers	Merged into Teamsters in 1973

Source: Gary N. Chaison, "Federation Expulsions and Union Mergers in the United States," *Relations Industrielles—Industrial Relations* 28 (March 1972):352–53. Reprinted with permission.

[a]In 1950 the Food, Tobacco, Agricultural, and Allied Workers amalgamated with the United Office and Professional Workers of America and the Distributive Workers Union to form the Distributive, Processing and Office Workers Union (DPOWU). The DPOWU merged into the RWDSU in 1954.

[b]In 1956, prior to their expulsion, the Laundry Workers International Union merged with the International Association of Dry Cleaning and Dye House Workers to form the Laundry, Dry Cleaning and Dye House Workers International Union (LDCDHW). The LDCDHW merged into the Teamsters in 1962.

remaining expelled unions reentered the federation or ended their independent existence by undergoing mergers.

Expulsion removes a union from the protection of the federation's no-raid agreement. Smaller unions have tended to be particularly vulnerable to the onslaught of raids by affiliates. After suffering through widespread raids, the Union of Mine, Mill and Smelter Workers merged into the affiliated Steelworkers, while for the same reason the Fur and Leather Workers was absorbed by the Amalgamated Meat Cutters and Butcher Workmen. In 1950, the Food, Tobacco, Agricultural and Allied Workers and the United Office and Professional Workers of America, facing membership declines, amalgamated with the Distributive Workers Union to form the Distributive, Processing and Office Workers Union. This new organization shedded much of the earlier communist influence among its leadership and entered the federation through absorption into the RWDSU.

In some cases federations chartered new unions to win over the membership of expelled unions. Merger into these federation-chartered rivals, following periods of intense rivalry, was the means for federation reentry for the ILA and the BC. In other instances, expelled unions ended their existence by merging into other, stronger expelled unions. The UE absorbed the FE, and the ILWU absorbed the Fishermen and Allied Workers.

The Teamsters grew rapidly outside of the federation, facing neither the challenge of a federation-created rival or substantial internal movements for reform or leadership change. Moreover, there were no affiliates capable of launching large-scale raiding campaigns in the union's jurisdiction. The Teamsters were in the position to absorb three other expelled unions (the American Communications Association, the Laundry Workers International Union, and the Dry Cleaning and Dye House Workers) which had suffered severe membership losses through raiding. Also, the Teamsters absorbed the Brewery Workers in 1973, but this was a unique situation—the agreement to merge had been the cause of rather than the result of the Brewery Workers' expulsion.

The flurry of merger activity after federation expulsion indicates the role of mergers in reducing the hazards of isolation. The heavily raided and weaker expelled unions were particularly merger prone and reached a safe haven through absorption either into affiliates in their jurisdiction or into stronger expelled unions. In effect, the federation expulsions served to create or intensify the conditions which act as motivators for merger, most visibly in the forms of declining memberships and financial difficulties. In many instances merger was the only alternative to eventual disbandment. On the other hand, the stronger expelled unions found themselves in the ideal position to absorb other expelled unions which could not survive outside the federation, meet the conditions for reaffiliation, or find a means to merge with an affiliate. In effect, federation expulsions gave rise to a significant subset of mergers with similar motivation and characteristics. The cause for merger was not found merely in the act of expulsion but rather in the vulnerability of the expelled unions.

Recent AFL–CIO Merger Policy

The federation's present policy regarding mergers among affiliates can be characterized as one of cautious assistance and encouragement. It is highly doubtful if the present federation could attempt to force affiliate mergers as the AFL once did, or entertain such radical plans of restructuring as once proposed by the amalgamationists.

During the twenty-year period of rivalry between the AFL and the CIO, the two federations chartered rivals to each others' affiliates. The eventual formation of the AFL–CIO in 1955 rested on the assurance that jurisdictions of affiliates would remain unchanged despite conspicuous duplication. Mergers would be encouraged but not forced; to force mergers would have been an intrusion into affiliates' autonomy. As a result of this policy, jurisdictional overlap has continued and intensified.[43]

The federation's constitution listed under its objectives and principles:

> to encourage the elimination of conflicting and duplicating organizations and jurisdictions through the process of voluntary agreements or voluntary merger in consultation with the appropriate officials of the Federation.[44]

At the time of the founding of the AFL–CIO, President George Meany emphasized the voluntary nature of mergers:

> we are going to try to bring unions together that are competing in the same field, and the merged federation, through its officers, are charged with the duty of trying to bring those organizations together, to get some kind of an agreement to merge if that is possible, but always with the definite and complete understanding that everything must be done by mutual agreement and by voluntary participation of each and every organization in whatever plan is brought forth to settle these problems.[45]

The AFL–CIO's posture became one of carefully and quietly encouraging mergers.[46] At the 1961 convention a resolution was presented for the "Establishment of a Department of Inter-Union Cooperation and Merger." The department would promote joint union efforts, establish interunion councils, and offer "guidance, counsel and technical assistance to international unions who are contemplating organic merger."[47] It would also carry out "the long range analysis of union and industrial trends to determine where organic merger of various international unions will become advisable, and the drafting of programs to lay the ground work for such mergers."[48]

The resolution was referred to the Executive Council and brought up again at the 1963 convention, but it was not adopted because the Executive Council said it was already being acted upon. Meany stated that the AFL–CIO leadership was constantly working on possible affiliate mergers:

> You don't get reports on it because when you attempt to get two unions together and you fail temporarily . . . there is no sense of reporting that fact, because it might in some way hinder your further efforts. But the officers . . . and myself and other members of the Council are constantly at this work.
>
> In fact, when I leave this rostrum at noon, I go back to meet the representatives of two unions that I first met back in 1955 for the purpose of trying to bring them together and we were not able to do so at this time.
>
> We have tried a couple of times since, and right here at this convention, because of circumstances that have developed, we are making another effort.[49]

At the next AFL–CIO convention, Meany reiterated his position and, in an often quoted statement, called for increased merger activity:

> I do not suggest that we deviate in any way from the principle that such [merger] action must be entirely voluntary. I do, however, strongly suggest that the responsible officers of many unions, who by all logic and common sense should merge, might take a broader view of the union as an instrument of progress for working people rather than an institution devoted to its own perpetuation for the sake of sentiment and tradition.[50]

Meany suggested that the need for mergers was most acute when two or more "static" unions—that is, unions that were not expanding—occupied a similar jurisdiction and did not have sufficient resources for organizing. He was critical of the use of absorptions by large unions to expand their jurisdictions. There was a need for "the consolidation of competing organizations as the way to more rational and effective trade union structure."[51]

In 1968, Lane Kirkland, then AFL–CIO secretary–treasurer and now president, stated that the federation was working on many mergers but added: "We can't force them; they must be voluntary."[52] As we will see later, affiliates have called on the AFL–CIO officers to act as intermediaries in arranging initial merger contacts and as mediators in merger negotiations. Attempts have been made to give a clearer definition and structure to these activities. In 1981, the federation's Executive Council established a committee to examine merger potential and assist merging affiliates. The reports and minutes of this committee suggest a somewhat more active federation role in affiliate mergers. The president of the AFL–CIO was urged to use former Executive Council members and other retired union officers as agents to encourage and assist in merger negotiations. In addition, a questionnaire was distributed to determine affiliates' interests in mergers and to "ascertain appropriate clusters and spheres of influence."[53] In 1984, the AFL–CIO's research director reported that several affiliate merger discussions were in progress and reiterated the federation's position that "union mergers tend to strengthen the entire labor movement. The trend is toward fewer, stronger and more diverse unions, and the AFL–CIO encourages that trend."[54]

In general, the federation still seems cautious about appearing too forceful or intrusive in encouraging mergers among affiliates. It continues to emphasize its role "to be helpful to the parties and to cajole and to persuade and to give technical assistance as they [affiliates] pursue their mergers."[55] On the other hand, there is a possibility that the federation will become more active in reviewing affiliate mergers, and may even refuse to recognize the mergers of unions in unrelated jurisdictions. In 1985, the AFL–CIO Committee on the Evolution of Work, consisting of twenty-seven top-level federation and affiliate officers, recommended that the only mergers that should be recognized are those in which the participating unions share a community of interest. Merging affiliates would have a community of interest if they have substantial overlap in their jurisdictions or have many members either in related industries or employed by the same conglomerate employers.[56] The committee proposed these guidelines to ensure that mergers "represent the optimum, beneficial combination."[57] The AFL–CIO officers were asked to carefully review each affiliate merger and ascertain the extent of the community of interest.[58] This policy could lead to a much closer scrutiny of mergers and the possible discouragement of some. However, the recent historical record indicates that it is unlikely that the federation would take strong actions, such as suspension or expulsion, against affiliates whose mergers were not deemed to be the best matches.

Frequency and Types of Mergers: 1890–1984

The preceding section reviewed some of the major historical forces shaping merger activity in the United States, including the drive for mergers of unions in related trades and the varied roles of the federations in mergers. At this point I turn to an examination of overall trends in merger forms and frequency.[59]

I developed a time series by identifying union mergers from such sources as merger chronologies, government directories of unions, the footnotes to union membership tables, and various lists of union names and name changes. The series covers the years 1890 to 1984. Prior to 1890, mergers were sporadic, and information tended to be incomplete.[60] The appendix to this volume contains the list of mergers which serves as the basis for the analysis and tables that follow.

The Frequency of Union Mergers

In the introductory chapter, I described the two basic forms of union mergers: the *amalgamation*, or fusion of two or more unions to form a new union, and the *absorption*, the merging of one union into another. Table 2–2 indicates the frequency of amalgamations and absorptions from 1890 to 1984. There were 183 mergers: 47 amalgamations and 136 absorptions. The absorptions combined 2 unions each. Among the amalgamations, 41 involved only 2 unions, 2 involved 3 unions each, 3 involved 4 unions each, and 1 joined together 5 unions.

A trend in merger frequency and type is apparent in table 2–2. In the 1890s, a period when many national unions were just being formed, there was only a moderate number of mergers. The turn of the century saw a relatively high level of merger activity with almost as many amalgamations as absorptions. This was an early move toward the combining of related trades. The number of mergers soon declined dramatically, with only four mergers from 1905 to 1914. From 1915 to 1919, there was a resurgence of mergers, primarily among smaller AFL affiliates absorbed by larger ones. This was part of the AFL's attempt to reduce the number of small, highly specialized unions.

The incidence of mergers declined after 1920 and varied from four to seven per five-year period until after World War II. In the postwar period there was increased merger activity, primarily in the form of absorptions. This trend accelerated sharply after the AFL–CIO consolidation (1955) and has remained at a high though fluctuating level through the present. In the last time period there was a sharp rise in the number of mergers. The factors contributing to this trend and the possibility of its continuation or acceleration will be discussed in detail in later chapters. At this point in my historical review it should be mentioned that many of these recent mergers were absorptions of small public employee unions or unions with narrow jurisdictions operating in declining industries.

Table 2–2
The Frequency of Union Mergers, 1890–1984 by Five-Year Periods

	Amalgamations	Absorptions	Total	Average Number of Mergers per Year
1890–1894	1	3	4	.8
1895–1899	2	2	4	.8
1900–1904	5	6	11	2.2
1905–1909	0	1	1	.2
1910–1914	1	2	3	.6
1915–1919	8	8	16	3.2
1920–1924	1	6	7	1.4
1925–1929	0	4	4	.8
1930–1934	3	2	5	1.0
1935–1939	1	5	6	1.2
1940–1944	0	4	4	.8
1945–1949	3	9	12	2.4
1950–1954	2	7	9	1.8
1955–1959	4	11	15	3.0
1960–1964	4	8	12	2.4
1965–1969	1	13	14	2.8
1970–1974	5	10	15	3.0
1975–1979	3	14	17	3.4
1980–1984	3	21	24	4.8
1890–1984	47	136	183	1.9

Source: Gary N. Chaison, "A Note on Union Merger Trends, 1900–1978," *Industrial and Labor Relations Review* 34 (October 1980):117–18.

Original Sources of Data:

1890–1972: Microfilming Corporation of America, *American Labor Unions' Constitutions and Proceedings: A Guide to the Microform Edition, part 1, 1836–1974* (Glen Rock, N.J.: MCA, 1975), pp. 1–41.

1890–1976: Gary M. Fink, ed., *Labor Unions* (Westport, Conn.: Greenwood Press, 1977), pp. 457–73.

1900–1930: American Federation of Labor, *Proceedings of the Fifty-First Annual Convention*, 1931, pp. 36–57.

1900–1932: Lewis L. Lorwin, *The American Federation of Labor: History, Policies, Prospects* (Washington, D.C.: The Brookings Institution, 1933), pp. 489–91.

1900–1935: Leo Wolman, *Ebb and Flow in Trade Unionism* (New York: National Bureau of Economic Research, 1936), pp. 173–97.

1935–1960: Leo Troy, *Trade Union Membership, 1897–1962* (New York: National Bureau of Economic Research, 1965), pp. A1–A51.

1956–1971: Lucretia M. Dewey, "Union Merger Pace Quickens," *Monthly Labor Review* 94 (June 1971):63–70.

1971–1978: Charles J. Janus, "Union Mergers in the 1970's: A Look at the Reasons and Results," *Monthly Labor Review* 101 (October 1978):13–23.

1979–1984: Larry T. Adams, "Labor Organization Mergers, 1979–1984: Adapting to Change," *Monthly Labor Review* 107 (September 1984):21–27.

Table 2–3 regroups the data into categories representing the three major periods in the history of the American labor movement. The first ends in 1935 with the passage of the Wagner Act, the major protective labor legislation, and the formation of the CIO. The second, 1936–1955, covers twenty years of

Table 2–3
The Frequency of Union Mergers, 1890–1984 by Major Periods

	Amalgamations	Absorptions	Total	Average Number of Mergers per Year
1890–1935	21	35	56	1.2
1936–1955	7	28	35	1.8
1956–1984	19	73	92	3.2
1890–1984	47	136	183	1.9

Source: Gary N. Chaison, "A Note on Union Merger Trends, 1900–1978," *Industrial and Labor Relations Review* 34 (October 1980):117–118. All rights reserved. Reprinted with permission.

widespread union and federation rivalry as well as rapid union growth. The third period, 1956 to 1984, covers the years since the founding of the AFL–CIO, a time of overall lowered union growth rates and the emergence of public sector unionism.

In the earliest time period there was a moderate level of merger activity, with a relatively high proportion (37.5 percent) of this activity in amalgamations. These were primarily the combinations of small craft unions which shared neighboring jurisdictions. Although the second period was marked by rapid union growth and changes in union structure, there was only a small increase in the average number of mergers per year. Eighty percent of these were absorptions. Since the formation of the AFL–CIO there has been a noticeable increase in merger activity; from 1956 to 1984, there were 92 mergers, about half of the total mergers since 1890. A very high proportion, 79 percent, were absorptions.

Table 2–4 indicates the affiliations of the merging unions during the three periods. In the first period, amalgamations often involved AFL affiliates either exclusively (11 cases) or with unaffiliated unions (7 cases). Affiliates were heavily involved in absorptions; in 17 cases affiliates absorbed each other and in 14 cases affiliates absorbed unaffiliated unions. In the years 1936 to 1955, there was a noticeable decline in the number of amalgamations, with those among affiliates exclusively dropping to 1 from the earlier figure of 11. There were 2 amalgamations among the CIO affiliates and none across the boundaries of the rival federations. There was also a substantial decline in the number of absorptions among the AFL unions (from 23 in the prior period to 5) as well as in the number of unaffiliated unions absorbed by AFL affiliates. On the other hand, the figures point to substantial merger activity among CIO affiliates; they absorbed each other in 8 cases and absorbed unaffiliated unions in 2 more. The trend from 1936 to 1955 may be interpreted as that showing that:

> [P]eriods of dual federations and extensive union organizing may not be conducive to any dramatic increase in the frequency of union mergers. Attention

Table 2–4
Affiliations of Unions Involved in Mergers, 1890–1984

Affiliation	1890–1935	1936–1955	1956–1984	Total
Amalgamations				
All AFL	11	1	—	12
All CIO	—	2	—	2
All AFL–CIO	—	—	14	14
AFL and unaffiliated	7	0	—	7
CIO and unaffiliated	—	1	—	1
AFL–CIO and unaffiliated	—	—	3	3
AFL and CIO	—	0	—	0
All unaffiliated	3	3	2	8
Total	21	7	19	47
Absorptions				
All AFL	17	5	—	22
All CIO	—	8	—	8
All AFL–CIO	—	—	35	35
Unaffiliated absorbed by AFL	14	7	—	21
AFL absorbed by unaffiliated	0	0	—	0
Unaffiliated absorbed by CIO	—	2	—	2
CIO absorbed by unaffiliated	—	0	—	0
CIO absorbed by AFL	—	1	—	1
AFL absorbed by CIO	—	0	—	0
Unaffiliated absorbed	—	—	26[a]	26
AFL–CIO absorbed by unaffiliated	—	—	1	1
All unaffiliated	4	5	11	20
Total	35	28	73	136
Total	56	35	92	183

Source: Gary N. Chaison, "A Note on Union Merger Trends, 1900–1978," *Industrial and Labor Relations Review* 34 (October 1980):117–118. All rights reserved. Reprinted with permission.

Note: Dashes indicate that there is no data for the cell.

[a]Includes cases in which AFL–CIO affiliates absorbed affiliates of the Assembly of Government Employees (AGE). These unions were counted as unaffiliated because they disaffiliated just before or at the time of merger.

must be focussed more during such periods on creating new unions to rival those in other federations than on reducing the number of affiliates. Mergers of affiliates from different federations would be discouraged and would thus be quite rare, particularly in the form of amalgamations. Finally, smaller unions might avoid the merger route, in either amalgamations or absorptions, if they see a possibility of renewed growth. The legislation of the 1930s and the rapid gains in organizing . . . may have pointed to such a possibility.[61]

In the post-1955 period, there was a high level of merger activity among AFL–CIO affiliates; 14 amalgamations and 35 absorptions involved affiliates exclusively. In addition, 2 affiliates amalgamated with unaffiliated unions, while 26 unaffiliated unions were absorbed by affiliates. Most of the 11 absorptions among only unaffiliated unions involved public sector unions or else were absorptions of expelled unions by other expelled unions (most notably by the Teamsters). In the accelerated merger trend of the post-1956 period, affiliates were often found as one or both merger partners; such cases accounted for 86 percent of the total. This may be the result of the previously described efforts of the AFL–CIO to encourage and assist affiliate mergers through informal methods. Also, many recent mergers involved unaffiliated public sector unions which were heavily raided and merged into affiliates in order to receive the protection of the AFL–CIO no-raid agreement.[62]

Unsuccessful Merger Attempts

It should be recognized that the figures in tables 2–2 to 2–4 represent only those merger attempts that were successful. It would be exceedingly difficult to compile comprehensive and accurate tabulations of unsuccessful merger efforts. Merger overtures and informal negotiations that fail are generally not acknowledged by the participating union officers.[63] We are usually only aware of those merger failures involving the largest unions or occurring during formal negotiations. For example, union records and newspaper articles indicate that among the recent unsuccessful merger negotiations were those between:

The Oil, Chemical and Atomic Workers and the Chemical Workers (1968) and the Rubber Workers (1975)

The American Federation of Teachers and the National Education Association (1974)

The International Longshoremens' and Warehousemens' Union and the Teamsters (1975)

The United Paperworkers and the Printing Pressmen (1975), and the Printing and Graphic Communications Union (1975), and the Chemical Workers (1977)

The United Shoe Workers of America and the Boot and Shoe Workers Union (1977)

The International Typographical Union and the Newspaper Guild (1982) and the Teamsters (1985)

The Retail, Wholesale and Department Store Union, the Retail Clerks, and the Amalgamated Meat Cutters (1979)

The Service Employees International Union and the Retail, Wholesale, Department Store Union (1982)

The Telecommunications' International Union and the American Federation of State, County and Municipal Employees (1985)

The Screen Actors Guild and the Screen Extras Guild (1982, 1984).

In some cases, there were series of unsuccessful merger attempts before there was a successful one. For example, the Brewery Workers failed in its attempt to merge into the Amalgamated Meat Cutters (1969) and the Machinists (1970) before it merged into the Teamsters in 1973.[64] The Insurance Workers' quest for a merger partner began in 1979, and took four years. The union held six sets of merger discussions with five different unions before it merged into the United Food and Commercial Workers in 1983. Finally, there have been some merger negotiations that seem to have an on-again, off-again status with with long recesses rather than any public declaration of failure. Major examples are the intermittent merger discussions between the Seafarers and the National Maritime Union, and between the Automobile Workers and the Machinists.

We can get a general approximation of the frequency of unsuccessful merger attempts when we examine some data from a survey conducted by Chaison in 1985.[65] The primary purpose of the survey was to record the impressions of officers of smaller unions (unions with less than fifty thousand members) regarding possible merger outcomes. However, one of the questions dealt with the frequency of successful and unsuccessful merger attempts in the past ten years. Completed questionnaires were received from officers of fifty of the 131 smaller unions. It was found that more than half of the respondents' unions had some form of merger experience in the past ten years. In about two-thirds of these merger cases (or one third of all respondents), the experiences included unsuccessful merger negotiations. There was a wide variety of unsuccessful merger attempts; five unions tried to amalgamate, three tried to absorb, six tried to be absorbed, and three tried to absorb and be absorbed. There is no reason to believe that less merger activity would be found for the larger unions, though I would expect to see more attempts to amalgamate and absorb and fewer attempts to be absorbed.

Anecdotal evidence and survey data point to a large number of unsuccessful merger attempts. It is quite possible that these cases even outnumber successful mergers. In the later analysis I will examine the reasons for the failure of merger negotiations, and by doing so I will discuss both the urge to merge (the motivation to merge) and the ability to merge (the extent to which barriers are overcome and mergers are consummated). If my analysis were confined solely to successful mergers, as in most empirical and case studies, my view of the merger process would be seriously incomplete.

The preceding sections briefly traced the historical dimensions of national union mergers in the United States. There were discussions of the mergers among the earliest unions, the movement for amalgamations of related trades, the short-lived campaign of the amalgamationists, and the role of the federations in affiliate mergers. I also profiled forms and frequency of union mergers over the past century, and then approximated the incidence of unsuccessful merger efforts. As I develop the model of the merger process in the following chapters, I will be using illustrations from this rich historical background.

Notes

1. Richard I. Kilroy, "Union Mergers and Transportation Labor in the 1980s." Paper presented at the Symposium on Transportation Labor Issues for the 1980s, Villanova University, Villanova,, Penn., May 17, 1982.

2. Edward B. Mittelman, "Trade Unionism (1833–1839)" in John R. Commons et al. (editors), *History of Labor in the United States*, vol. I (New York: Macmillan, 1918), pp. 335–623.

3. Selig Perlman, *A History of Trade Unionism in the United States* (New York: Macmillan, 1922), p. 40.

4. Philip Taft, *The A.F. of L. in the Time of Gompers* (New York: Harper, 1957), p. 2.

5. Norman J. Ware, *The Labor Movement in the United States, 1860–1895* (New York: D. Appleton & Co., 1929), p. 167.

6. Philip Taft, *Organized Labor in American History* (New York: Harper & Row, 1964), p. 58.

7. Theodore W. Glocker, "Amalgamation of Related Trades in American Unions," *American Economic Review* 5 (September 1915):554; Gary M. Fink, *Labor Unions* (Westport, Conn.: Greenwood Press, 1977), p. 325.

8. Lloyd Ulman, *The Rise of the National Trade Union* (Cambridge, Mass.: Harvard University Press, 1955), p. 4.

9. Ware, *op. cit.*, pp. 228–29; J.B. Andrews, "Nationalization, 1860–1877" in John R. Commons et al. (editors), *History of Labor in the United States*, vol. II (New York: Macmillan, 1918), pp. 168–69.

10. Taft, *Organized Labor In American History*, p. 147; Fink, *op. cit.*, p. 222.

11. The major discussion of the amalgamation of unions in related trades is found in Glocker, *op. cit.* In 1915 Glocker defined amalgamations of related trades as unions that "unite only part of the trades in an industry" as opposed to the craft unions (organizations of workers "requiring identical skill and training") or those other unions "claiming jurisdiction over all trades in an industry." Aside from being formed by mergers, amalgamations of related trades were said to also arise from the extension of union jurisdictions (p. 554). In this study I examine the merger route for creating unions of related trades.

12. Glocker, *op. cit.*, p. 555; Ulman, *op. cit.*, p. 324.

13. Ulman, *op. cit.*, p. 322.

14. Glocker, *op. cit.*, p. 560. Reprinted with permission.

15. Ibid., pp. 560–62.

16. For a discussion of federations and alliances as alternatives to amalgamations, see Glocker *op. cit.*, pp. 565–66; and Ulman, *op. cit.*, p. 324.

17. Irving Bernstein, "Union Growth and Structural Cycles" in *Proceedings of the Seventh Annual Meeting of the Industrial Relations Research Association* (Madison, Wis.: Industrial Relations Research Association (IRRA), 1954), p. 219.

18. Taft, *Organized Labor In American History*, p. 463; John T. Dunlop, "Past and Future Tendencies in American Labor Unions," *Daedalus* 107 (1978):81.

19. John T. Dunlop, "Structural Changes in the American Labor Movement and Industrial Relations System" in Richard L. Rowan (editor), *Readings in Labor Economics and Labor Relations*, 3d ed. (Homewood, Ill.: 1976), p. 146.

20. For discussions of the policy of craft autonomy, see Selig Perlman and Philip Taft, *History of Labor in the United States, 1896–1932* (New York: A.M. Kelley, 1966), p. 353; and Taft, *Organized Labor in American History*, p. 463.

21. Taft, *The A.F. of L. in the Time of Gompers*, p. 185.

22. David Brody, *Workers in Industrial America* (New York: Oxford University Press, 1980), p. 80.

23. The resolution was made at the 1899 convention of the AFL. Lewis L. Lorwin, *The American Federation of Labor: History, Politics and Prospects* (Washington, D.C.: Brookings Institution, 1933), p. 67.

24. Ibid., pp. 339–40.

25. Ibid., p. 69.

26. *Idem.* Also see Taft, *Organized Labor in American History*, p. 272.

27. The statement was made in the Scranton Declaration. Lorwin, *op. cit.*, p. 69.

28. Taft, *The A.F. of L. in the Time of Gompers*, p. 197.

29. American Federation of Labor, *Proceedings of the Twenty-fifth Convention, 1905* (Washington, D.C.: AFL, 1905), p. 23.

30. Perlman and Taft, *op. cit.*, pp. 360–61.

31. Ibid., p. 361.

32. *Idem.*

33. Perlman and Taft, *op. cit.*, pp. 359–60; Walter Galenson, *The United Brotherhood of Carpenters: The First Hundred Years* (Cambridge, Mass.: Harvard University Press, 1983), pp. 99–104, 107–12.

34. Leo Wolman, *Ebb and Flow in Trade Unionism* (New York: National Bureau of Economic Research, 1936), pp. 194–97.

35. Taft, *The A.F. of L. in the Time of Gompers*, p. 21. Also see Lorwin, *op. cit.*, p. 343.

36. For discussions of the amalgamationists, see Edward B. Mittelman, "Basis for the American Federation of Labor Opposition to Amalgamation and Politics at Portland," *Journal of Political Economy* 32 (February 1924):86–100; Taft, *A.F. of L. in the Time of Gompers*, pp. 453–56; Lorwin, *op. cit.*, pp. 214–16.

37. The resolutions were opposed in an AFL Executive Council report entitled "Evolution of the Trade Union Movement," which was accepted by unanimous vote. *Report of the Proceedings of the Forty-Third Annual Convention of the American Federation of Labor, 1923*, pp. 37–39, 165, 169, 172, 265–68.

38. Taft, *A.F. of L. in the Time of Gompers*, p. 456

39. *Report of the Proceedings of the Forty-Third Annual Convention of the American Federation of Labor, 1923*, p. 267. The statement continues in an extremely hostile tone:

> In this they [the amalgamationists] serve well the employers who would again assume complete mastery over the destinies of the wage earners. The purpose and aim of the destructionists, as well as their standing within our communities, is no less savory than that of private detectives who would sell the soul of their fellow man for the jingle of gold. In the religious world such men are excommunicated. In the political world such men are ostracized from society, if not treated more severly [sic] through the operation of laws related to treason. In the industrial world we have tolerated them altogether too freely. These sinister agents, propagandists and destructionists of [sic] a foreign foe to our American institutions, should be singled out wherever found and the light of day should be thrown upon their nefarious work. Likewise, employers, frenzied in their blindness for wealth and gold, and who, for a moment find encouragement and hope and give passive if not active support to this and similar movements which seek to distract attention and divide labor's forces, may well hesitate. They should realize that to destroy the evolutionary process of progress, advancement and application of the ideals of democracy and of the golden rule in all relations of mankind is but to hasten revolutionary tendencies with all that these great social revulsions impress so tragically upon mankind. The trade autonomy declarations of the 1901 convention [the Scranton Declaration] are therefor [sic] reaffirmed.

In many ways the amalgamationists were more than just a movement for political action and structural rearrangement. They posed a challenge to basic tenets of the AFL and traditional unionism of that time. For example, Brody (p. 88) noted that in the 1930s: "Industrial unionism was directed only at the mass production industries, not, as the amalgamation movement of the 1920s, *at the entire economy*" (emphasis added). It was recalled that such a strong industrial unionist as John L. Lewis had even opposed the amalgamationists.

40. Lorwin, *op. cit.*, p. 342.

41. This section is derived primarily from Gary N. Chaison, "Federation Expulsions and Union Mergers in the United States," *Relations Industrielles—Industrial Relations* 21 (March 1972):343–61.

42. AFL–CIO, *Proceedings of the AFL–CIO Tenth Constitutional Convention, 1973* (Washington, D.C.: AFL–CIO, 1973), pp. 50, 177–78. It was also argued by the federation that expulsion of the Brewery Workers before it joined the Teamsters would permit some of its locals to secede and return to the federation. Twenty-two Brewery Workers locals with ten thousand members refused to join the Teamsters and became directly chartered locals of the AFL–CIO. Charles Janus, "Union Mergers in the 1970s: A Look at the Reasons and Results," *Monthly Labor Review* 101 (October 1978):20.

43. Arthur J. Goldberg, *AFL–CIO: Labor United* (New York: McGraw-Hill, 1956), pp. 230–31; Chaison, *op. cit.*, p. 344.

44. *AFL–CIO Constitution*, article II, section 8, in Goldberg, *op. cit.*, p. 237. Also see *Agreement for the Merger of the American Federation of Labor and the Congress of Industrial Organizations* (February 19, 1955), section 2(d).

45. AFL, *Proceedings of the Constitutional Convention, 1955* (Washington, D.C.: AFL, 1955), p. 451.

46. "Bigger Unions Will Pack a Bigger Wallop," *Nation's Business* (May 1973):51.

47. The resolution was proposed by five members of the International Chemical Workers Union. AFL–CIO, *Proceedings of the Fourth Constitutional Convention*, vol. 1 (Washington, D.C.: AFL–CIO, 1961), p. 709.

48. *Idem.*

49. AFL–CIO, *Proceedings of the Fifth Constitutional Convention*, vol. 1 (Washington, D.C.: AFL–CIO, 1963), pp. 331–33.

50. AFL–CIO, *Proceedings of the Sixth Constitutional Convention*, vol. 1 (Washington, D.C.: AFL–CIO, 1965), p. 21.

51. *Idem.* Meany's influence on mergers was said to be very strong. Presidents of affiliates indicated that Meany often endorsed merger arrangements and pointed out arguments in support of mergers, though his public stance continued to be one of "relative unawareness." "Heavy Increase in Merger Negotiations," *BNA Daily Labor Report*, April 29, 1975, pp. c1–5.

52. Quoted in James P. Gannon, "Union Mergers: Labor Organizations Show Mounting Interest in Combining Forces," *Wall Street Journal*, March 7, 1968, p. 1.

Over the years, Kirkland made numerous statements favoring mergers of affiliates. For example, when addressing the 1978 convention of the Bakery and Confectionery Workers, Kirkland said:

> There have been a number of union mergers in recent years in fields where members have a deep community of interests. And I know of none that has failed to improve the position of workers involved in organizing, administration, collective bargaining and legislation and political action and all other areas in which unions must engage today.

Proceedings of the Convention of the American Bakery and Confectionery Workers International Union, 1978 (Washington, D.C.: ABCWIU, 1978), p. 484.

At the 1981 convention of the American Federation of Television and Radio Artists, Kirkland stated that merged unions were stronger, more efficient, and better able to serve their members. *BNA Daily Labor Report*, August 3, 1981, p. A1.

53. *AFL–CIO Merger Committee Report* (July 3, 1981), p. 1; *AFL–CIO Merger Committee Report* (February 23, 1983), p. 1. For a resolution encouraging increased merger activity through the services of this committee, see AFL–CIO, *Proceedings of the Fourteenth Constitutional Convention* (Washington, D.C.: AFL–CIO, November 1981), pp. 358–60.

54. Rudy Oswald, "New Directions for American Labor," *The Annals of the American Academy of Political and Social Science* 493 (May 1984):147.

55. "Kirkland Discusses Issues Facing Labor," *AFL–CIO News*, April 6, 1985, p. 2.

56. AFL–CIO Committee on the Evolution of Work, *The Changing Situation of Workers and Their Unions* (Washington, D.C.: AFL–CIO, February 1985), pp. 30–31.

57. Ibid., p. 33.

58. Ibid., pp. 33–34. To be considered as sharing a community of interest with other unions in an industry, the affiliate should have either 20 percent of its members

employed in the industrial category, or its members in that category should constitute at least 20 percent of the AFL–CIO members in that category. Unions meeting one of these criteria will have a presumptive community of interest. Other unions will have an opportunity to demonstrate a community of interest. Where there is no community of interest the AFL–CIO Executive Council reviews the situation before approval of the merger is granted.

59. This section is derived primarily from Gary N. Chaison, "A Note on Union Merger Trends, 1900–1978," *Industrial and Labor Relations Review* 34 (October 1980: 114–20. The tables are revisions and extensions of the tables found in the article and have been reprinted with permission.

60. For descriptions of the sources of the data, see ibid., p. 115.

61. Ibid, p. 118.

62. Larry T. Adams, "Labor Organization Mergers, 1979–1984: Adapting to Change," *Monthly Labor Review* 107 (September 1984):23–24; Leo Troy and Neil Sheflin, "The Flow and Ebb of U.S. Public Sector Unionism," *Government Union Review* 5 (Spring 1984):21–22.

63. Gary N. Chaison, "A Note on the Critical Dimensions of the Union Merger Process," *Relations Industrielles–Industrial Relations* 37 (1982):203–04; Adams, *op. cit.*, p. 26.

64. Ibid., p. 204.

65. Gary N. Chaison, "Union Merger Outcomes: The View From the Smaller Unions," Clark University Graduate School of Management Working Paper No. 85–103 (Worcester, Mass.: Clark University, 1985), pp. 9, 17.

3
The Motivation to Merge

My model of the merger process places the motivating factors in a crucial role as the driving force behind mergers. The ability to overcome merger barriers is a function of not only the height of the barriers but also the relative strength of the motivating forces. Seemingly inconsequential barriers may become formidable when the motivation to merge is weak. Conversely, the highest barriers have been overcome by unions with exceptionally strong motivation. Moreover, we will see that the motivating factors are not always felt in their full force but can be redirected through forms of alliances which serve as merger alternatives.

Contemporary unions seldom disband, but rather the difficulties that may have once finished off a union now act as the motivation to merge.[1] At first glance, the most visible factors would seem to be membership decline and financial difficulty.

Membership Decline and Financial Difficulty

Membership decline and financial difficulty are usually cited as the major causes of union mergers. The case of the dying union moving toward merger was described by one union officer:

> In the most unfortunate situation a union can face, a merger may be the only way to ensure its survival. A dying union that is rapidly losing members because of job loss or defections to other organizations may be forced to seek a merger to continue at all. Its revenue base may be too small to enable it to carry out any of the tasks necessary to represent its members. In this case, a merger is a desperation move.[2]

Decline in membership and financial difficulty are clearly interrelated and operate in a vicious circle. As membership falls for whatever reason, the union's income through dues also declines. Adequate funds can no longer be devoted to organizing because the scarcity of resources forces the union to choose between servicing the present membership or recruiting new members. Unions are basically political organizations, and elected officers tend to direct expenditures toward the present (and voting) members. Organizing staff are soon laid off, organizing drives are abandoned, and the union finds itself unable to reverse the decline in membership. As a consequence, the financial problems are further intensified, additional staff and funding cuts occur, and the cycle of decline continues. While membership decline and financial difficulty are problems that compound each other, the question remains whether they are primary motivating forces behind mergers or common symptoms of other underlying forces.

Union Mergers and Membership Change

General descriptions of union mergers point to a major role for membership loss in the decision to merge. Examples abound of declining membership before merger. In 1948, the Mine, Mill and Smelter Workers had 114,000 members, but this fell to 75,000 twenty years later when it was absorbed by the Steelworkers.[3] The membership of the Hosiery Workers dropped from 50,000 before World War II to 5,000 in 1965, when it was absorbed by the Textile Workers.[4] The membership of the Insurance Workers fell from 24,000 in 1970 to 15,000 in 1983, when it was absorbed by the United Food and Commercial Workers.[5] The National Association of Government Employees' membership fell from 200,000 in 1978 to 100,000 by the end of 1982, when it was absorbed by the Service Employees International Union.[6]

Similarly, the Glass and Ceramic Workers had fallen from 43,000 members in 1972 to 15,000 a decade later when it merged with the Aluminum, Brick and Clay Workers.[7] The Ohio Civil Service Employees lost half of its membership in the 8 years prior to its absorption by the American Federation of State, County and Municipal Employees.[8] Additional examples are found in the preceding chapter's description of the membership losses and subsequent mergers of several unions expelled from federations. While there certainly is a great deal of anecdotal evidence of the role of membership decline, we have to turn to a longitudinal study to determine if we are seeing a characteristic of some, most, or all merging unions.

In 1981, I analyzed the changes in the membership of unions involved in mergers since 1900.[9] After the investigation of several data sources, 142 union mergers were identified: 106 absorptions and 36 amalgamations. It was possible to locate membership figures for most of the merging unions. However, there were methodological problems in comparing membership data, primarily because unions differed in their definition of the "dues-paying member" and in the compilation and timing of membership reports.[10] Accordingly, a decision was made to dichotomize the variable of union growth into the categories of "decrease or no change" and "increase." Membership changes were calculated for five-year periods to provide some recognition of the time lag between the initial attempt to merge and the actual consummation of the merger. It seemed reasonable in most cases that the five-year period prior to the merger would include any membership changes which prompted the merger.

The analysis indicated that about half of the merging unions experienced a decrease or no change in membership five years prior to merger. This was primarily a characteristic of the absorbed or amalgamating unions. Only 28 percent of the absorbing unions had declining or unchanged membership prior to merger. The rates for absorbed or amalgamating unions were 64.4 percent and 60.6 percent, respectively. In light of these figures, it was concluded that there was hardly overwhelming support for any characterization that absorbed or amalgamating unions are "dying" organizations in terms of membership change. More than a third of the absorbed and amalgamating unions had actually grown in the period five years prior to merger.

The analysis also failed to find any significant relationships between membership changes for different types of merging unions. Periods of overall union expansion accounted for 79.9 percent of all merging unions, and 77.9 percent, 77.8 percent, and 85.2 percent of absorbed, absorbing, and amalgamating unions, respectively. It had been suggested that unions most compelled to merge would be those with declining or static membership during periods of overall membership increase. Membership declines would seem most discouraging when unions in general were growing. A union's poor condition might seem less serious in a period of overall union decline. The analysis indicated that the most frequent form of merger was that of a declining amalgamating or absorbed union during periods of increases in overall union membership. However, such cases represented only 46.3 percent and 50.6 percent of the total amalgamating and absorbed unions, respectively. Thus, the suggested relationship appears to be only a frequent rather than a predominant characteristic of mergers.

A major finding of the survey was that absorbed and amalgamating unions often had declining or unchanged premerger membership, while absorbing unions were generally growing prior to merger. But as I already noted, these relationships were far from pervasive; more than a third of the absorbed and amalgamating unions grew prior to merger and more than a quarter of the absorbing unions declined. Furthermore, the other predicted trends in growth and mergers were either not detected or were quite weak when they did appear. The only conclusions I can reach from the data analysis is that membership decline or a static state are common though certainly not predominant characteristics of merging unions.

Financial Difficulties of Merging Unions

A frequently cited reason for merger is the poor financial condition of the involved unions. For example, officers may claim that they are seeking a merger partner because their union lacks funds to pay full-time staff and officers, cannot afford to hold a convention, or is unable to process grievances to arbitration because it cannot cover the legal expenses. As I noted earlier in this chapter, financial difficulty can be both the cause of and result of a declining or static membership.

There are numerous examples of premerger financial difficulty. In the decade prior to its absorption, the Sleeping Car Porters' cash receipts, cash on hand, and assets fell by more than 80 percent.[11] The Stone Workers was operating at a deficit and was forced to lay off staff prior to its merger. Most Stone Workers locals had assets of less than $1,000.[12] The Mine, Mill and Smelter Workers was, in the words of its secretary–treasurer, "pretty broke" before it was absorbed.[13] Before it merged, the Bakery and Confectionery Workers was forced to reduce officers' salaries and other union expenses.[14] The Pulp, Sulphite and Paper Mill Workers faced serious financial problems and had to increase its per capita tax several times before its amalgamation.[15]

While there seem to be many highly visible cases of merging unions with financial problems, it is nevertheless difficult to conclude that this is a widely shared condition of merging unions or that these problems were a prime motivating force behind mergers. First, there is no generally accepted means for evaluating the financial health of a union or comparing the health of one union with that of another.[16] Even if some standards could be agreed upon, important measurement problems would remain. Union accounting practices tend to be seriously deficient and often apply procedures and standards which accountants consider to be unacceptable.[17] Moreover, union financial structures differ significantly in regard to the type and use of assets and investments, the degree of reliance on per capita taxes as a source of income, and the nature of liabilities.

One could always argue that the best sign that a union is in serious financial difficulty is not necessarily the low levels of cash reserves or dues income, but rather the sale of fixed assets, the declining proportion of income from dues, and the inability to increase salaries for officers and staff. A case could also be made that economic adversity should only be guaged in relation to conditions of earlier periods rather than measured in any absolute sense. It could be that some unions, perhaps the smallest ones, have learned to survive and function in a lean state, with an ongoing austerity program and minimal funding for such functions as organizing, research, lobbying, and labor education. Major union activities may be carried out by a devoted corps of volunteers on the local level.

In many cases it could be difficult to find a clear and direct link between the figures in a union treasurer's report and its ability to carry out its activities. As Strauss observed:

Can financial data be used to measure union performance? Company comptrollers make great use (and misuse) of financial analysis to pinpoint inefficiencies within their organizations. Unfortunately, financial analysis is far less useful in evaluating the efficiency of service organizations such as unions, particularly since expenditures measure only input, not output (performance). Moreover, cost efficiency may correlate rather poorly with organizational effectiveness.[18]

In summary, one must be wary of assigning too great a role to financial difficulty in the union's decision to merge. Extreme cases of financial adversity will always be found, particularly among the very small absorbed unions. However, for the remaining unions one would have to determine on a case-by-case basis, first, whether the deterioration in financial condition significantly changed the ability to organize, negotiate, and provide satisfactory levels of representation, and then whether these changes prompted the search for a merger partner.

It would be tempting to first say that many if not most unions merge because they are incapable of growing and/or improving their poor financial health. I could then add the caveat that these conditions are difficult to measure and not universally shared. However, this simplification, though widely found in research on union mergers, creates two problems. First, it leads one to neglect the multitude of factors than can bring about these conditions. In the final analysis, when there is membership decline and financial difficulty, these may not be the true motivating factors but rather symptoms or surface manifestations of other problems leading to union mergers. Second, there may be some important factors which lead to merger but which do not reveal themselves as membership decline and financial difficulty. The following sections explore the underlying motivating forces faced by amalgamating, absorbed, and absorbing unions.

The Motivation to Merge for Absorbed and Amalgamating Unions

Technological Change

Probably the most frequently mentioned motivation for union mergers is the need to reduce the adverse impact of technological change on union growth and financial conditions. Technological change threatens the employment of union members and thus jeopardizes the survival of the union as a representative institution.[19] Mergers are aimed at absorbing the impact of technological change rather than preventing its introduction or continuation. As Coady noted:

> In a number of cases, merger has been recognized as the only course of action offering even a minimum of protection to the officers and members of unions

in industries swept by technology. Accordingly, while the immediate prospects for the remaining members of a dying union may not be dramatically
improved by merger, those members do at least obtain the benefit of a
stronger, more viable and broader based organization attempting to relocate
them in the industrial world. For the merging union itself and its officers, absorption into a larger organization must in some cases be a more encouraging
prospect than final dissolution.[20]

Several writers have documented the connection between technological
change and the propensity to merge; illustrations of the impact of this factor
are certainly not difficult to find.[21] A major example is found in the printing
industry where technological change is said to diminish union bargaining
power by decreasing the skill content of jobs and thus making workers more
easily replaced during strikes.[22] Technological change also blurred the lines
between traditional printing crafts, so unions found themselves in intense
disputes over the right to organize as well as the assignment of work.[23] At the
same time, there developed a large nonunion sector utilizing the new
technology. Employers in this sector strongly resisted union organizing in an
effort to avoid higher wage levels and restrictive work practices. More
employers also began to operate in a national rather than localized market,
and printing locals, which traditionally enjoyed a high degree of autonomy in
negotiations, found it difficult to adjust to the broader based bargaining.[24] As
the bargaining relations and crafts changed in the printing industry, unions
turned toward merger as a means to adapt, with the eventual goal of a single
multicraft union capable of militant organizing and broad-based bargaining.

Boundaries of traditional crafts were also eroded by technological change
in the railroads. For example, new work processes prompted the absorption
of the Transport Communications Employees Union (TCEU) into the Brotherhood of Railway and Airline Clerks (BRAC) in 1969. The two unions once
represented separate crafts, but new jobs were created that combined
elements of the two. A 1966 Supreme Court decision in the Union Pacific
case gave the railroad the right to decide whether TCEU or BRAC members
were given the new jobs. Grievances arose and it appeared to the unions that
the best way to resolve the jurisdictional dispute was through a merger.[25]

Mergers among some of the craft unions in the construction industry
were also motivated by changes in work processes. For example, the loss of
members' craft identities was the principal factor behind the United Weldors
merger into the Operating Engineers in 1969, and the absorption of the
Lathers into the Carpenters in 1979.[26]

In conclusion, technological change has had a substantial impact on the
"job territories" of craft unions. New work processes threatened the institutional survival of these unions by reducing the employment opportunities of
members, creating possibilities for union rivalry, and placing unions at a disadvantage in bargaining. The shrinking membership base and competitive

organizing often resulted in membership declines and financial difficulties. When faced with these problems smaller unions often sought to be absorbed into the larger unions against which they had been unable to compete for members. On the other hand, amalgamations tended to be among unions facing similar dilemmas and which were of comparable size, in neighboring jurisdictions, and in industries such as printing where constant technological change had erased many of the distinctions between crafts by creating new jobs which crossed craft boundaries.

Narrow or Overlapping Jurisdictions

The historical review in chapter 2 mentioned that early unions tended to adopt narrow organizing jurisdictions and that in the years of rivalry between the AFL and the CIO there emerged numerous affiliates with overlapping jurisdictions. A prerequisite to the merger of the federations was agreement that unions could join the new federation with their jurisdictions intact.[27] While there was some encouragement for a merger movement among duplicate and narrowly based unions, the actual number of mergers has generally been considered to be disappointing.[28]

Jurisdictional problems have provided a powerful incentive for union mergers. Some unions found themselves incapable of growing because they were boxed into narrow jurisdictions. Others faced membership declines because they had to share portions of their jurisdiction with several unions. Glocker described the jurisdictional dilemma in his early article on the incidence of amalgamations of related trades:

> When two related trades are organized into separate unions, each demands a careful demarcation of its work and a strict observance of the boundaries thus set. Such a rigid division causes great inconvenience both to employer and employee and in many instances is impractical. If after long negotiation a satisfactory dividing line is fixed, the adoption of new methods of production is apt soon to upset the arrangement. The result is an endless controversy with all the disastrous consequences which follow in the trail of such internal conflicts.[29]

There exists an obvious link between jurisdictional difficulties and technological change. New work processes blur craft lines, forcing unions to share organizing territories and creating jobs which fall under several unions' jurisdictions. Moreover, unions with narrow jurisdictions face an immediate and severe threat because they stake their futures on the continuation of a particular craft or work process, and technological change can dramatically reduce or even eliminate their organizing base. The way out of the crisis brought about by narrow or overlapping jurisdictions, and intensified by technological change, is amalgamation or absorption.

The Lack of Economies of Scale in Union Operations

The inability to attain economies of scale in union operations is said to be a frequent cause of mergers, particularly the absorptions of smaller unions. For example, Dewey noted that an important factor behind mergers was:

> the increasing cost of maintaining a union headquarters and staff. This burden is particularly acute for small, and even medium sized, unions that are expected to provide the same array of services as larger unions—organizing, negotiation guidance, arbitration assistance, research and education programs, strike benefits and lobbying efforts.[30]

Several writers have suggested that unions below some minimum size have difficulty carrying out their representative, organizing, and administrative activities.[31] Smaller unions may not be able to hire full-time staff to combat employers' unfair labor practices,[32] provide educational programs for members and officers,[33] lobby effectively, if at all, or cover their legal expenses.[34] Moreover, the costs of providing the basic services and maintaining a union have increased with inflation.[35] As Coady noted:

> It hardly need be stated that inflation and the rising cost of nearly everything affect unions just as much as they do any other large organization. The result, from the union point of view, is a choice between attempting to increase revenues, on the one hand, and attempting to cut costs without a drop in the quality of services provided, on the other. In the face of this choice, several small unions and some large ones have opted for mergers, thereby reducing administrative inefficiency and duplication, and increasing strength and effectiveness in dealing with employers. While smallness itself may not provide an incentive to merger, the institutional problems which attend smallness almost certainly have and will continue to do so.[36]

Large size is widely seen as an advantage to unions.[37] The point at which a union becomes large enough to achieve significant economies of scale has been increasing because of the greater expense of maintaining a headquarters and paying officers and staff, as well as the rising expectations that workers have about the quantity and quality of services that their unions should provide. At present there appears to be a general consensus that many unions with less than 50,000 members are not achieving economies of scale in thier operations.[38]

The United Furniture Workers is a typical union lacking economies of scale. With a membership of 35,000 primarily low-paid workers, the union has a small treasury. It has to spend about half of its income on organizing and is said to have difficulty attracting organizing staff because of relatively low salaries. Its leaders have considered mergers with the Steelworkers and the Carpenters, but reportedly have felt that an absorption might terminate leadership positions and also dilute the militant character of the union.[39]

In depressed industries, such as shoe manufacturing, unions find their membership falling to the point where economies of scale soon becomes a pressing problem. In 1979, the United Shoe Workers, with 27,000 members, merged into the Amalgamated Clothing and Textile Workers Union. The Shoe Workers' general secretary–treasurer stated that foreign imports had severely reduced the employment of his union's membership. It found itself in the position where it could not afford to hire new organizers or lobby effectively against imports.[40]

The lack of economies of scale is frequently related to the other motivating factors. For example, a narrow jurisdiction coupled with declining membership employment caused by technological change may place a union in a position where growth is highly unlikely. The lack of economies of scale soon becomes a pressing problem as the costs of union operations rise and these costs cannot be met with the income from members' dues.

The Need to Increase Bargaining Power

It has almost become traditional for union officers to state that the principal reason for mergers is to increase bargaining power. Officers claim that mergers will lead to the coordination of negotiations and enhance the ability to strike for unions dealing with either the same employer or employers operating in the same or related industries. In smaller unions it is argued that absorption into a large union leads to improved contract negotiations and administration because of economies of scale, the availability of a larger and more specialized staff, and access to a greater strike fund. While many claims may be highly exaggerated and serve primarily to rally membership support for merger, there are some cases where the desire to increase bargaining power figured largely in the reasons for merger.

The need to enhance bargaining power was a major force behind the formation of the Amalgamated Clothing and Textile Workers Union. The first official act of the new union was to declare a boycott against the J.P. Stevens Company, an employer against whom the predecessor unions had fought in a long and bitter dispute. The amalgamation created a vertically integrated union with presumably increased leverage in negotiations and the possibility of effective strike or boycott action. Workers producing fabric and those converting fabric into clothing would now belong to the same union.[41]

Negotiating and striking ability also played a prominent role in the efforts for a merger between the American Federation of Television and Radio Artists and the Screen Actors Guild. The two unions struck together in 1980 against the movie industry and there was a possibility that one union might ratify the new contract while the other rejected it. As a result, one union's members would have to cross the other's picket lines. This was complicated by the fact that about 40 percent of the SAG members were also in AFTRA.

While the two unions have discussed merger on several occasions since 1940, the first major steps toward an eventual merger were made in 1981, when they established joint bargaining structures and simultaneous contract ratification procedures.[42]

In a later chapter I will examine the question of whether mergers actually increase bargaining power and striking ability. At this point, note that these factors act as major motivating forces primarily when potential merger partners deal with the same employer(s) or operate in the same or neighboring industries. However, it should also be recognized that in practically all mergers, officers claim that there is some significant link between merger and enhanced bargaining power. Often, this is done to sell the merger by assuring the membership that it is in keeping with the primary goals of the union and will directly benefit them.

Merger, Reorganization, or Diversification by Employers

Employer mergers, reorganizations, and diversifications have created pressures for union mergers when unions felt that these employer actions placed them at a disadvantage in collective bargaining and organizing. Major examples are found in the railroad and printing industries.

In the railroad industry, the large number of company mergers in the past twenty years, along with technological change and the general decline in the industry, resulted in a 60 percent drop in employment and substantial union membership loss. These were the primary motivating forces behind the merger of four unions to form the United Transportation Union in 1969[43] as well as the absorption of the Railway and Airline Supervisors into the Brotherhood of Railway and Airline Clerks in 1980.[44]

It was mentioned in an earlier section of this chapter that employer reorganization and the development of a substantial nonunion sector in the printing industry caused a number of union mergers. As employer resistance to unionization grew and organizing became more difficult in the restructured industry, unions sought mergers to restore their countervailing power.[45] It was believed that larger unions, perhaps eventually a single unified printing union, would be better able to coordinate bargaining, end wasteful jurisdictional disputes, and launch major organizing campaigns. In printing, changes in employer structures seemed to necessitate changes in union structures.

The transformation of an industry has been identified as a motivating force behind mergers. For example, the absorption of the United Packinghouse, Food and Allied Workers into the Amalgamated Meat Cutters and Butcher Workmen in 1968 was largely in reaction to the changing character of their principal industry. Several meat-packing companies were taken over by conglomerates, while at the same time major meat packers began to decrease the size of production facilities and move many operations to rural areas. Small, nonunion companies began to capture an increasing share of the market. The merging unions were also concerned about a trend toward the centralization of meat-cutting operations by food chains and the subsequent elimination of the jobs of butchers in retail stores.[46] Merger was seen as a way to adjust to these new developments and reduce the difficulties in coordinating bargaining and organizing efforts.

Employer mergers were behind the absorption of the International Jewelry Workers by the Service Employees International Union in 1980. It was believed that the absorption would enhance the union's ability to negotiate and organize in an industry where small jewelry firms had been taken over by conglomerates.[47]

Employer diversification was cited as a reason for starting merger negotiations between the Paper Workers and the Oil, Chemical and Atomic Workers in 1980. There were many common employers in the two unions' primary jurisdictions; one study indicated that fifty-four companies negotiated with both unions. The unions' officers concluded that it was only sensible for their organizations to work together, reduce the number of field representatives, and coordinate collective bargaining.[48]

A final example of the impact of changing employer operations is the Barbers and Beauticians and Allied Industries International Association's absorption by the United Food and Commercial Workers in 1980. A main reason for the merger was the former's inability to organize chain beauty shops and barber shops that were starting to replace independent shops. The United Food and Commercial Workers already represented employees in the malls and department stores where the new beauty and barber shops are located.[49]

Employer mergers, reorganizations, and diversifications appear to be closely related to other motivating factors. My examples show that changes in employer structure threaten unions' ability to effectively organize and bargain, and also intensify the difficulties associated with narrow or overlapping jurisdiction or the lack of economies of scale in union operations. It appears that changes on the employer's side do not directly lead to a union seeking a merger but do intensify the impact of the other motivating factors.

Protection against Raids

It was mentioned earlier that AFL–CIO affiliates are bound by the federation's no-raid agreement and are required to refrain from raiding (attempting to attain the representation rights to each other's members). Article XX (Settlement of Internal Disputes) of the AFL–CIO Constitution states:

> Each affiliate shall respect the established collective bargaining relationship of every other affiliate. No affiliate shall organize or attempt to represent employees as to whom an established collective bargaining relationship exists with any other affiliate.[50]

If an affiliate claims that there is a violation of this section, the federation attempts to mediate the dispute. If this fails, a hearing is held before an impartial umpire, who is empowered to make a determination. An affiliate that is adversely affected by such a determination may appeal to a subcommittee of the AFL–CIO Executive Council. If an appeal is not filed, or is filed and rejected, and the affiliate does not comply with the determination, it may then be denied use of federation facilities and services, may lose any protection under federation policies and provisions (for example, the protection of the no-raid agreement), and may also be expelled.[51]

Affiliated unions remain free to raid nonaffiliates, and vice versa, unless they enter into their own individually negotiated no-raid agreements. Some unions, particularly those outside of the federations, have reacted to heavy raiding by seeking a merger partner. In the historical review in chapter 2, there was a description of the raiding campaigns frequently launched against unions expelled from federations because of communist domination, leadership corruption, or dual unionism. In reaction to their vulnerable condition, most of the expelled unions sought the protection of absorption into other more powerful expelled unions or into affiliates operating in their jurisdiction. This latter alternative could only occur after the expelled union had rid itself of its communist or corrupt leadership or had left its dual federation.[52]

Protection against raids was also behind several recent mergers. A major example is the absorption of the Civil Service Employees Association of New York State (CSEA) into the American Federation of State, County and Municipal Employees (AFSCME) in 1978. As a large unaffiliated public sector union, the CSEA faced intense raiding from AFL–CIO affiliates. A short time before signing the merger agreement, the CSEA had lost a raid from the Public Employees Federation, an organization composed of the New York State United Teachers and the Service Employees International Union (SEIU). The raided bargaining unit consisted of 45,500 professional, scientific, and technical employees. As soon as the CSEA became part of AFSCME, it was protected against raids from the SEIU and other affiliates because it was covered by the AFL–CIO no-raid agreement.[53]

The need for protection against raids was also the principal consideration in the absorption of the unaffiliated National Association of Government Employees and the affiliated Service Employees International Union. The two unions were often rivals in organizing federal employees. The SEIU's president remarked: "The merger strengthens both unions and brings to a halt the debilitating raiding between NAGE, SEIU and other AFL-CIO unions."[54]

The size, potential wealth, and unaffiliated status of many state-level public sector unions seem to have made them particularly vulnerable to raids. For example, in 1983, legislation was passed in California permitting agency shop provisions in public sector collective agreements. Under the agency shop, all employees in bargaining units are either required to pay dues to the union that represents them if they decide to join it, or pay an agency fee if they decide not to join it. The possibility of receiving these substantial funds did not go unnoticed by several organizing unions. The fifty-thousand-member California State Employees Association faced severe raiding, so rather than concentrate its efforts and resources on defensive actions, it decided to merge into an AFL–CIO affiliate. It considered merger proposals from AFSCME, the Communications Workers of America, the United Automobile Workers, and the SEIU. In 1984, it merged into SEIU. It was predicted that without the merger, the California State Employees Association would have had to spend about $2 million to defend its bargaining unit. At the time of the merger, the union's president said it will "no longer have to divert precious resources to fight off other unions."[55]

Other Motivating Factors

In addition to those factors just described, there are three conditions, though of lesser importance, that motivate unions to merge.

Reunification after Schism. Among some earlier unions, schisms occurred because of philosophical or personal differences between leaders, or animosity between skilled and less skilled members. These divisions often ended with reunification through amalgamation when the dispute was resolved or when the seceding group found it too difficult to survive on its own. For example, in 1903, a merger reunited the two teamster unions after a schism in 1902.[56] In 1900, an amalgamation, mediated by the AFL, provided for the reunification of the painters unions after a six-year separation.[57]

Influencing the Terms of Future Mergers. There are instances when a union may enter into a merger primarily to affect the terms of future mergers. For example, it is believed that the Bakery and Confectionery Workers' (BC) absorption into the Teamsters in 1968 was used as a tactic by the former to gain some leverage in its merger negotiations with the American Bakery and Confectionery Workers (ABC), an AFL–CIO rival. Shortly after the BC merged into the Teamsters as an autonomous division, it started intensive merger negotiations with the ABC. A year later the ties with the Teamsters were severed and the two bakery unions amalgamated.[58]

The Continued Employment and Increased Compensation of the Officers of a Dying Union. It has been argued by Brooks and Gamm that officers of unions faced by severe membership decline and financial adversity see absorption as a far better alternative than the disbandment of their union. "Merger into a larger union guarantees the officers and staff continued employment, almost always at more favorable terms than in the original unions."[59] Northrup also observed: "When large unions absorb smaller ones, they provide guaranteed employment and pensions for the officers of the absorbed union at a higher rate than they were receiving."[60] Certainly, future employment and compensation possibilities are an important consideration in the decision to merge into a union, to merge with one particular union as opposed to another, or to finally accept a merger offer after other motivating factors have been salient for a long time. It is doubtful, however, that officers' interests are a prime factor in the initial urge to merge; rather, they probably intensify the force of other factors. We will see in the next chapter that the personal employment goals of officers are more often a barrier to merger than a motivating factor. It is much easier for dissatisfied officers to block a merger than for officers attracted to a lucrative postmerger deal to push a merger through in the absence of other motivating factors.

The Motivation to Merge for Absorbing Unions

The motivating factors described thus far relate to unions considering the possibility of being absorbed or entering into amalgamations. In the case of the *absorbing* union, the merger is often motivated by the need for growth and diversification.

There have been numerous recent critiques of American labor unions' desire and ability to recruit new members. Faced with a declining proportion of the labor force that is organized, unions often seem unable to launch large scale, coordinated organizing campaigns. The decline in success rates in the certification elections through which unions gain bargaining rights is continuing with apparently little chance of a major reversal.[61] Craft and Extejt claim that:

> Unions have traditionally been rather unclear and imprecise on organizing priorities in terms of long range opportunities or goals. . . . It would appear that unions do little hard assessment of organizing activity to better determine how to invest resources for the biggest payoff to the union in terms of its objectives.[62]

Most unions carry out the organizing function in a decentralized way, directing their efforts at individual work groups. There is an emphasis on proselytizing, on face-to-face communication with workers to convince them of the benefits of unionism.[63] This traditional form of organizing is time consuming and expensive, calling for the investment of considerable human and financial resources for incremental gains in membership. For some unions a much faster and less expensive alternative is absorbing small unions, literally "organizing unions" rather than organizing workers.[64] This strategy can also be used to expand an organizing jurisdiction. The absorbing union selects some occupational groupings related to that of its present membership. It then seeks to absorb unions already in those fields in order to gain a foothold in the jurisdiction as well as staff and officers experienced in representing those workers.[65]

One of the earliest unions to use absorption to widen a jurisdiction was the Painters. Formed in 1887, the union initially represented painters but over the years it expanded to cover all workers in the painting, paper hanging, and decorative arts trade. In its early years it absorbed a number of small unaffiliated unions, including the United Scenic Artists, the National Paperhangers Association, and the National Union of Sign Painters. In 1915, it absorbed the Amalgamated Glass Workers International Association, a small union of stained and decorative glass workers. During the 1930s, the Painters began organizing workers involved in paint and varnish manufacturing, and linoleum, carpet, and soft tile laying.[66]

The United Steelworkers of America provides a recent example of a major union using absorptions for diversification. The Steelworkers' jurisdiction has taken on a conglomerate form as the union reacted to the expanding employer operations by absorbing unions with members in such industries as chemicals, metals, mining, and stone cutting.[67] This diversification through merger was much faster than the organization of new members and for a time served as an important means for the union's growth.[68] The Steelworkers' financial resources made it attractive to unions seeking to be absorbed; it is usually able to offer generous salaries and pensions to the officers and staff of the absorbed unions.[69]

Between 1965 and 1974, the Steelworkers' membership increased by about 25 percent and it is estimated that about three-quarters of these new members were gained from absorbed unions.[70] At one point in the mid-1970s, the secretary–treasurer of the Steelworkers claimed that his union could double its size by merging with other unions in its jurisdiction.[71] The Steelworkers suffered severe membership losses from 1978 to 1984, primarily because of the declining steel industry, and in 1984, a Committee on the Future Directions of the Union recommended that it add new members by absorbing unions. The committee went so far as to list 20 AFL–CIO affiliates with fewer than 100,000 members apiece that could be potential merger partners.[72]

The mergers of the Laborers International Union provide another recent example of diversification through absorption. The union's president stated that his union had absorbed the Stone Cutters to "provide an organizational base" in that industry, and had absorbed the Mail Handlers as a first step toward "massive organizing activity for the federal, city and state employees."[73] While the major organizing campaigns in the new jurisdictions did not fully materialize because of the lack of funds, the Laborers did find that the absorptions saved considerable time and effort in establishing and staffing new divisions within their union for workers in diverse industries.[74]

In conclusion, absorbing unions find that mergers can provide a fast and relatively inexpensive means for union growth and a particularly effective strategy for diversification. Absorbing unions gain instant members along with the staff and local structures needed for continued representation and possible future organizing. However, it should be recognized that absorption results in individual rather than aggregate union growth. New union members are not organized; members are merely transferred from one organization to another. New growth will occur only if the absorbing union, after achieving a foothold in a new jurisdiction, then decides to exploit this situation and organize additional workers. Such membership gains were not apparent for the Steelworkers and the Laborers, but this was because attention and resources had to be redirected to pressing organizing and negotiating problems in their principal jurisdictions.

An Overview of the Motivating Factors

What can we conclude about the reasons for union mergers? First, it would appear that membership decline and financial hardship are symptoms of motivating factors, and relate more to absorbed and amalgamating unions than to absorbing ones. Membership decline and financial hardship are clearly interrelated and tend to compound each other. They can be difficult to measure in either absolute or relative terms and are not universally shared by merging unions. It is only by looking beyond these two surface characteristics that we see the primary forces that motivate unions to merge.

Second, there appear to be distinct differences between the motivation to merge for absorbed and amalgamating unions on the one hand, and for absorbing unions on the other. Unions absorb primarily for aggrandizement, quick membership gain, and jurisdictional diversification. In contrast, most unions seek to be absorbed or amalgamate with each other for purposes of institutional survival in the face of technological change, narrow or overlapping jurisdictions, the lack of economies of scale, and bargaining difficulties. This is not to say that survival is not behind the mergers of absorbing unions; rather these unions pursue mergers as part of a long-term survival strategy, a recognition of the need for greater size, and a wider membership base. Absorbed and amalgamating unions are reacting more to an immediate need.

Third, most mergers are probably caused by combinations of factors, some contributing to or intensifying others, and some developing from a common source. For example, in one case technological change can simultaneously alter the work of a union's membership, create overlapping jurisdictions with other unions, lead to raiding campaigns and other jurisdictional disputes, and eventually cause membership decline and financial adversity. For another union, overlapping jurisdictions and technological change may merely limit the potential for growth, but as the cost of union operations rises, this can result in a lack of economies of scale. In still another instance, technological change and a narrow jurisdiction combined with employer diversification can place a union at a substantial disadvantage in organizing and negotiating. In these examples it is the combined force of the motivating factors that drives a union to seek possible merger partners. However, whether or not a merger actually occurs also depends on the strength of the merger barriers, which is discussed in the next chapter, and the presence of merger alternatives, as reviewed in the following section.

Alliances as Merger Alternatives

At this point in the development of the model it is important to recognize that there are alliances between unions which may act as merger alternatives by satisfying the motivation to merge. For some unions, the drive to merge can be rechanneled through institutional arrangements which are more easily entered into and require less of an organizational change than mergers.

In a sense, membership in a federation can alleviate some of the pressures for merger by protecting affiliates from raids, assisting in the coordination of bargaining, and providing services such as research and lobbying, which smaller unions might not be able to afford on their own.[75] Various interunion arrangements also reduce the need to merge. Among such arrangements are no-raid agreements, coordinated organizing campaigns,[76] and forms of coalition bargaining where a group of unions "bargain with a multi-plant, multi-union employer on a joint basis."[77] However, it is in the self-governing and multipurpose alliances that unions devise a structure specifically to resolve problems that might otherwise force them to seek a merger partner.

Although many contemporary studies of union mergers devote little if any attention to alliances,[78] their role was clearly outlined by Glocker seventy years ago in his study of amalgamations of related trades.[79] Unions in related craft jurisdictions had to decide on an appropriate structure for joining together.

> Should the government by which . . . related trades are organized be a centralized amalgamation practically identical to that of the national craft unions which it replaces or should it be a loose alliance or federation in which the national craft unions continue to retain their existence?[80]

Glocker reviewed the various stages of union cooperation, from the least to the most formal, and suggested that "higher stages of efficiency" are reached in alliances "when government machinery is provided to carry out the terms of the agreement"[81] for cooperative action as opposed to those situations when there is only an agreement for joint action, such as arrangements for the coordination of strikes.

More recently, Dewey suggested a direct relationship between alliances and mergers. In her chronicle of merger activity from 1956 to 1971, she showed that several unions entered into bargaining or organizing alliances specifically to resolve those pressing problems that might otherwise have forced a merger. Some unions hoped that the urge to merge would be relieved permanently while others used an alliance as a first step toward an eventual amalgamation.[82]

The complex causal relationships between alliances and mergers is illustrated by the case of the Stone, Glass and Clay Coordinating Committee (SGCCC). In 1961, this alliance was formed among nine national unions to deal with issues of mutual concern in their industry, primarily to study and lobby regarding restrictions on imports and the banning of nonreturnable bottles.[83] In the later 1960s the president of the Glass Bottle Blowers suggested the SGCCC members explore the possibility of a merger; in 1968, with the encouragement of AFL–CIO, a meeting of interested unions was held. The sessions were chaired by federation officers.[84] In 1970, a tentative merger agreement was entered into by six SGCCC members: the United Stone and Allied Product Workers; the International Brotherhood of Pottery and Allied Workers; the Glass Bottle Blowers Association; the Cement, Lime and Gypsum Workers International Union; the United Glass and Ceramic Workers; and the Window Glass Cutters League of America.[85] Some mergers did eventually occur but not in the form of the broad amalgamation first envisioned by the AFL–CIO and many of the alliance's unions. In January 1971, the United Stone and Allied Product Workers was absorbed by the Steelworkers. Four years later two other SGCCC unions merged: the Window Glass Cutters League was absorbed by the Glass Bottle Blowers Association. In 1976, the Pottery and Allied Workers was absorbed by the Seafarers International Union but this was dissolved when it failed to produce the organizing gains that the unions had expected.[86]

The SGCCC was formed primarily for lobbying purposes but the member unions and the AFL–CIO hoped that participation in the alliance would build sufficient trust for an amalgamation of the numerous unions operating in the stone, glass, and clay industry. In other instances, alliances have been created to lessen the desire to merge. A recent example of this is the coalition formed among some smaller (less than 50,000 members) affiliates of the AFL–CIO. In 1980, it was reported that officers of these unions believed that they lacked sufficient influence in the federation's policy-making. They also claimed that they faced serious problems as employee representatives because of their poor financial condition. Most of these unions were opposed to mergers and felt that an alliance would increase their influence with the federation and enable them to reach economies of scale in operations.[87] In effect, these smaller unions used an alliance in order to achieve the benefits of larger size without having to alter their structures to the degree that might be called for in an amalgamation or absorption.

In our merger model, alliances can either lead to or away from mergers. They can be devised as alternatives to merger in the hope that organizing, bargaining, or economies-of-scale problems can be resolved through structural arrangements that do not threaten the independence of participating unions. Alternatively, alliances can be used to demonstrate the mutuality of interests of the member unions and build the trust needed for the subsequent negotiation of a merger.[88]

Conclusions

In this chapter I have reviewed the factors motivating union mergers. It was seen that membership loss and financial difficulty are primarily symptoms of motivating factors. The desire to amalgamate or be absorbed can be the result of:

Technological change

Narrow or overlapping jurisdictions

A lack of economies of scale in union operations

The need to increase bargaining power

Employer merger, reorganization, and diversification

The need for protection against raids.

Factors of less importance are the attempts to (1) unify a union after schism, (2) influence the terms of a future merger, and (3) continue the employment and raise the compensation of the officers of dying unions.

Absorbing unions are motivated by the need for union growth and diversification. The merger is part of an organizing strategy directed at long-term institutional survival, in contrast to the more immediate survival needs behind amalgamations and absorptions.

It was shown that union alliances can serve as either a prelude to or an alternative to mergers. Some may smooth the way toward merger by building trust between union officers and members while others may satisfy the motivating forces which might otherwise have led to the search for a merger partner.

There are three elements that interact with each other in the premerger period. This chapter described the first two—the motivational forces pushing a union toward merger and the alliances which can serve as alternatives or preludes to merger. The next chapter examines the third element, the force created by the barriers to merger.

Notes

1. George W. Brooks and Sara Gamm, "The Causes and Effects of Union Mergers with Special Reference to Selected Cases in the 60's and 70's" (Washington, D.C.: U.S. Department of Labor, Labor Management Services Administration, September 1976), p. a3.

2. Richard L. Kilroy, "Union Mergers and Transportation Labor in the 1980s" (paper presented at the Symposium on Transportation Labor Issues for the 1980s, Villanova University, Villanova, Penn., May 17, 1982), p. 207. Reprinted with permission.

3. Gideon Chitayat, *Trade Union Mergers and Labor Conglomerates* (New York: Praeger, 1979), p. 44; Lucretia M. Dewey, "Union Merger Pace Quickens," *Monthly Labor Review* 94 (June 1971):70.

4. "Steps Toward Union Mergers," *Monthly Labor Review* 90 (March 1967):iii.

5. Larry T. Adams, "Labor Organization Mergers, 1979–1984: Adapting to Change," *Monthly Labor Review* 107 (September 1984):22.

6. Ibid., p. 24.

7. Ibid., p. 25.

8. Ibid., pp. 24–25.

9. Gary N. Chaison, "Union Growth and Union Mergers," *Industrial Relations* 20 (Winter 1981):98–108.

10. Ibid., pp. 100–1. For a discussion of the problems encountered in the collection and comparison of union membership data, see Gary N. Chaison, 'A Note on the Limitations of Union Membership Data," *Industrial Relations* 23 (Winter 1984): 113–18.

11. This information is contained in the LM2 Reports of the Brotherhood of Sleeping Car Porters on file at the U.S. Department of Labor.

12. Michael A. Coady, "Trade Union Mergers and Their Significance in the Canadian Union Movement" (Toronto: unpublished LL.M. dissertation, Osgood Hall Law School, 1976), p. 54.

13. Ibid., pp. 44–45.

14. Chitayat, *op. cit.*, p. 100.

15. Ibid., p. 115.

16. Leo Troy, "American Unions and Their Wealth," *Industrial Relations* 14 (May 1975):134–44; Elisabeth Allison, "Financial Analysis of the Local Union," *Industrial Relations* 14 (May 1975):145–55. A recent discussion of the financial position of the labor movement is found in Neil Sheflin and Leo Troy, "Finances of American Unions in the 1970s," *Journal of Labor Research* 4 (Spring 1983):149–58.

17. Ronnie Jon Burrows, "Accounting and Reporting Practices of National Labor Unions" (University Park: unpublished Ph.D. dissertation, Pennsylvania State University, May 1980).

18. George Strauss, "Introduction: Symposium—Union Financial Data," *Industrial Relations* 14 (May 1975):132. Reprinted with permission.

19. Coady, *op. cit.*, pp. 39–44.

20. Ibid., p. 43. Reprinted with permission.

21. For example, see: Adams, *op. cit.*, p. 25; Coady, *op. cit.*, pp. 39–47; Patrick Elias, "Trade Union Amalgamations: Patterns and Procedures," *Industrial Law Journal* (September 1973):125–26; Harry Graham, "Union Mergers," *Relations Indus-*

trielles—Industrial Relations 25 (1970):553; A.H. Raskin, "What Happened to Labors' Merger Movement?" *Challenge* 14 (September–October 1965):26–29. For a view that technological change accounts for relatively few union mergers, see Brooks and Gamm, *op. cit.*, p. a56.

22. "Text of Lithographers President Brown's Address to Atlanta Merger Information Conference: July 17, 1971," *The International Bookbinder* (July–August 1971):3.

23. Adams, *op. cit.*, p. 26; Louise D. Walsh, "A Study of the Proposed Merger of the International Typographical Union and the Newspaper Guild: 1974–1983" (Ithaca, N.Y.: unpublished M.S. thesis, Cornell University, January 1985), pp. 66–73; Michael Wallace, "Responding to Technological Change in the Newspaper Industry: A Comparison of the United States, Great Britain, and the Federal Republic of Germany" in *Thirty-seventh Annual Proceedings of the Industrial Relations Research Association* (Madison, Wis.: IRRA, 1985), pp. 326–28.

24. Brooks and Gamm, *op. cit.*, p. 20. The changing nature of the industry was reviewed by a vice president of the International Typographical Union in "Allan J. Heritage Presents Case for Merger in his Address to International Mailers Union Convention," *Typographical Journal* 73 (September 1978):6.

25. Kilroy, *op. cit.*, pp. 209–10.

26. "Developments in Industrial Relations," *Monthly Labor Review* 102 (October 1979):73.

27. *Agreement for the Merger of the American Federation of Labor and the Congress of Industrial Organizations* (February 9, 1955), Sections 2(c)–(d).

28. Dewey, *op. cit.*, p. 63.

29. Theodore W. Glocker, "Amalgamation of Related Trades in American Unions," *American Economic Review* 5 (September 1915):56–62. Reprinted with permission.

30. Dewey, *op. cit.*, p. 64. Bok and Dunlop stated: "The problem of achieving economies of scale applies to international unions as well as local units. The membership must be large enough to permit the bulk of the locals to achieve a size that will support the necessary number of full-time officials. The union must also be large enough to finance a field staff that can give adequate support and service to all its locals. In addition, its headquarters must be able to maintain a group of specialists with experts in legal matters, education organizing, research, and so forth." Derek C. Bok and John T. Dunlop, *Labor and the American Community* (New York: Simon and Schuster, 1970, p. 55).

31. For example, see Chitayat, *op. cit.*, pp. 7–8; Herbert R. Northrup, "Reflections on Bargaining Structure Change" in *Proceedings of the Twenty-Sixth Annual Meeting of the Industrial Relations Research Association, 1973* (Madison, Wis.: IRRA, 1974), pp. 137–38; J. David Edelstein and Malcolm Warner, *Comparative Union Democracy: Organization and Opposition in British and American Unions* (New York: Halsted Press, 1976), p. 347, Bok and Dunlop, *Labor and the American Community*, p. 155.

32. Charles J. Janus, "Union Mergers in the 1970s: A Look at the Reasons and Results," *Monthly Labor Review* 101 (October 1978):14.

33. Kilroy, *op. cit.*, pp. 205–06.

34. Ibid., p. 207.

35. Philip Taft, "Internal Union Structure and Functions" in Gerald G. Somers (editor), *The Next Twenty-Five Years of Industrial Relations* (Madison, Wis.: Industrial Relations Research Association, 1973), pp. 1–2.

36. Coady, *op. cit.*, p. 25. Reprinted with permission.

37. Elias, *op. cit.*, p. 125.

38. For example, see A.H. Raskin, "Changes That are Spurring Labor Union Merger Talks," *New York Times*, August 16, 1977, p. D5; Philip Shabecoff, "Big Labor, Little Labor," *New York Times*, May 11, 1980, p. 19.

39. William Serrin, "Transplanted Union Tries to Survive," *New York Times*, March 27, 1984, p. A14.

40. "Merger is Voted," *The United Shoe Worker* 23 (January–February 1979):3.

41. "A Labor Merger Aimed at the South," *Business Week* (February 23, 1976): 29. Also see "The All Out Campaign Against J.P. Stevens," *Business Week* (June 14, 1976):28–29.

42. Aljean Harmetz, "Two Actors Unions Edging Toward Merger," *New York Times*, September 8, 1981, p. C7; Chester L. Migden, "Looking Toward Merger," *Screen Actor* (Winter 1980–1981):48; "Forging a Future," *Screen Actor* (Winter 1980–1981):43.

43. Brooks and Gamm, *op. cit.*, p. d5.

44. "Developments in Industrial Relations," *Monthly Labor Review* 103 (September 1980):61.

45. Brooks and Gamm, *op. cit.*, p. 90.

46. Dewey, *op. cit.*, pp. 65–66.

47. "Jewelry Workers Union Votes Merger with Service Employees," *Daily Labor Report*, May 9, 1980, p. A2.

48. "Paper and Oil Unions Talk Conglomeration," *Business Week* (May 26, 1980):52–53.

49. "Developments in Industrial Relations," *Monthly Labor Review* 103 (March 1980):57; Adams, *op. cit.*, p. 22.

50. *Constitution of the American Federation of Labor and Congress of Industrial Organizations*, article XX, section 2.

51. Ibid., article XX.

52. Gary N. Chaison, "Federation Expulsions and Union Mergers in the United States," *Relations Industrielles—Industrial Relations* 21 (March 1972):343–61. The unaffiliated Allied and Technical Workers also sought absorption into the Steelworkers as a means to gain protection against raids from affiliates. Coady, *op. cit.*, p. 68.

53. Janus, *op. cit.*, p. 21; Joseph C. Goulden, *Jerry Wurf: Labors' Last Angry Man* (New York: Atheneum, 1982), p. 286.

54. John J. Sweeney as quoted in "Merger of NAGE, Service Employees," *Labor Relations Reporter* (December 20, 1982):312. Also see "NAGE to Affiliate with SEIU, Become Part of AFL–CIO," *Government Employee Relations Report* (December 6, 1982):5; "Service Employees and NAGE Merge, Forming Union of 780,000 Members," *Governmeent Employee Relations Report* (December 27, 1982):8–9.

55. Adams, *op. cit.*, p. 24; "CSEA, Nation's Premier Independent Union Affiliates with SEIU," *Service Employee* 43 (February 1984):3. Protection against raiding was also a factor in the absorption of the Ohio Civil Service Employees Association into the American Federation of State, County and Municipal Employees. Prior to the merger, the OCSEA has faced a rival organizing campaign from an alliance of the Council of Public Workers and the Communication Workers of America. "AFSCME and OCEA Finish Process of Affiliation," *Government Employee Relations Report*

(June 6, 1983):1191. Also see Leo Troy and Neil Sheflin, "The Flow and Ebb of U.S. Public Sector Unionism," *Government Union Review* 5 (Spring 1984):47.

56. Gary M. Fink (ed.), *Labor Unions* (Westport, Conn.: Greenwood Press, 1977), p. 370.

57. Ibid., p. 272.

58. Chitayat, *op. cit.*, p. 94; Dewey, *op. cit.*, p. 66.

59. Brooks and Gamm, *op. cit.*, p. A23.

60. Northrup, *op. cit.*, p. 138.

61. For example, see Joseph B. Rose and Gary N. Chaison, "The State of the Unions: United States and Canada," *Journal of Labor Research* 6 (Winter 1985): 97–111.

62.

63. James A. Craft and Marian M. Extejt, "New Strategies in Union Organizing," *Journal of Labor Research* 4 (Winter 1983):30; Charles B. Craver, "The Current and Future Status of Labor Organizations," *Labor Law Journal* 36 (April 4, 1985):216.

64. Gideon Chitayat, "Mergers of Trade Unions" (Philadelphia: unpublished Ph.D. dissertation, University of Pennsylvania, 1975), p. 223.

65. Bok and Dunlop, *op. cit.*, p. 157. Also see Brooks and Gamm, *op. cit.*, p. A9; Adams, *op. cit.*, p. 26.

66. Fink, *op. cit.*, p. 273.

67. Chitayat, *Trade Union Mergers*, p. 12. A recent review of the state of the Steelworkers emphasized the diversity of the union's present jurisdiction and concluded that the Steelworkers "should explicitly define its jurisdiction to embrace *any* unorganized workers *anywhere* in the Western Hemisphere." United Steelworkers of America, *Forging a Future: Report of the Convention Committee on the Future Directions of the Union, 22nd Constitutional Convention* (1984), pp. 14–15.

68. Ibid., p. 24.

69. Brooks and Gamm, *op. cit.*, p. a63.

70. Chitayat, *Trade Union Mergers*, p. 130. Also see Brooks and Gamm, *op. cit.*, p. e1.

71. Coady, *op. cit.*, p. 24.

72. United Steelworkers of America, "Forging a Future," pp. 20–23.

73. Chitayat, *Trade Union Mergers*, p. 82.

74. Ibid., p. 87.

75. For example, A.H. Raskin has argued that "the security engendered by the keep-out arrangement [the AFL–CIO no-raid agreement] has reinforced the determination of tired and aging leaders to shun mergers or any other change that would cut short their tenure." Raskin, *op. cit.*, p. 28.

76. Descriptions of these interunion arrangements are found in: John T. Dunlop, "Structural Changes in the American Labor Movement and Industrial Relations System" in *Proceedings of the Ninth Annual Meeting of the Industrial Relations Research Association* (Madison, Wis.: IRRA, 1956), pp. 16–20; Marten S. Estey, "The Strategic Alliance as a Factor in Union Growth," *Industrial and Labor Relations Review* 8 (October 1955):41–53.

77. William N. Chernish, *Coalition Bargaining* (Philadelphia: University of Pennsylvania Press, 1969), p. 3. Chernish recognizes that coalition bargaining has some-

times served as an alternative to merger. "In a sense, coalition bargaining has permitted a limited temporary merger among divergent interest unions for special purposes: attempts to bargain with new strength where weaknesses have prevailed without the sacrifices of leadership, patronage and potential for withdrawal" (p. 259).

78. Gary N. Chaison, "A Note on the Critical Dimensions of the Union Merger Process," *Relations Industrielles—Industrial Relations* 37 (1982):202–3.

79. Glocker, *op. cit.*, pp. 554–75.

80. Ibid., p. 557.

81. Ibid., p. 565.

82. Dewey, *op. cit.*, p. 64.

83. *Proceedings of the Nineteenth International Convention of the American Flint Glass Workers Union* (1975), pp. 55–56.

84. *International Officers Report of the Glass Bottle Blowers Association* (1969), p. 5.

85. Dewey, *op. cit.*, p. 67.

86. Janus, *op. cit.*, p. 15.

87. Shabecoff, *op. cit.*, p. 19.

88. Kilroy, *op. cit.*, p. 25.

4
The Barriers to Merger

hether or not a union will merge is determined by the countervailing forces of the motivations and barriers to merger and the extent to which these forces are reduced or redirected by union alliances. It was suggested in the historical review in chapter 2 that merger barriers are frequently powerful and that many, perhaps a majority of merger attempts end in failure. Before I examine these barriers, it would be useful to briefly describe the merger negotiation process. It is along the path of these negotiations that the various forms of barriers are encountered.

Merger Negotiations

Most unions follow similar steps when negotiating a merger.[1] In terms of both procedures and documents, the negotiations for the AFL–CIO merger in 1955 served as the basic model for merging unions for the past thirty years.[2] In all likelihood, the federations at that time adopted the merger procedures that had been used successfully by their affiliates.

Figure 4–1 lists the sequence of steps in merger negotiations and approvals. Although not indicated in the diagram because of its rarity, in a few cases early membership approval was sought at a convention through a resolution that authorized the union's officers to seek merger partners and enter into mergers. This may be done when a large union launches a program of expansion through absorption. For example, a 1976 convention resolution of the Steelworkers enumerated the benefits of past mergers and authorized the officers "to explore merger possibilities and to consummate those mergers which are in the best interests of the union."[3] Constitution clauses may also give wide latitude to union officers in arranging and approving a merger, provided that the merger does not require the amendment of other portions of the constitution.[4] These provisions are most meaningful for absorbing unions. Amalgamating and absorbed unions often have their constitutions altered substantially through the compromises made in merger negotiations.

Initial Contact between Union Officers

↓

Executive Board or Council Approval
to Establish Merger Committee

↓

Merger Negotiations

↓

Approval of Merger Documents
by Executive Board(s) or Council(s)

↓

Approval of Merger Documents by Membership through Delegate Vote
at Special Convention, National Referendum, or Local Referendums

↓

MERGER

Figure 4–1. Steps in Initiating Merger Negotiations and Approving Merger Proposals

At the earliest stages of merger negotiations, union officers make initial, informal contacts with each other to explore merger possibilities. This can occur at the numerous occasions when officers meet, such as AFL–CIO conventions, meetings of federation departments or governing bodies, or bargaining or lobbying conferences. The exploratory merger discussions are usually kept secret so that they will not be seen as failures if nothing further develops.[5] If there is a mutual feeling that merger is both possible and desirable, the merger effort will be publicized and officers will ask their respective executive councils or boards to select members for a merger committee. The joint merger committee (sometimes called a "unity committee") is comprised of key officers and meets to prepare drafts of the following merger documents:

1. *The merger agreement.* This describes the principles and conditions of the merger, including, for example, the forms and composition of governing structures, the status of locals and members, and the organization's new name and headquarters.

2. *The merger implementation agreement.* This agreement lists the actions necessary to implement the merger, such as disposing of properties, combining of funds, employment or retirement of staff, and establishment of union governing bodies until the election of officers at the first convention of the merged union. The implementation agreement and the merger agreement are frequently combined into a single document.

3. *The proposed constitution of the new union.* In an amalgamation a great deal of time and effort goes into drafting the new union's constitution. An absorption generally requires only minor amendments to the

absorbing union's constitution, designating the special status, if any, of the absorbed union's members, officers, staff, and governing structures.[6]

If negotiations are successful, the merger committee will approve the act of merger in general and the merger documents in specific. The documents are then presented to the executive boards or councils of the involved unions for their approval. The proposals and agreements can pass this stage without amendments or can be referred back to the merger committee for renegotiation and amendments before they will satisfy the board or council members. The documents are then presented to the membership for discussion and approval. This is usually done in a combination of ways, including special local meetings, regional or national conventions, the mailing of notices and sample merger documents, and announcements in union periodicals, often in a special merger edition.

Merger proposals are presented to the membership on a take-it-or-leave-it basis, without an opportunity for modification or rejection of clauses.[7] Proposals for amalgamation are subjected to a referendum among union members or a vote of delegates at a special merger convention. Absorbed unions follow a similar practice. Absorbing unions will not have a requirement for membership approval if the leadership has a prior mandate to seek merger partners and if the merger does not entail changes in the absorbing union's constitution. If the absorbing union's constitution is changed, as in the creation of a special division to accommodate the absorbed union, membership or convention delegate approval will be required.

Most unions need only a simple majority of those voting when there is approval of mergers by members or convention delegates. In some cases, a larger majority is necessary. For example, the Oil, Chemical and Atomic Workers requires two-thirds of convention delegate votes, while the constitution of the Screen Actors Guild calls for a 60-percent vote of the membership for merger approval.[8]

The procedures for entering into a merger are frequently found in a general form under union constitutional provisions for changing union structures or disbanding the organization. In rare cases, the constitution will contain a specific merger clause. For example, article XIX of the constitution of the Amalgamated Clothing and Textile Workers Union states:

ARTICLE XIX
Mergers and Consolidations

The President and Secretary–Treasurer, with the approval of the General Executive Board, may propose and negotiate mergers and/or consolidations . . . with labor organizations whose objectives are compatible with those of ACTWU set forth in Article III [the general objectives of the union]. Notwithstanding any other procedure provided in the Constitution for ratification of such merger or mergers, upon the approval by the General Executive Board the Secretary–Treasurer shall cause to be published and distributed to all members the terms and conditions of such merger. Thereupon each local union, at a regular or special meeting called for such purpose, after no less than fifteen (15) days notice that such proposed merger shall be considered thereat, shall vote upon such merger by secret ballot after full opportunity afforded at such regular or special meeting for discussion of the terms and conditions of such proposed merger. The secretary of each local union shall certify results of such secret ballot vote to the Secretary–Treasurer and shall preserve the ballots and attendance list of such meeting. Upon receipt of certifications that a majority of those voting after notice and opportunity for discussion, have by secret ballot approved the terms and conditions of such proposed merger, the Secretary–Treasurer shall cause to be issued a certification of merger and such merger shall be effective as of the date of such certification. In the event such merger requires amendment of the Constitution the procedures provided herein for ratification of such merger shall supercede the provisions of Article XV [the procedures for amending the constitution].[9]

The process for approving a merger can also be described in the concluding sections of a merger or implementation agreement. For example, the following steps were specified in article X of the merger agreement for the absorption of the Insurance Workers International Union (IWIU) into the United Food and Commercial Workers (UFCW):

ARTICLE X

Following approval of this agreement by the General Executive Board of the IWIU, the IWIU convention currently scheduled to be held during June 1983, shall vote to authorize the conducting of a referendum of those persons it represents for purposes of collective bargaining. Following such convention action by the IWIU, this agreement shall be submitted to a referendum vote of employees represented by the IWIU. Following referendum approval, this agreement shall be submitted to the International Executive Board of the UFCW. If this agreement is approved by the IWIU convention, the IWIU referendum, and the UFCW International Executive Board, it shall become effective on the first day of the month immediately following approval by the UFCW International Executive Board. If this agreement is not so approved, it shall be null and void and of no effect.[10]

There are a few important procedural variations that can occur during merger negotiations. First, there may be a negotiated "prelude" to the merger. The parties may be so reluctant to commit their organizations to a merger that they will only enter into a "trial affiliation." This is a type of alliance with a set expiration date (in one case it was eighteen months); it is subject to further evaluation and approval by officers and members before being converted into a merger.[11] Some unions may also ask for a no-raid agreement or cooperative organizing pact as a demonstration of mutual trust before a formal merger proposal can be agreed to or even negotiated.[12] Finally, unions may carry out several simultaneous sets of merger negotiations. A union seeking to become absorbed may try to have potential merger partners compete among themselves to see which can offer the best terms.[13] When there are multiple negotiations, the discussions may be overlapping but only one proposal at a time is voted on by the membership. As we will see later, this can create membership dissension as supporters of one merger partner try to block the consideration of another's proposal.

Along the path to merger, unions can encounter several barriers; some may only seem to make negotiations or approvals more difficult, while others can quickly prove fatal to the merger effort. As one might expect, the barriers found at earlier stages must be overcome for the later ones to be reached. Merger attempts have failed because of internal opposition, external opposition, and institutional differences.

Internal Opposition

Important merger barriers often develop within unions negotiating to amalgamate or to be absorbed. Opposition from the incumbent leadership may arise at the earliest stages of merger negotiations—the points of initial contact and the establishment of formal negotiating committees. Membership opposition forms at the later stages, usually after officers have completed negotiations and proposals are presented for membership approval.[14]

Opposition from Union Leaders

Perhaps the most common barrier to union merger is officer opposition. In their case studies, Brooks and Gamm found that merger negotiations were often successful because officers wanted them to be. Some mergers which might have seemed justified on purely economic grounds floundered during negotiations because of officer opposition. If officers did not want the merger, it would never reach the membership for their consideration. Alternatively, if officers supported a merger, agreement was reached in negotiations and officers tried to sell the proposal to the membership.[15]

The primary reason for officer opposition is the pursuit of their economic and political self-interest. National officers would understandably oppose mergers that they believed would cause them to lose status, power, and prestige, or reduce their salaries and benefits.[16]

Local leaders have opposed mergers that they feared would result in local mergers and the possible elimination of their positions. Even when local mergers are not required as part of the proposed national merger, local leaders may believe that the change would still decrease their power and status. They may suspect that they will become officers in a national organization with expanded governing structures plus new political alliances and power centers. The merged union would have a greater number of local leaders and consequently there would be more political competition in the local leaders' rise to national-level positions.[17]

Local leader opposition generally forms when the merger proposal is at the final stages of negotiations or presented to the membership. National union leaders have been a more potent source of opposition to merger because of their direct involvement in merger negotiations.

The strongest national officer opposition may come from both the newest and the most tenured union officers. On the one hand, mergers can be difficult in unions with older leaders who feel the bitterness of past rivalries, have a deep sense of tradition, and believe that too much of their union's identity and history would be lost in the merger. They may be closest to retirement and would probably expect to gain the least from the merger in terms of positions or increased salaries or benefits. On the other hand, young officers might block mergers because they feel a need to establish a record of their own before ending their position through a merger or before negotiating to share power in the merged union.[18]

Officer opposition has proved fatal to numerous merger efforts. For example, in 1975, the United Papermakers and Paperworkers tried to negotiate a merger with the Printing and Graphic Communications Union. The president of the latter union wanted to serve as president of the new union, with the leader of the Paperworkers serving as "general president." This was rejected as being unworkable, although merger negotiations continued for several more years.[19]

The sense of pride that officers of the Pulp, Sulphite and Paper Mill Workers Union felt in their union's history proved to be the major obstacle in an attempt to merge with the Paperworkers. It was reported that the long-time president of Pulp, Sulphite refused to negotiate any merger agreement that he thought would submerge the identity of his union. It was only after he left office in 1965 that the merger negotiations could resume in earnest, although at the time they proved unsuccessful for other reasons and the unions did not merge until 1972.[20] Similarly, in the amalgamation that formed the United Food and Commercial Workers, an agreement to merge was only possible after the retirement of the Meat Cutters' president, age seventy-six, who for many years had opposed the merger.[21]

In 1976, a proposal to merge the Rubber Workers and the Oil, Chemical and Atomic Workers failed because of a disagreement over which union's leaders would step aside. Merger talks were revived in 1980 because officer succession was no longer a major issue. As one Rubber Workers officer commented, "Those people aren't around any longer. The time is right."[22]

While officer turnover can clear the path to merger, there have also been cases where the emergence of new officers only served to increase opposition. For example, in 1981, there were unsuccessful merger discussions between the Amalgamated Clothing and Textile Workers Union and the International Ladies Garment Workers Union. It was reported that a major barrier to merger was the age of the unions' officers. The leaders of both unions were fairly young and they could not decide who would be the president of the new union.[23] A recent change in officers was also said to have blocked the recent efforts of the Rubber Workers to negotiate a merger with the United Automobile Workers.[24]

Merger opposition can come from an incumbent officer, either younger or older, who faces a serious election challenge. The open support of a merger could be used by opponents as political ammunition in the election campaign. They would claim that the reelection of the incumbent would be a vote to end the union as an independent organization.[25] As a result, only the most secure union leaders could enter into negotiations for their union to amalgamate or be absorbed. Other officers might have to oppose merger openly, even if they personally believed that a merger would benefit the union and its members.

Finally, it should be mentioned that officers may oppose mergers for reasons other than the furtherance of their self-interest, or because of union politics or traditions. Some merger proposals may be unattractive in a financial sense. A union being considered for absorption may be too small to generate the dues income needed to cover its operating expenses, particularly if there is little chance of raising dues and there are guarantees of continued officer and staff employment after the merger.

Both absorptions and amalgamations could require the continuation of generous officer and staff pension plans, and these might be seen as prohibitive expenses. All merger proposals raise some financial questions and are evaluated on a cost/benefit basis. Officers ask if the amalgamated union will be financially sound, or if the absorbed union will create a burden on the absorbing union's treasury. However, except for extreme cases, the financial aspects are seldom cut and dry. As we saw in chapter 3, union financial health is often subjectively evaluated and difficult to forecast. There is always a possibility that financial concerns will be used as a justification by some officers who reject a merger for more personal and political reasons. They may exaggerate the conditions of potential amalgamation or absorption partners because financial problems would seem to be a more rational and responsible reason for rejecting the merger. Their decision would gain wider acceptance among other officers, union staff, and members than if it were a transparently political or personal move. Consequently, aside from the extreme cases where a merger partner would be an obvious financial drain, it may be difficult to determine the real importance of the financial considerations behind officer opposition.

Membership Opposition

In recent years there has been an increased assertiveness on the part of union members. This has taken many forms, including strikes during the term of collective agreements, opposition to incumbent officers, contract rejections, and union decertifications.[26] It can also appear as membership opposition to mergers.

Union members are generally informed by their leaders of a potential merger at the later stages of negotiations, either when the final issues are being discussed or when a tentative proposal has been agreed to by the officers and must be presented to the membership for approval. Opposition develops if the members of a union to be absorbed or amalgamated believe that their interests and identity will be submerged in the merger partner. For example, there would tend to be apprehension if a small craft union were being absorbed into a much larger industrial union and the smaller union's members could find little that was familiar with the new governing and bargaining practices. In contrast, an absorbing union's members rarely oppose merger because the process has much less effect on their union. An exception might be found if they believed that the terms offered to the absorbed union (for example, the degree of autonomy in bargaining or governance, or the salaries to be paid officers and staff) were too generous and would give the absorbed union's members and officers a favored status within the union.

Membership opposition to merger is expressed in a variety of ways. Antimerger committees may carry out extensive campaigns aimed at passing convention resolutions which reject the merger agreement. Sometimes candidates may even run against the promerger union officers. Locals may threaten to disaffiliate if the merger goes through. There have also been instances where members (sometimes in conjunction with local officers) have sought and received court orders blocking the proposed merger because it was not carried out in accordance with the requirements of the union's constitution. They usually rest their case on those sections of the union constitution dealing with the time limits and methods for notifying members of important union business, or the procedures for dissolving or altering union governing structures.

A strong and particularly well organized form of membership opposition can occur when a union considers proposals from alternative merger partners. The members may form competing groups, each supporting one of the merger candidates and urging the rejection of the others. In these campaigns, the opposition tends to be directed against specific merger terms, rather than the merger act in general, with critical comparisons made between the different proposals. It is often claimed that one proposal will result in the submergence of interests while another guarantees continued and fair representation in bargaining and union decision making.

Membership opposition was found in even the earliest of mergers. For example, in his history of the United Brotherhood of Carpenters, Galenson mentions that during the Brotherhood's absorption of the Order of Carpenters in 1888, some dissenting members of the Order managed to get a temporary injunction against the merger. However, this injunction was later dissolved and the merger went through, with 3,500 members in twenty-five locals entering into the Brotherhood.[27]

As illustrations of the effectiveness of more recent membership opposition, I will briefly review the attempted merger of the Screen Actors Guild and Screen Extras Guild, and that of the Telecommunications International Union and the American Federation of State, County and Municipal Employees.

In the widely publicized merger attempt of the Screen Actors Guild (SAG) and the Screen Extras Guild (SEG, an organization of stuntpeople and extras), membership opposition was well organized. In a 1982 membership vote, the merger proposal was favored by 56 percent of the voters, but 60 percent was needed for approval. Two years later another vote was held but only 52 percent supported the merger, although it had been approved by the union's board of directors by a vote of seventy to one.[28]

The opposition formed an association called "AWAG" (Actors Working for an Actors' Guild) and claimed that the merger would cost actors' jobs and submerge their interests in a broader based union. It was argued that the actors would find little benefit and much harm in the merger. Actors would compete with extras for work and the increased wages of extras might reduce overall employment opportunities in the industry. There were also objections to extras sitting on the SAG board of directors and participating in decisions about the wages and working conditions of actors.[29]

The promerger group, called "CAM" (Caucus of Artists for Mergers), distributed a twenty-two page *Merger Primer* and the SAG leadership prepared special merger issues of the *Screen Actors News*. They claimed that the merger would create rather than reduce job opportunities for SAG members. It was also stated that the merger would protect wages, expand SAG's jurisdiction, and serve as an important step toward the eventual formation of one union for all performers, with the next merger involving the American Federation of Radio and Television Artists. A major point often repeated in the promerger campaign was that SAG and SEG already had overlapping memberships and jurisdictions.[30] The majority of extra players were also SAG members; SAG represented all extras in New York, Philadelphia, Boston, Washington, D.C., and Baltimore, while SEG represented extras in Los Angeles, San Diego, San Francisco, Las Vegas, and Hawaii.[31]

In the SAG–SEG merger efforts, lines were clearly drawn between the merger proponents and opponents. However, as I noted earlier, sometimes membership opposition is not antimerger but instead is directed against the terms offered by one competing merger candidate while supporting the terms of another. A recent illustration is found in the attempt of Telecommunications International Union (TIU) to be absorbed by the American Federation of State, County and Municipal Employees (AFSCME).[32] The unaffiliated TIU had received merger proposals from AFSCME, the Communications Workers of America (CWA), and the International Brotherhood of Electrical Workers (IBEW). These three unions are all affiliates of the AFL–CIO. In December 1983, the TIU officers recommended that their union merge into AFSCME, and this was approved by the union's executive committee. A special convention was called for early 1984 to vote on the merger with AFSCME.

However, in reaction to complaints from dissident TIU members, a district court judge issued a temporary restraining order postponing the convention until the membership was more fully informed of the merger's implications. The order stated that before such a convention could be held, the TIU must fully disclose to its members the terms of the merger, allow ninety days after the disclosure for membership debate over alternative merger proposals, and permit locals to carry out membership referendums so that delegates to a special convention could be better informed of the members' preferences. The judge felt that the membership had not received the full details about the AFSCME merger. While they did receive a letter from the TIU's president about the proposal, they were not given copies of the draft merger agreement or AFSCME's constitution. A fact sheet on the merger was prepared but not distributed, and members were not told about the competing merger proposal from the CWA. There were also some inaccuracies in the merger information provided by the TIU's officers.

The TIU's leaders responded that they would distribute the required information (including the details of the CWA proposal) and that local meetings would be scheduled. They saw the opposition to merger as a last ditch CWA effort to prevent the TIU from joining an AFL–CIO affiliate. An assistant to the TIU's president claimed that the CWA had been raiding his union and that this would end when and if the TIU was absorbed by an AFL–CIO affiliate such as the AFSCME and consequently covered by the AFL–CIO no-raid agreement. While the leader of the opposition within the TIU admitted that he favored the CWA, he said that many in the TIU objected to the manner in which the AFSCME proposal was being presented. A petition signed by a large number of members protested the AFSCME merger and wanted more time for the examination of other merger proposals. A large New York City local which favored the CWA even went so far as to disaffiliate.[33]

In November 1984, the courts ruled that TIU could finally hold a convention to further explore its merger options. At a special convention during the following month the delegates voted to conduct a membership referendum only on the question of the merger with AFSCME. In early 1985, this referendum was carried out and nearly 60 percent of the TIU members voted against the merger. The CWA and IBEW saw this as an encouraging sign and launched campaigns to separately absorb any of the TIU's locals that were willing to disaffiliate from their parent union.[34]

The merger attempts between SAG and SEG and between TIU and AFSCME suggest the potential forcefulness and complexity of membership opposition to mergers. These are extreme cases of member reactions against merger proposals. While all merger attempts arouse some member opposition, this is usually expressed by individual speakers or small caucuses at local meetings or union conventions. The fear of submergence of interests and the distrust of officers negotiating the merger have to be intense and widely shared for opposition to become so well organized and effective that the merger is blocked.

External Opposition

Opposition from Federations and Affiliates

Although most opposition to merger is generated within the involved unions, there are instances in which important barriers are formed by federations and their affiliates. This can take place when a proposed merger is between an affiliate and an unaffiliated union which had once been expelled. A federation would strongly oppose the return of an expelled union through a merger if that union could not meet the criteria necessary for reentry. These criteria might include changes in jurisdiction or leadership, or the end of a raiding campaign. If a merger is agreed to without the necessary changes, the merging affiliate would find itself faced with federation suspension or expulsion.

Reasons for Opposition. Pressure to block a merger or punish a merging affiliate might come from other affiliates which feel threatened because their jurisdictions overlap with that of the unaffiliated union. They would argue that the merger was being used as a quick and indirect route to affiliation and the subsequent legitimation of the outside union's jurisdiction. They would point out that the new union's jurisdiction would be protected from encroachment after the merger because it would then be covered under the federation's no-raid agreement. This reasoning was behind the moves to stop the 1972 absorption of District 50, Allied and Technical Workers, an unaffiliated union, into the Steelworkers, an AFL–CIO affiliate. The Oil, Chemical and Atomic Workers claimed that the merger would conflict with their jurisdiction and protested to the AFL–CIO Executive Council. Another affiliate, the Utility Workers Union, was opposed to the merger because District 50 had thirteen thousand members in public utilities. The AFL–CIO Building and Construction Trades Department protested that many District 50 members were construction workers and that the absorption could create jurisdictional disputes between the Steelworkers and the federation's construction unions. Despite these objections, the AFL–CIO decided not to oppose the merger.[35]

The Proposed ITU–Teamster Merger. The recent merger attempt of the International Typographical Union (ITU) and the Teamsters is worth reviewing in detail because it illustrates the strength and direction of federation opposition as well as the exceptional lengths that union officers and members will go to block a merger.

Technological change and overlapping union jurisdictions have recently created intense pressures for mergers in the printing industry. The AFL–CIO through its president, Lane Kirkland, has promoted the eventual formation through merger of a single affiliated union in printing. At the same time, the International Brotherhood of Teamsters, expelled from the AFL–CIO in 1957 because of leadership corruption, has shown a keen interest in absorbing the declining printing unions. A clash between merger goals of the federation and the Teamsters found the International Typographical Union caught in the middle. The merger attempt between the ITU and the Teamsters is so complicated that it is best described in chronological order.

September 1982. The ITU and the Newspaper Guild had been discussing a possible merger since 1973. Talks were broken off in 1981, in disagreement primarily over issues of dues structure and local autonomy. Negotiations resumed in early 1982, and by September an agreement had been reached to amalgamate and form a "Media Employees International Union." This merger agreement would have to be approved by special conventions and membership referendums to be held in 1983.[36]

August 1983. Teamster President Jackie Presser addressed the ITU convention in San Francisco and urged the delegates to reject the merger agreement with the Guild and to merge with the Teamsters instead. The ITU–Guild merger resolution was defeated by a three-to-two margin. (It had been endorsed earlier by the Guild.) At the convention, the ITU officers were also given a mandate to discuss merger with the Graphic Communications International Union (GCIU), itself recently formed by an amalgamation. However, Joe Bingel, the ITU president, said that such talks would have to wait until meetings with Teamsters were held.[37]

October 1983. One week before the AFL–CIO convention, Bingel announced that substantial progress was being made toward a merger with the Teamsters. These negotiations were being carried out despite warnings from Kirkland that the federation would oust the ITU if it merged with the Teamsters. The federation continued its efforts to build one big union in printing and during the AFL–CIO convention Kirkland met with Bingel and the officers of two other printing affiliates, the GCIU and the Guild. Little progress was made toward a merger.[38] The meetings were described as "exploratory" and the parties agreed to meet again, though no date was set.[39]

November 1983. Robert S. McMichen, at the time the ITU's first vice president, defeated Bingel in the election for the Union presidency by a vote of 26,885 to 21,935. McMichen opposed a merger with the Teamsters, instead favoring one with an affiliated union. Bingel challenged the election results, claiming that some ITU locals had improperly used dues to assist McMichen's campaign. The union's canvassing board upheld these charges and set the election aside. McMichen then filed election objections with the U.S. Department of Labor. A repeat of the election was recommended by the ITU canvassing board, but Bingel and the other officers supporting a Teamsters merger wanted the election postponed until the Department of Labor ruled on McMichen's objections. If these complaints were upheld, the Department of Labor would then supervise the election.[40]

After his election was challenged and set aside, McMichen was dismissed from his vice presidency. However, he soon found a place on the AFL–CIO payroll as chairman of a committee promoting the mergers of printing affiliates.[41] For the next few months, the results of the ITU officer election remained contested and merger negotiations were carried out with the GCIU.

March 1984. The negotiations between the ITU and the GCIU broke down. The ITU claimed that the GCIU negotiators refused to put any of their merger terms in writing. The GCIU president responded that the ITU was trying to involve his union in a "bidding war" with the Teamsters over the terms of the merger agreement and that he would not engage in "collective bargaining" over the merger terms.[42]

April 1984. The Teamsters and the ITU announced that they had agreed to merge. Under the proposed agreement, the ITU would become "an autonomous trade division within the . . . [Teamsters] pursuant to the . . . [Teamsters] constitution."[43] The division would be headed by a trade division director appointed by the Teamster president, although the ITU officer structure would also "remain in place."[44]

Following the merger announcement, the AFL–CIO announced it was disappointed that the ITU leaders had rushed into an agreement with the Teamsters without seriously considering a merger with the GCIU. The Federation believed that the ITU members were being denied the opportunity to fairly decide whether the Teamsters or the GCIU could best serve their interests.[45] The Teamster president, however, claimed that the proposed merger would "preserve traditions and enhance economic benefits by joining the nation's oldest trade union [the ITU] and the nation's largest union [the Teamsters]."[46]

McMichen and his supporters formed a committee within the ITU to campaign against the merger with the Teamsters and to promote a merger with the GCIU. Calling itself the "Committee for One Big Union," it published a newsletter and distributed posters with the slogan "Labor Strength Plus Respect," an obvious reference to the Teamsters' poor public image. The campaign literature emphasized that a merger with the Teamsters would result in expulsion from the AFL–CIO. The committee also distributed portions of the Teamsters' constitution which they believed to be undemocratic and in conflict with the ITU constitution.[47] At the same time, the incumbent ITU officers held regional meetings to present the case for the merger with the Teamsters.[48]

May 1984. McMichen supporters obtained a court injunction blocking the ITU–Teamsters merger referendum which had been scheduled for May 16. The referendum would have to wait until the final resolution to the challenges to the ITU officer elections.[49]

June 1984. The earlier ITU election was nullified by the Department of Labor because of charges of illegal campaigning on both sides, primarily the promotion of candidates through publications supported by union dues. A supervised election was conducted in June.[50]

July 1984. In the ITU election McMichen defeated Bingel by a vote of 28,167 to 15,296. McMichen's slate of officers was also victorious and took a majority of the seats on the union's five-member executive board.[51] McMichen's victory statement emphasized the important role that the merger negotiations had played in the election:

> This victory says three things to us. First, that the members of the ITU cherish our long democratic tradition and will never allow it to be put up for sale. . . . Second, our victory shows that the overwhelming majority of the ITU members have no desire to be absorbed by the Teamsters union. Third, the vote indicates a clear interest in pursuing merger with the Graphic Communications International Union—our most logical, natural ally. We plan to pursue and, we hope in time, to consummate the merger with GCIU, or if that is not possible, with another union in the mainstream of U.S. and Canadian labor. Finally, we restore to this union our proud tradition of open debate and democratic rule.[52]

August 1984. Bingel asked the Department of Labor to nullify the results of the officer elections on the grounds that the McMichen campaign had received illegal assistance from the AFL–CIO.[53]

September 1984. The objections to the officer elections were dismissed and McMichen and the other officers were sworn in. However, the dispute over the ITU–Teamster merger was still not resolved. Merger supporters claimed that a referendum petition had been signed by 178 local unions and therefore the ITU constitution required that the merger proposal be subjected to a vote. Moreover, Teamster leader Presser stated that his union's agreement with the ITU was "not null and void" despite McMichen's election. He said the Teamsters would "not walk away from our friends and our commitments."[54]

The ITU convention set a ninety-day time limit for McMichen and the other officers to negotiate a merger within the Graphic Communications International Union. If an agreement could not be reached the ITU would have to conduct a referendum on the Teamsters' merger offer.[55]

November 1984. The ITU officers claimed that the Teamsters, unable to complete the merger, were resorting to a raiding campaign. ITU bargaining units were raided in Cleveland and Columbus, Ohio, as well as in Montreal and Toronto. The AFL–CIO said it found the situation "a serious matter and is monitoring it."[56] One observer compared the raid to a takeover on Wall Street, with the Teamsters first attempting a friendly takeover, but then going after the ITU's largest and most available units.[57]

December 1984 to February 1985. Faced with the ninety-day negotiations deadline, the ITU and GCIU negotiating committees were able to work out an agreement for amalgamation. In late December, the ITU's officers announced that they had reached a "sound basis" for merger and by early January they submitted a merger proposal to their executive boards for approval.[58] A membership referendum was scheduled for April. The Teamsters' president, believing that his union would finally be blocked from absorbing the ITU, was very critical and called the agreement a "sell out" reached through "secret meetings" and "side deals."[59]

March 1985 to June 1985. In mid-March, the GCIU board voted to reject the proposed merger with the ITU, apparently because they were dissatisfied with the financial projections based on the ITU's membership. The April 1 referendum among ITU and GCIU membership was cancelled. The Teamsters issued a statement commending this action and indicating that it would renew its efforts to merge with the ITU. The ITU–Teamsters merger proposal would now be presented to the ITU membership for their approval.[60]

August 1985. A referendum was finally held among the ITU's membership. The merger with the Teamsters was rejected by a two-to-one margin (17,547 in favor and 34,234 against). McMichen stated: "We're confident that this strong vote will put the Teamster affair well behind us."[61]

The ITU–Teamsters merger effort, with all its twists and turns, was only briefly outlined here. It serves as a vivid illustration of the combined influence of a variety of sources of opposition to merger. Internal opposition came from the ITU membership and leadership which supported an alternative merger proposal. The major source of external opposition was the federation. The internal and external opposition were clearly interrelated, with the federation openly encouraging the officers and members who campaigned against the merger. While such strong and direct federation opposition is rare, it could be expected in this case because of the important implications of an ITU–Teamsters merger. First, the merger would be a major setback in the federation's attempt to eventually shape a series of mergers combining affiliates in the printing industry. Second, the federation had to maintain its policy of opposing mergers between affiliates and expelled unions, or else such unions could use merger as a route to reentry and subsequent protection under the no-raid agreement.[62] As we saw in the historical overview in chapter 2, the federation expelled the Chemical Workers for joining with the Alliance for Labor Action and the Brewery Workers for merging into the Teamsters. It would have little alternative than to expel the ITU, even if it had only joined in a loose affiliation with the Teamsters.

Opposition from Other Unions

In some cases, a union will end its merger overtures or negotiations because they interfere with the merger plans of another union and could disturb friendly or strategic relations. Many unions have entered into joint organizing and no-raid pacts and would not want to pursue mergers that would antagonize allies and jeopardize these agreements. This is often a matter of the costs of ending these relationships outweighing the benefits of the merger.

The situation of the Brewery Workers is an excellent illustration of the triangle of relationships found when there is merger opposition from other unions. In 1971, the Brewery Workers faced simultaneous raiding campaigns and pressure to be absorbed from the Teamsters. At that time the Brewery Workers was also attempted to merge into the Amalgamated Meat Cutters and Butcher Workmen. The Meat Cutters and the Teamsters had signed a no-raid agreement and the absorption into the Meat Cutters would have protected the Brewery Workers from further Teamster raids. Accordingly, the Teamsters opposed the merger and the Meat Cutters backed off rather than severely strain their relationship with the Teamsters. The president of the Brewery Workers reported to his union's convention on his negotiations with the Meat Cutters:

> We met at the Meat Cutters' Headquarters and examined their facilities, their methods of operation, their bookkeeping system, membership record system, departmental operations, etc.

After exploring their facilities, we met in their Executive Board Room and after preliminary discussions, we were informed that one of their Vice Presidents had contacted a Vice President of the Teamsters about our merger discussions and possibilities. They were informed by the Teamsters that any merger that took place between our organizations would be considered a very unfriendly act and it would disrupt entirely the friendly relations that existed with the Meat Cutters, their Mutual Aid and Assistance Pact, their joint organizing endeavors, their joint bargaining efforts, etc. in various plants and industries. As a result of this development, they felt it would be futile to continue discussions since obviously the risk was too great and they didn't want to become involved in jurisdictional warfare, in addition to losing the good relationship they had with the Teamsters for many years. Discussions at this point were broken off without any thought or hope in the future of resuming same. In other words, the issue was no longer alive and should be forgotten. Fini.[63]

The Teamsters' intervention was also said to be partially behind the unsuccessful merger negotiations in 1970 between the Brewery Workers and the International Association of Machinists.[64] Left with few alternatives, the Brewery Workers were finally absorbed into the Teamsters in 1973.

Institutional Differences

Merger negotiations require that unions reconcile numerous institutional differences and that they meld administrative, governing, and bargaining structures and practices. In both amalgamations and absorptions, the parties must reach agreement on such issues as:

The composition of the executive board and its members' duties, responsibilities, and terms of office

The salaries and benefits of the officers and staff members

The transfer and consolidation of properties, titles, rights, obligations, and debts, as well as the pension and health care plans of employees

The merging of locals, districts, regional divisions, and state councils, as well as union departments

The method of dues calculation and the division of dues receipts between locals, intermediate bodies, and the union headquarters

The continuation, titles, and editorships of union periodicals

The degree of autonomy that locals will exercise in determining bargaining issues, ratifying contracts, and calling strikes

The combining of bargaining units.[65]

Amalgamating unions must also agree on the name of the new union, the location of the headquarters, the frequency of conventions, the selection of convention delegates, and the provisions of the new union's constitution.

In DeCenzo's study of an attempted amalgamation of two unions in the foundry and metal fabrication industries, it was found that merger negotiations failed because of disagreement over officers' positions in the new union, the amount of dues, the new union's name, and the location of union headquarters.[66] Walsh reported that among the major issues blocking the merger of the International Typographical Union and the Newspaper Guild were the computation of dues and the degree of local autonomy in negotiations.[67] The dues structure was an issue that could not be resolved in the 1980 merger discussions between the Steelworkers and the Insurance Workers.[68] The following year, merger discussions between the Insurance Workers and the International Ladies Garment Workers Union broke down partly because the parties could not agree on the number of Insurance Workers delegates to be seated at the ILGWU convention.[69] Dues were a major issue when the Retail, Wholesale and Department Store Union bowed out of the 1979 merger talks that combined the Retail Clerks and the Meat Cutters to form the United Food and Commercial Workers.[70]

A variety of institutional differences have been brought up in the intermittent merger negotiations between the United Automobile Workers and the Machinists (IAM). One problem is resolving the role of locals in bargaining. The IAM gives considerable freedom to locals in bargaining, with regional officers directing negotiations. In contrast, the UAW's top officers play a central role in negotiations in major bargaining units. These differences would have to be overcome if there were a merger and any subsequent move to regional negotiations in industries where there are UAW and IAM units. Another important issue is the selection of officers in the new union. UAW officers are elected at the union's convention and represent workers in specific districts. IAM vice presidents are elected on an at-large basis at their convention and then are assigned territories.[71]

Officer selection was also a problem in the merger negotiations between the International Chemical Workers and the United Rubber Workers. The executive board of the Rubber Workers is composed primarily of local presidents elected by the union membership. In the Chemical Workers, elected convention delegates rather than the membership vote for board members.[72]

Sometimes there is a long list of insurmountable institutional differences. For example, it was reported that no agreement could be reached on a merger between the Rubber Workers and the Oil, Chemical and Atomic Workers because of differences in:

> per capita taxes, staff salaries, the manner in which vacancies in elected offices will be filled, the appointment of convention committees, the number of

districts and their regional boundaries, the duties of the secretary–treasurer, the selection of the Canadian district director, . . . the creation of uniform local bylaws.[73]

Institutional differences are often at the root of the officer and membership opposition discussed in earlier sections. Officers may resist mergers when they disapprove of arrangements which threaten their status, power, or tenure in the merged union. Among these threats are changes in titles and terms of office, the degree of local union autonomy, and the composition and authority of executive boards. Members may feel that their interests are being submerged if the resolution of institutional differences means that the other union's practices and structures are the ones most often retained. For example, Walsh believes that an obstacle to the proposed merger of the ITU and Newspaper Guild was that the structures described in the merger document were very similar to the Guild's existing structure. The merger looked more like an absorption than an amalgamation; it seemed to the ITU's members that the creation of the new union would not combine the features of both predecessor unions but rather would continue the Guild at the cost to ITU.[74]

It is important to recognize that in many unsuccessful merger negotiations, failure stems not from the negotiating committees' inability to devise compromise solutions to the problems of institutional differences, but rather from a belief that any compromise that could be reached by the two negotiating teams would arouse strong opposition from other officers and the members. In the final analysis, the resolution of institutional differences has to be within the boundaries of what is acceptable and capable of winning approval at executive board meetings, conventions, and membership referendums. The joining of union structures may often be more of a political than a technical problem and we must consider this dimension when trying to understand why merger-negotiating committees are not more flexible or innovative in resolving institutional differences.

Conclusions

This chapter examined the major forms of merger barriers. Leadership opposition is usually the earliest barrier and often the most formidable one; if officers object to a merger, the membership will seldom have a chance to consider it. Union officers may oppose a merger at the early stages because of combinations of personal, political, and financial reasons. Even if officers favor the merger in principle, it remains for them to devise solutions to the problems of the institutional differences. When and if merger negotiations are successful, the proposal is presented to the membership and acceptance is encouraged. It is at this stage that membership opposition may emerge, either because of some strongly emotional reasons (such as the attachment to the union's history and traditions or a general fear of submergence in the merged union) or because of concerns over such institutional arrangements as the new dues structure or the degree of local autonomy in negotiations. In some cases, membership opposition forms because of the support of an alternative merger candidate. Finally, at either the time of merger negotiation or ratification, the opposition from another union or a federation can also appear, and although this is not a frequent barrier, it has been fatal to merger efforts.

At this point in the development of my model of the merger process, I have outlined the dimensions of the two forces in the premerger stage—the motivation to merge and the barriers to merger. It was emphasized that the roles of the barriers and motivation are most meaningful when viewed in relation to each other. For example, a merger will be consummated if the officers are strongly motivated, even when there is significant and organized membership opposition and major institutional differences. Negotiations may have continued for years with little progress, until the motivating factors become so strong that the leaders of one or both of the merging unions are spurred on to make greater compromises on institutional differences and to launch a campaign to counter membership opposition. In another case, the motivation to merge may remain unchanged, but barriers are lowered as the leaders opposing merger retire or as the institutional differences between the potential merger partners are slowly eliminated through changes in their constitutions or their general practices and policies. In short, whether or not there is a merger is determined by the balance between the motivating factors and the barriers rather than just their individual importance.

In chapter 3 we saw that alliance can satisfy the motivation to merge and serve as a substitute for merger. Alliances can also diminish the barriers to merger by reducing the distrust among the unions' members and officers and by showing that joint action in a formal structure does not necessarily entail the loss of power or prestige, or the submergence of members' interests. Alliances can also eliminate some institutional differences between potential merger partners by creating common organizing and bargaining structures and by putting officers and members in the position where they can try out new institutional arrangements.

When barriers are overcome and the merger is approved and completed, we enter into the postmerger stage. As we will see in the next chapter, the arrangements and compromises needed to arrive at a merger shape the character of the new amalgamated union or the fate of the absorbed union.

Notes

1. For a comprehensive case study of a union merger negotiation, see Louise D. Walsh, "A Study of the Proposed Merger of the International Typographical Union

and the Newspaper Guild" (Ithaca, N.Y.: unpublished M.S. thesis, Cornell University, January 1985).

2. George W. Brooks and Sara Gamm, "The Causes and Effects of Union Mergers with Special Reference to Selected Cases in the 60's and 70's" (Washington, D.C.: U.S. Department of Labor, Labor Management Services Administration, September 1976), pp. a25, b20.

3. *Proceedings of the 1976 Convention of the United Steelworkers of America*, p. 467.

4. For example, see *United Food and Commercial Workers—Constitution, 1983*, p. 7 (article 1).

5. Larry T. Adams, "Labor Organization Mergers, 1979–1984: Adapting to Change," *Monthly Labor Review* 107 (September 1984):26.

6. These documents are described in Brooks and Gamm, *op. cit.*, p. a26.

7. Gideon Chitayat, "Mergers of Trade Unions" (Philadelphia: unpublished Ph.D. dissertation, University of Pennsylvania, 1975), p. 227.

8. "Paperworkers, Oil Workers Merger," *Labor Relations Reporter,* September 2, 1985, p. 10; "Screen Extras Merger," *Labor Relations Reporter,* March 26, 1984, p. 259.

9. *Constitution of the Amalgamated Clothing and Textile Workers Union, 1981*, pp. 65–66.

10. *Merger Agreement Between the Insurance Workers International Union and the United Food and Commercial Workers*, September 30, 1983, p. 14.

11. "AFGE Considering Trial Affiliation with Air Traffic Specialists Union," *Government Employee Relations Report*, June 13, 1983, pp. 1234–35.

12. No-raid agreements were signed prior to the absorption of District 50 into the Steelworkers and the amalgamation of the two bakery unions. Gideon Chitayat, *Trade Union Mergers and Labor Conglomerates* (New York: Praeger, 1979), pp. 144, 162–63. A no-raid agreement was also signed in the preliminary negotiations for merger between the International Typographical Union and the Newspaper Guild. Walsh, *op. cit.,* p. 79.

13. For example, see "Interunion Rivalries Exacerbated as Parties Vie for 45,000 Member Independent Telephone Union," *Daily Labor Report*, August 13, 1984, pp. c1–c3.

14. In rare cases, membership opposition may appear early when union leaders ask convention delegates for a mandate to explore merger possibilities. This could create a dangerous situation for union officers who face a contested election at the convention and would be open to charges that they are seeking to dismantle the union.

15. Brooks and Gamm, *op. cit.*, p. a24.

16. Chitayat, "Mergers of Trade Unions", p. 174; Walsh, *op. cit.*, p. 188; Derek C. Bok and John T. Dunlop, *Labor and the American Community* (New York: Simon and Schuster, 1970), p. 155; Jerry Wurf, "Labor's Battle with Itself," *Washington Post*, October 14, 1973, p. c3.

17. Gary N. Chaison, "Local Union Mergers: Frequency, Forms and National Union Policy," *Journal of Labor Research* 4 (Fall 1983):325–38; Michael J. Coady, "Trade Union Mergers and Their Significance in the Canadian Union Movement" (Toronto: unpublished LL.M. dissertation, Osgood Hall Law School, 1976), p. 235.

18. Chitayat, "Mergers of Trade Unions," p. 228; Coady, *op. cit.*, p. 212; "Bigger Unions Will Pack a Bigger Wallop," *Nation's Business* (May 1973):51; "The Urge to Merge Hits Unions Again," *Business Week*, April 20, 1968, p. 62.

19. Chitayat, "Trade Union Mergers and Labor Conglomerates," p. 121.

20. Ibid., p. 114.

21. "Why Unions are Going the Merger Route," *U.S. New and World Report* (June 4, 1979):62.

22. "Unions for Rubber, Oil and Paper Workers Talk About a Merger," *Wall Street Journal*, April 15, 1980, p. 10.

23. Damon Stetson, "Can One Union Label Cover Two Garment Worker Groups?" *New York Times*, November 30, 1980, p. E6. The emergence of new top officers also inhibited merger negotiations in the late 1960s between pulp and paper unions. See Harry Graham, "Union Mergers," *Relations Industrielles—Industrial Relations* 25 (1970):565.

24. "Merger Talks," *Labor Relations Reporter*, March 22, 1982, p. 259.

25. Gary N. Chaison, "Comment: Union Merger Process and the Industrial Environment," *Industrial Relations* 17 (February 1978):120.

26. Jack Barbash, *The Elements of Industrial Relations* (Madison, Wis.: University of Wisconsin Press, 1984), p. 73.

27. Walter Galenson, *The United Brotherhood of Carpenters: The First Hundred Years* (Cambridge, Mass.: Harvard University Press, 1983), p. 55.

28. "Screen Extras Merger," p. 259.

29. "Dear Guild Members, We Urge You To Vote *Against* the SAG/SEG Merger" Actors Working For an Actors' Guild (AWAG) leaflet (1984); "AWAG—Actors Working for an Actors Guild" AWAG leaflet (1984), p. 2.

30. "Merger Can Work for Union," *Screen Actor News* 15 (January 1984):2; "Most Frequently Asked Questions," *Screen Actors News* Winter 1984, 7; "The SAG/SEG Merger Issues: Majority Report—The Truth About Merger," (leaflet, 1984), p. 3; "The Merger Issue," *Screen Actor News* (January 1984):1.

31. *Screen Actors Guild—Screen Extras Guild Merger Primer*, p. 2; "Merger Can Work for Both of You", *Screen Actor News* (Hollywood: Screen Actors Guild, January 1984), pp. 2–3.

32. For discussions of the initial opposition to this merger, see "Interunion Rivalries Exacerbated as Parties Vie for 45,000 Member Independent Telephone Union," pp. c1–c3, d1–d19; "Court Blocks Scheduled Vote on Merger Between Telecommunications Union, AFSCME," *Daily Labor Report,* February 16, 1984, pp. a1–a3; "Recommendations on Merger Expected at Telecommunications Union Convention," *Daily Labor Report*, December 21, 1984, pp. a8–a9; "Independent Phone Union Will Vote Next Month on Merger with AFSCME," *Daily Labor Report*, December 22, 1984, p. a10.

33. "10,000-member Union Joins CWA," *AFL–CIO News*, June 22, 1985, p. 6.

34. "Independent Telephone Union Rejects AFSCME: CWA and IBEW Vow to Continue Organizing Drive," *Daily Labor Report*, March 6, 1985, p. A11; "CWA's Victory in New York," *Labor Relations Reporter*, June 24, 1985, pp. 146–147.

35. Chitayat, *Trade Union Mergers and Labor Conglomerates*, pp. 33–35.

36. For a discussion of the background to the attempted merger between the ITU and the Newspaper Guild, see Walsh, *op. cit.*; "Terms of Merger of Newspaper Unions," *Labor Relations Reporter*, September 20, 1982, p. 52; "Guild and Typographical Union Make Papers in Merger Talks," *Daily Labor Report*, November

26, 1974, p. A1; "Typographical Union and Newspaper Guild Fail to Reach Merger Agreement, End Talks," *Daily Labor Report*, April 13, 1981, pp. A1–A2.

37. "Typographical Union to Open Merger Talks With Teamsters," *Daily Labor Report*, September 28, 1983, p. a9; Walsh, *op. cit.*, pp. 165–72.

38. "Typographical Union Chief Complains to Kirkland: Urges Teamsters Reaffiliation," *Daily Labor Report*, October 12, 1983, p. A10.

39. "Printing Industry Union Officials Meet to Discuss Possible Merger," *Daily Labor Report*, October 26, 1983, p. A5.

40. "Talks Advance on Merger of Printers Into Teamsters Union," *New York Times*, February 21, 1984, p. A19.

41. "Teamsters Merger Plans with ITU Presenting Challenge to AFL–CIO," *Daily Labor Report*, April 11, 1984, p. A7.

42. "Agreement of Merger of Teamsters, Typographers," *Labor Relations Reporter*, April 2, 1984, p. 274.

43. "Merger Agreement Between International Typographical Union and the International Brotherhood of Teamsters," *Daily Labor Report*, April 11, 1984, p. E1.

44. Ibid., p. E2.

45. "Agreement on Merger of Teamsters, Typographers," p. 274. Federation opposition also occurred in Canada. The Canadian branches of the ITU were affiliated with the Canadian Labor Congress and that federation's president, Dennis McDermott, urged the ITU membership to vote against the merger with the Teamsters. "Typographers Urged to Reject Merger with Teamsters," *Canadian Labor* 29 (April 1984):3.

46. "Agreement on Merger of Teamsters, Typographers," p. 274.

47. "Committee Formed to Battle Proposed ITU–Teamsters Merger," *Daily Labor Report*, April 9, 1984, pp. A8–a9; "Battle Over Proposed Teamster–ITU Merger," *Labor Relations Reporter*, April 16, 1984, pp. 313–14: "Merger Between International Typographical Union and the International Brotherhood of Teamsters," p. e1.

48. "Committee Formed to Battle Proposed ITU–Teamsters Merger," p. a8; "Protest Over ITU Presidential Election," *Labor Relations Reporter*, August 13, 1984, p. 288.

49. "Election of ITU President," *Labor Relations Reporter*, August 6, 1984, p. 271; "Judge Bars Teamster, ITU Merger Until U.S. Rules on Election," *Wall Street Journal*, May 2, 1984, p. 60; Leonard M. Apcar, "ITU Agrees to Hold Rerun of Election, Supervised by U.S.," *Wall Street Journal*, May 7, 1984, p. 10.

50. "Printers to Pick Union President," *New York Times*, June 26, 1984, p. a13.

51. "ITU's Leader Appears Defeated in Voting," *New York Times*, July 27 1984, p. b11; Wilfred List, "Typographers New President Fought Merger," *Toronto Globe and Mail*, August 1, 1984, p. m5.

52. "Election of ITU President," p. 272. Reprinted with permission.

53. "Protest Over ITU Presidential Election," p. 289.

54. "Typographical Union Officer Election," *Labor Relations Reporter*, September 10, 1984, p. 25.

55. "Typographical Workers Union to Vote March 27 on Merger With Graphic Union," *Daily Labor Report,* January 23, 1985, p. A6.

56. "Labor Letter," *Wall Street Journal*, November 27, 1984, p. 1.

57. Gregory Stricharchuk, "Tying the Knot: With Ranks Thinning, Unions Seek Mergers to Retain their Clout," *Wall Street Journal*, January 18, 1985, p. 1.

58. "Merger Terms Worked Out by Leaders of Typographical, Graphic Workers Unions," *Daily Labor Report*, January 10, 1985, p. A10; "Printing Trades Unions Draft Plan for Merger," *AFL–CIO News*, January 12, 1985, p. 1; "ITU Leader Urges Members to Support Merger Accord," *AFL–CIO News*, January 19, 1985, p. 4.

59. "Typographical Workers Union To Vote March 27 on Merger With Graphic Union," p. A6; "Graphic Union Board Sets Vote on Merger with ITU," *AFL–CIO News*, February 16, 1985, p. 4.

60. "Typographical Union Members Seek Injunction to Block Merger Vote," *Daily Labor Report*, February 6, 1985, p. A11; "Graphic Union Board Rejects Merger with Typographical Union," *Daily Labor Report*, March 15, 1985, p. A14; "Developments in Industrial Relations," *Monthly Labor Review* 108 (May 1985):48; "Printing Unions Cancel Merger Vote," *AFL–CIO News*, March 16, 1985, p. 3.

61. "Printers' Union Rejects a Teamster Merger," *New York Times*, August 29, 1985, p. A21; "ITU Rejects Link with Teamsters, Still Seeks Merger," *Wall Street Journal*, August 29, 1985, p. 12.

62. The opposition to the merger between the affiliate (the ITU) and the expelled nonaffiliate (the Teamsters) is expressed in a recent interview with Lane Kirkland. "Kirkland Discusses Issues Facing Labor," *AFL–CIO News*, April 6, 1985, p. 2.

63. *Report of Karl F. Feller, International President to the Delegates to the Fortieth Convention of the International Union of United Brewery, Flour, Soft Drink and Distributive Workers*, September 1971, p. 46.

64. Ibid., p. 134.

65. For a list of the issues covered in merger negotiations, see David D. DeCenzo, "Union Merger Negotiations" (Morgantown: unpublished Ph.D. dissertation, University of West Virginia, 1981), p. 55. A discussion of the inability of two unions to resolve institutional differences in merger is found in Walsh, *op. cit.*, pp. 101–15.

66. DeCenzo, ibid., p. 67.

67. Walsh, *op. cit.*, pp. 89–175.

68. "Failure of IWIU–Steelworker Merger," *Labor Relations Reporter*, June 2, 1980, p. 89; "Developments in Industrial Relations," *Monthly Labor Review* 105 (October 1982):45.

69. "Union Merger Failure," *Labor Relations Reporter*, June 1, 1981, pp. 99–100.

70. "Why Mergers Tempt the Labor Unions," *Business Week*, January 14, 1980, p. 30.

71. "Merging Old Rivals into the Mightiest U.S. Union," *Business Week* (October 20, 1980):106.

72. Stricharchuk, *op. cit.*, p. 8.

73. Janus, "Union Mergers in the 1970's: A Look at the Reasons and Results," *Monthly Labor Review*, 101 (October 1978):17.

74. Walsh, *op. cit.*, p. 184.

5
The Integration of Union Governing Structures

In chapters 3 and 4 I examined the relationship between the motivations and barriers to merger. In the premerger stage, complex and lengthy negotiations are often needed before there is an agreement that satisfies the motivation to merge and overcomes merger barriers. The compromises found in the merger agreement are shaped by the forces acting for and against merger and can call for varying degrees of integration of governing structures in the postmerger union. In this chapter, I examine the way in which postmerger arrangements reflect the premerger situation.[1] I also review some results from a recent survey of local union mergers, an important form of postmerger integration.

Integrating Governing Structures

The principal study of union mergers and integration of union governing structures was completed by Chaison in 1982. It was hoped that the development of a typography of postmerger arrangements would be useful to "unions contemplating mergers, entering into merger negotiations and even at impasse in such negotiations."[2] The analysis was based on the degrees of integration presented in figure 5–1. The various degrees were differentiated by the union structures and the transitional character of the postmerger arrangements.

Amalgamations range from complete or near complete fusions of the involved unions, to only moderate degrees of integration, to loosely federated structures that many even resemble alliances more than mergers. At one extreme, absorptions can be complete and instantaneous mergers. Other absorptions can create semi-autonomous divisional structures and some may only be affiliations of smaller unions with larger ones. Most amalgamations and absorptions fall between the extremes in figure 5–1 and require only the partial combining of unions. In the following sections I describe and illustrate merger variations and then relate the degree of integration to the conditions prior to the merger.

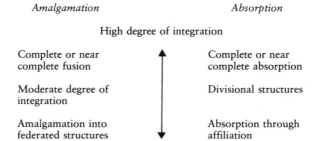

Source: Gary N. Chaison, "Union Mergers and the Integration of Union Governing Structures," *Journal of Labor Research* 3 (Spring 1982):142. Reprinted with permission.

Figure 5–1. Degrees of Integration of Union Governing Structures

Amalgamations

Fusion

It is a common practice in amalgamations to create additional governing positions to assure the continued employment of some or all of the merging unions' officers. This can be effective in overcoming resistance to merger. In complete fusions (a rare variation) there are no additional positions, while in near complete fusions, a small number of positions are created but these are eliminated after a short transitional period usually lasting until the first postmerger convention.

In both complete and near-complete fusions, the amalgamated union's first constitution serves to reaffirm the singular identity of the new union. All members of the premerger unions are treated as equal and full members of the new union. Officer positions are open to all possible candidates rather than allocated on the basis of prior union membership. Mergers are forced among local bodies that overlap in jurisdiction, as well as union departments which provide duplicate services. There are no divisional structures or separate dues schedules, conventions, or election procedures based on premerger membership. A possible exception might be the continuation of pension or benefit plans, but this is because of the difficulty in transferring to other plans. Future officers or staff would be covered under newly created plans which are standardized throughout the amalgamated union.

A high degree of integration was found in the 1959 amalgamation of the Insurance Agents' International Union (IAIU) and the Insurance Workers of America (IWA) to form the Insurance Workers International Union (IWIU).

The unions stated that they had "agreed to consolidate and merge both organizations to create a *single* International Union for insurance agents and insurance workers," to merge into *"one, single, consolidated* labor organization" (emphasis added).[3] The merger agreement allocated officer positions on the basis of prior union membership. The IAIU president would serve as the new union's president, and the IWA president would be the secretary–treasurer. However, these positions were to last for only two years until the second convention, at which time elections would be open regardless of past membership. All property, rights, funds, and debts of the unions were transferred to the merged organization. The unions' members were deemed to be members of the IWIU and all of their employees became employees of the new organization. The constitution provided for only one local union in any designated city or area and required that locals attempt to merge. Power was given to the IWIU General Executive Board to carry out local mergers whenever this was deemed appropriate.[4]

A fairly high degree of integration after a brief transitional period was also apparent in the 1982 amalgamation of the Aluminum, Brick and Clay Workers (Aluminum) and the United Glass and Ceramic Workers (Glass) to form the Aluminum, Brick and Glass Workers International Union (ABGW). Aluminum had a larger membership than Glass, as was evident in the initial division of officer positions. For the one-year transitional period before the 1983 convention, the president and secretary–treasurer of Aluminum received similar positions in the new union. Special positions were created for the president, secretary–treasurer, and executive vice president of Glass. However, rather than becoming a continuing feature, these special positions were set to expire upon the retirement, death, or removal of the incumbents. The ABGW would have twenty-nine vice presidents (nineteen from Aluminum and ten from Glass) but this was to last only until the 1985 convention. At that convention there were no requirements that candidates for any particular position had to be prior Glass or Aluminum members.[5]

All properties, rights, funds, and debts were transferred from Aluminum and Glass over to the ABGW. The merger agreement guaranteed that the merger would not terminate the employment of Aluminum and Glass staff members. All locals and districts were rechartered (but not forced to merge) and the members in good standing of both unions became members of the ABGW.[6]

Moderate Degrees of Integration

Most amalgamations call for only moderate degrees of integration of union governing structures. There is usually an expanded governing structure in place during a transitional period (sometimes called the "stability period") lasting until the first or second convention. This provides for continued employment of most premerger union officers. Officers close to retirement may be offered special pensions or short-term positions as consultants. Key officer positions are generally filled in accordance with formulas based on the merging unions' sizes. The unions often pledge that for some period of time they will make an effort to see that officer nominations for particular positions will be filled by persons from one or the other of the predecessor unions. After the transitional period, the size of the governing structure is reduced and nomination requirements based on past union membership are phased out. The eventual size and composition of the governing bodies are stated in the merger agreement or union constitution, rather than being left open to members and officers during the postmerger period.

Amalgamations with only moderate degrees of integration usually do not require widespread mergers of locals, although a few may encourage mergers of locals below a certain size. Frequently, collective bargaining councils or craft conferences are established to preserve the craft identities of the premerger unions. However, these bodies usually have little authority in the administration of the new union, while their activities are confined to negotiations and contract enforcement.

When unions settle for moderate degrees of integration, they often recognize that a complete or near fusion could not be accomplished immediately or even in the near future. This is illustrated by the 1983 amalgamation of the International Printing and Graphic Communications Union (Printing) and the Graphic Arts International Union (Graphic) to form the Graphic Communications International Union (GCIU). While the unions stated that they wished to achieve "complete organic merger," they recognized the need from a transitional period with special procedures. At the effective date of merger the GCIU was to have a president (the past Graphic president), a president emeritus (the past Printing president), a secretary–treasurer (the past Printing secretary–treasurer), and an executive vice president (the past Graphic executive vice president). The new union started with fifteen vice presidents—eight from Printing and seven from Graphic.[7] The merger agreement specified that the period until 1992 (ten years after the merger) would be a "transitional period to allow for gradual full integration while accommodating the interests of various segments of the membership."[8] There was a schedule for the attrition of positions, which eliminated the executive vice president's position by 1984 and five vice presidents' positions over a ten-year period. An "attrition principle" was also used to reduce the size of the general board; transitional board positions would not be filled upon the death or retirement of the incumbents.

Moderate degrees of integration were also required in the 1976 merger of the Amalgamated Clothing Workers of America (ACWA) and the Textile Workers Union of America (TWUA) to form the Amalgamated Clothing and Textile Workers Union (ACTWU). The two organizations were joined together under a new constitution. The positions of president and sectretary–treasurer were filled by the ACWA general president and the ACWA secretary–treasurer, respectively. The TWUA general president became the senior executive vice president and the TWUA secretary–treasurer became the executive vice president. The new union had forty-six vice presidents—the twenty-six ACWA vice presidents and the twenty TWUA vice presidents. These positions were later subject to election at conventions, but the parties pledged to "make their best effort" to continue the allotment of positions by prior union membership.[9] On the effective date of the merger, both unions' properties, rights, funds, and debts were transferred to the ACTWU. All prior employees of the ACWA and TWUA continued in their positions and were deemed to be employees of the ACTWU. Local unions and joint boards received a charter from the ACTWU and all past members of the unions become ACTWU members.[10]

Under the 1978 ACTWU constitution, there was a reduction in vice presidents from forty-six to forty-four.[11] The position of senior executive vice president was made transitional and scheduled to end in 1982, six years after the merger.[12]

Arrangements similar to those for ACTWU were used in the 1979 amalgamation between the Retail Clerks International Union and the Amalgamated Meat Cutters and Butcher Workmen to form the United Food and Commercial Workers International Union (UFCW). The allocation of initial governing offices was determined by past union positions. The Retail Clerks' president became the UFCW president and the Meat Cutters' secretary–treasurer became the UFCW secretary–treasurer. Executive vice president positions were created for the Meat Cutters' president and the Retail Clerks' secretary–treasurer. There were forty-eight vice presidents in the new union; twenty-five from the Retail Clerks and twenty-three from the Meat Cutters. All international officers would sit on an International Executive Board, but their voting strength would be proportional to the membership of their earlier union. The parties pledged themselves "to use their best efforts" to achieve results in officer nominations and elections at the first regular convention (1983) which would conform to the agreed upon allocation of officer positions.[13]

The merging unions wished to retain their prior geographic divisions, though they did merge some of their departments. All local unions could keep their charters and would become bodies of the UFCW. Local mergers were encouraged but would remain voluntary. The merger agreement stated that in recognition of "diverse practices" and "the inherent difficulties of substantial and precipitate change," locals would be permitted to retain some provisions regarding officers, elections, and funds which were inconsistent with the merged union's constitution.[14]

In keeping with the common practice in amalgamations, the employees of the Retail Clerks and the Meat Cutters were deemed to be employees of the

UFCW. Pension, insurance, and employee benefit plans were to be continued. All members of the Retail Clerks and the Meat Cutters would become UFCW members on the effective date of the merger. The two unions' properties, funds, obligations, and liabilities were transferred to the UFCW.

Amalgamation into Federated Structures

The lowest degree of integration occurs when amalgamating unions adopt federated structures. This variation has often been used to provide continued representation for craft groups in divisions with full-time officers and staff. The divisions elect their own officers and are usually given a role in negotiations and contract enforcement. A large number of new officer positions are created for divisions; few of these positions are transitional. Officers carrying the titles of "assistant president" or even "president" administer the affairs of the divisions. These officers also serve on the amalgamated unions' executive council. An officer from one of the larger division s serves as a "general president."

In federated structures, the divisions may hold conventions or craft conferences shortly before their parent union's convention. Activities at these meetings include officer elections, the determination of negotiation policy, and the passing of resolutions related to the division's interests.

A federational structure was used in the 1971 merger combining five postal unions into the American Postal Workers Union. The new union retained the craft identities of the predecessors by creating several divisions: the Clerk Craft Division, the Motor Vehicle Service Craft Division, the Special Delivery Messengers Craft Division, and the Maintenance Craft Division. Each division elected officers from among its own members and maintained a separate craft council. Nominating and election procedures varied among the divisions. Craft conventions met prior to the general APWU convention and were convened by each division's president.[15]

The governing positions of the APWU consisted of a general president, a general executive vice president, and the general secretary–treasurer. The federated structure resulted in a governing body of exceptional size, with a National Executive Board of forty-seven members.[16] This was not merely a transitional arrangement devised to ease the way to eventual integration; it reaffirmed and perpetuated craft identities and interests despite the merger of the unions.

Absorptions

Complete Absorptions

A high degree of integration of governing structures occurs in complete absorptions when one union becomes an indistinguishable part of another. In these mergers, the absorbed union's properties, rights, funds, and debts are transferred to the absorbing union. The absorbed group's members and staff join those of the absorbing union. Local mergers may be forced if there is substantial regional overlapping or many small locals. On the national level, there are no surviving governing structures of the absorbed union. Its officers are pensioned off, retained as consultants for short periods, or provided with employment in the absorbing union.

The complete absorption is exemplified by the merger of District 50, Allied and Technical Workers into the Steelworkers in 1972. Under the merger agreement, all District 50 locals were issued Steelworkers charters and governed by the Steelworkers' constitution and by-laws. After a brief transitional period, the officers of these locals had to be elected in accordance with Steelworker requirements. While locals previously in District 50 could retain their records, properties, and funds, these became subject to provisions of the Steelworkers' constitution and by-laws. The absorbing union received "all powers, rights, privileges, authority, duties and responsiblities" in regard to collective bargaining.[17]

The employees of District 50 became Steelworkers employees with full rights and obligations. The District 50 international president, international vice president, international secretary–treasurer, and general council became employees of the Steelworkers, and arrangements were made for their retention as consultants after voluntary retirement.[18]

The absorption of District 50 is indicative of the Steelworkers' practice of absorbing unions into a highly integrated structure. The union's first president, Philip Murray, was opposed to having his union's membership extend outside the steel industry. In 1944, he was finally persuaded to let his union absorb the Aluminum Workers of America, but only under the condition that it not form a separate entity within the Steelworkers. This established the Steelworkers' policy of absorbing unions "completely."[19] Recently some officers of the Steelworkers have suggested that the absorption approach should be more flexible and that an absorbed union should be able to retain "some measure of its own identity." Such arrangements would be needed if the Steelworkers were to reverse membership declines and diversfy its jurisdiction by attracting large numbers of absorption partners.[20] The recently proposed absorption of the Upholsterers International Union may indicate a shift toward mergers with low degrees of integration. The Upholsterers would form a division with its own headquarters and director. Autonomy of its local unions was also assured.[21] This form of absorption is discussed next.

Absorption through Divisional Structures

In this form of merger the absorbed union becomes a separate division, although its assets and liabilities are usually transferred to the absorbing union.

Some divisional arrangements entail separate constitutions, executive boards, and conventions. Others may provide less autonomy; meetings of local officers or delegates are only for the purpose of proposing broad resolutions, which are then submitted to the absorbing union's executive council.

Divisions are frequently headed by a full-time staff member appointed by the officers of the absorbing union, although in those few instances where there is greater autonomy, divisions conduct their own elections of officers. In either case, the division head has only the authority to direct the division's affairs on behalf of the officers or executive council of the absorbing union.

Divisional structures are not designed for transitional purposes. Rather, they serve to recognize, in a limited way, the special interests and identity of the membership of the absorbed union.

In 1979, a divisional arrangement was devised for the absorption of the Wood, Wire and Metal Lathers by the United Brotherhood of Carpenters and Joiners. The Carpenters created a Lathing Subdivision consisting of all former Lathers local unions. The subdivision's activities are supervised by the past general president of the Lathers, who assumed the title of assistant to the general president of the Carpenters. The general secretary–treasurer of the Lathers also became an assistant to the general president of the Carpenters and moved to a position within the Carpenters' Training and Apprenticeship Division. The international representatives of the lathers were integrated into the staff of the Carpenters. All past members of the Lathers were guaranteed full rights, privileges, and benefits as members of the Carpenters.[22]

The erosion of the lathers' craft status was the prime motivating factor behind their union's absorption. As a result, the merger agreement emphasized the retention of lathers' work: "Carpenters assure and guarantees that the craft of lathing will be continued and preserved";[23] "Collective bargaining relationships between Lathers Local Unions and employers which deal solely with the lathing trade shall be continued."[24]

A unique aspect of the Lathers/Carpenters agreement is that some issues which would have served as merger barriers were unresolved at the time of merger, probably because the Lathers were so strongly motivated to merge. For example, in regard to the merger of locals, the agreement only states that "an appropriate time will be agreed upon for consideration of . . . small local unions."[25] As for fringe benefit plans of officers and staff, it was agreed that they "must be further considered and discussed on a case by case basis."[26] The parties stipulated that if there were a dispute about the merger during a one-year transition period, it would be arbitrated by the AFL–CIO president or the president's designee.[27]

A typical divisional structure was also used in the 1978 absorption of the United Shoe Workers of America into the Amalgamated Clothing and Textile

Workers Union. The Shoe Workers was reconstituted the Shoe Division. Its Shoe Workers president and secretary–treasurer became ACTWU vice presidents, and the ACTWU pledged to make an effort at its next two conventions to have these two officers nominated and elected to their positions. The Shoe Worker vice presidents were designated as regional directors of the Shoe Division and given six-year terms of office.[28]

At the effective date of the merger all properties, rights, assets, and obligations of the Shoe Workers were transferred to the ACTWU. The positions of Shoe Workers' employees were continued and arrangements were made for integrating their pension, insurance, and benefit plans with those of ACTWU employees.[29]

The Shoe Division is directed and administered by a director and assistant director, but this is done "on behalf of, in consultation with and under the supervision of the President and Secretary–Treasurer of the ACTWU."[30] The director and assistant director's duties include supervising, hiring, and discharging field staff, convening meetings, and advising and consulting with locals. However, these officers must make periodic reports to the ACTWU officers and can approve strikes only "after prior consultation and approval of the President and Secretary–Treasurer of the ACTWU."[31] At the time of the merger, the general president and general secretary–treasurer of the Shoe Workers became director and assistant director, respectively, and were given six-year terms of office. "[A]fter the sixth anniversary of the effective date the Director and Assistant Director shall be appointed from the Shoe Division by the President and Secretary–Treasurer with the approval of the General Executive Board."[32] The clauses of the merger agreement which established the Shoe Division and its officers' positions were deemed to be in effect for ten years after the effective date of merger, at which time they would then be treated as parts of the constitution and subject to amendment. This last procedure is a fairly common safeguard in the establishment of divisions. It alleviates fears on the part of the absorbed union that the division could be altered or eliminated soon after merger if the majority of the absorbing union's members voted for a constitutional amendment to do so.

A typical divisional arrangement was also used for the 1983 absorption of the Insurance Workers International Union into the United Food and Commercial Workers. A Professional, Insurance and Finance Divison was established. The Insurance Workers' president became the division's associate director, with the union's secretary–treasurer and three vice presidents serving as his assistants. An Insurance Workers Advisory Committee was also created, staffed largely by the Insurance Workers' past officers. If division positions became vacant, the UFCW president would consult with the Advisory Committee before naming a successor, who must be from the insurance industry. The division holds a conference every three years.[33]

Absorption through Affiliation

An affiliation provides a way for an absorbed union to maintain a low degree of integration within the absorbing union. The absorbed union, often called the "affiliate," is set up as an autonomous local, district, or division. It retains its constitution and the right to collect dues, hire staff, and elect officers. Affiliates are free to establish their own bargaining policies and are unrestricted in their ability to declare work stoppages. For the right of affiliation, the union pays a per capita fee to the absorbing union and in return receives a subsidy to cover its organizing, bargaining, and administrative expenses. In many cases, the merger agreement can be terminated by either party after a specified time period.

Although they enjoy substantial autonomy, unions in affiliate status are nonetheless considered to have become part of the absorbing union. Consequently, if the absorbing union is covered by a no-raid pact, such as that of AFL–CIO affiliates, the absorbed union would be protected as soon as the merger became effective. Historically, this has been a frequent reason for absorptions through affiliation, and most recently this merger route has become attractive to unaffiliated public sector unions which need protection from raiding campaigns.[34]

The largest absorption through affiliation was the 1978 merger of the Civil Service Employees Association (375,000 members) into the American Federation of State, County and Municipal Employees (1,250,000 members). The CSEA was chartered as Local 1000 of AFSCME and was permitted to retain its jurisdiction over public employees in New York State. The CSEA continued to be governed by its own constitution, and it retained the right to:

> establish its own dues structure, elect its own officers, hire its own staff, make its own decisions regarding contracts and economic action, engage in political activity consistent with its own principles and policies, and retain such professional and other related services as it sees fit.[35]

The CSEA was required to pay a per capita tax of $2.90 per member per month to AFSCME and most of this fee was returned ($2.65 for the first year of the affiliation and later $2.40) in order to assist the CSEA in its representation and organizing activities. The CSEA retained its name and all property rights. It was permitted to select two international vice presidents for the AFSCME governing body.[36]

The Special Case of the Local Union Merger

Local mergers play a unique role as part of the motivation to merge, as a formidable merger barrier, and as a means for the postmerger integration of governing structures. In chapter 3 we saw the motivational aspect; some mergers were aimed at achieving economies of scale in union operations, partly through the combining of small locals.[37] In chapter 4, we saw that officer and member resistance to local mergers can form an important merger barrier, and that merger proposals have been contested and merger negotiations ended at impasse over the issue of whether locals should be forced or merely encouraged to merge.[38] Finally, earlier sections of this chapter indicated that extensive local mergers were generally not required in national union mergers except where there was a high degree of integration of governing structures. Despite its apparent importance, little was known about the dimensions of local merger activity until recently.

In 1982, I conducted a survey on local union mergers which dealt in part with the relationship between national and local mergers.[39] A questionnaire was mailed to the secretaries of the 184 national unions and employee associations that had local structures. Information was sought on the number and forms of local mergers, specific merger requirements, and parent union assistance in local mergers. Seventy-one usable responses were received for a response rate of 38.6 percent.[40]

There was a highly skewed distribution for the frequency of local mergers. Forty-three of the respondents (60.6 percent) indicated they had had at least one local merger in the past five years. A total of 1,885 local mergers were reported but a large proportion of these were in a few active unions. There were five respondents with over one hundred local mergers each, and these unions accounted for about two-thirds of the total mergers.

An analysis of the results indicated that many local mergers occur independently of national mergers. Only two of the five most active unions (those with more than one hundred local mergers) had been through national level mergers; the other three unions were using local mergers to develop wider bargaining structures in the construction industry or to achieve economies of scale in reaction to recent and severe membership declines.[41] The two active national unions which had undergone mergers accounted for 712 local mergers or 37.8 percent of the total cases. One of these unions had been created through an amalgamation (it had 255 local mergers in the five-year period) and the other recently absorbed another union (457 local mergers). Both are typical of national mergers being carried out with high degrees of integration. The national officers were active in local mergers by meeting with local officers, addressing local meetings, aiding in the combining of local funds, providing model merger agreements, and serving as mediators and arbitrators in local merger negotiations.

There were 6 less active responding unions that had undergone national level mergers. Three were involved in absorptions and had 90, 8, and 5 local mergers, respectively, while 2 unions formed by amalgamations had 32 and 10 local mergers. There were 5 local mergers in a union that was formed by amalgamation and later absorbed another union. The officers of these 6 merged national unions generally provided lesser degrees of assistance in local mergers.

The survey results illustrate the variations in local merger activity among merged national unions. The most active unions had apparently launched major campaigns to integrate postmerger governing structures. The other respondents were refraining from promoting extensive local mergers. There may be two primary reasons for the latter's policy. First, and most obvious, there may have been little need for local mergers. For example, this might be the case for merging industrial unions where locals do not overlap. Second, for some unions there could have been a need for local mergers but this may have been countered by strong resistance from local officers and members. If this occurred, there would be no requirement for local mergers in the national merger agreement and national officers would do little to promote them for fear of arousing local officers and members. In summary, the variations in local merger activity after national mergers reflect both the strength of local mergers as a barrier and the importance of local mergers as a motivating force behind the national merger. As a consequence, local merger activity (or the lack of it) provides an important link between premerger forces and postmerger integration.

Conclusions

It has been emphasized that mergers are not necessarily complete and immediate fusions of unions. Our analysis of merger agreements provided numerous illustrations of the possible degrees of postmerger integration of union governing structures. The degree of integration is the result of the give and take of merger negotiations; consequently it is shaped by the relative strengths of the motivation and barriers to merger. If merger barriers are not offset by a sufficiently high motivation to merger, these barriers will have to be resolved in negotiations if a merger is to be consummated. An effective way to resolve the barriers, particularly officer and membership resistance, is through structures requiring low degrees of integration.

Divisional structures or forms of affiliation are often proposed to overcome the resistance from the absorbed union's members. These arrangements, as well as the amalgamations into federated structures, are used to gain the acceptance of the merger proposal by assuring union members that their special needs and identity can be protected within larger unions. In addition, structures with low degrees of integration have positions that continue the tenure of officers and staff and these positions go far to alleviate their resistance to merger. Finally, lowered degrees of integration would help resolve institutional differences which create political and technical barriers to merger. Affiliations require few if any changes in the absorbed union's governing structure or administrative procedures. In divisional arrangements and amalgamations into federated structures, the merging unions are not required to undergo any radical changes.

The premerger conditions, as measured by the opposing forces of motivation and barriers to merger, can be closely linked to the postmerger structures agreed to by the negotiating unions. In this chapter I identified the varied degrees of integration of governing structures; in the next one I examine the possible merger outcomes and explain how they relate to postmerger integration and premerger forces.

Notes

1. The analysis of integration in this chapter is derived from Gary N. Chaison, "Union Mergers and the Integration of Union Governing Structures," *Journal of Labor Research* 3 (Spring 1982):139–52.

2. Ibid., p. 140.

3. "Merger Agreement," *Proceedings of the First Constitutional Convention of the Insurance Workers International Union*, 1959, p. 181.

4. Ibid., p. 181; "GEB Approves Merger," *The Insurance Agent* (March 1959):1.

5. *Merger Agreement of the Aluminum, Brick and Clay Workers' International Union and the United, Glass and Ceramic Workers of North America*, July 27, 1982.

6. Idem.

7. *Agreement for Merger: International Printing and Graphic Communications Union and the Graphic Arts International Union*, May 1983.

8. Idem., p. 5.

9. "Agreement and Plan of Merger and Consolidation," *The Advance* (March 1976):4–8.

10. Idem.

11. *Constitution of the Amalgamated Clothing and Textile Workers Union, as amended*, 1978, p. 13.

12. Ibid., p. 20.

13. *Merger Agreement of the Retail Clerks International Union and the Amalgamated Meat Cutters and the Butcher Workmen*, (1979).

14. Ibid., p. 7.

15. *Constitution and Bylaws of the American Postal Workers Union*, 1971.

16. Idem.

17. *Merger Between the United Steelworkers of America and the International Union of District 50, Allied and Technical Workers of the United States and Canada*, April 24, 1971.

18. Idem. Another illustration of a high degree of integration is found in the 1979 absorption of the 3,100-member International Mailers Union (IMU) by the 81,300-member International Typographical Union (ITU). The merger agreement stated that IMU members would become ITU members and be governed by its constitution.

Principal IMU officers became ITU representatives and all IMU funds were transferred over to the ITU general fund. However, local mergers were "entirely at the option of the involved local union." *Merger Agreement: International Typographical Union and International Mailers Union,* (1979).

19. George W. Brooks and Sara Gamm, "The Causes and Effects of Union Mergers with Special Reference to Selected Cases in the 60's and 70's" (Washington, D.C.: U.S. Department of Labor, Labor Management Services Administration, September 1976), p. E2–3.

20. *Forging a Future: The Report of the Convention Committee of the Future Directions of the Union, Twenty-second Constitutional Convention of the United Steelworkers of America,* September 24–28, 1984, p. 21.

21. "Steelworkers, Upholsters Shape Proposal for Merger," *AFL–CIO News,* April 6, 1985, p. 3; "Merger Approval for USW–Upholsters," *Labor Relations Report,* July 29, 1985, p. 263.

22. *Agreement of Affiliation: United Brotherhood of Carpenters and Joiners of America and the Wood, Wire, Metal Lathers International Union,* April 13, 1979.

23. Ibid., article I.

24. Ibid., article II.

25. Ibid., article III.

26. Ibid., article VII.

27. *Idem.* Arbitration of disputes over the interpretation of merger agreements is also specified in the agreements for the absorption of the United Shoe Workers of America by the Amalgamated Clothing and Textile Workers Union (1979) and for the amalgamation forming the Amalgamated Clothing and Textile Workers Union (1976).

28. "Agreement and Plan of Merger," *The United Shoe Worker* (November 1978):1.

29. *Idem.*

30. Ibid., p. 7.

31. Ibid., p. 9.

32. Ibid., p. 8.

33. "Merger of UFCW, Insurance Workers," *Labor Relations Reporter,* September 12, 1983, pp. 34–35.

34. Leo Troy and Neil Sheflin, "The Flow and Ebb of U.S. Public Sector Unionism," *Government Union Review* 5 (Spring 1984):20–21.

35. "CSEA–AFSCME Affiliation Agreement," *Civil Service Leader,* May 5, 1978, p. 8.

36. *Idem.* AFSCME also used an affiliation arrangement to absorb the Ohio Civil Service Employees Association. "Affiliation Brings AFSCME Strength to 50,000 in Buckeye State," *Public Employee* (September 1983):1; "AFSCME and OCSEA Finish Process of Affiliation," *Government Employee Relations Report,* June 6, 1983, pp. 1190–91.

37. Gideon Chitayat, "Mergers of Trade Unions" (Philadelphia: Ph.D. Dissertation, University of Pennsylvania, 1975), pp. 205–6; Brooks and Gamm, *op. cit.,* pp. B68–73.

38. For example, local mergers was one of the issues leading to the breakdown in merger negotiations between the International Longshoremens' and Warehousemens'

Union and the Teamsters in 1973. "Bigger Unions Will Pack a Bigger Wallop," *Nations' Business* (May 1973):52.

39. Gary N. Chaison, "Local Union Mergers: Frequency, Forms and National Union Policy," *Journal of Labor Research* 4 (Fall 1983):325–38.

40. For a discussion of the methodology, see ibid., pp. 328–29.

41. These unions are discussed in greater detail in ibid., pp. 330–31.

6
Merger Outcomes

U nions seem to have the greatest of expectations when they enter into mergers. They hope to reverse a declining trend, eliminate a persistent problem, or build a path to a brighter future. The expected merger outcomes are usually stated in the vaguest terms. For example, union officers have claimed that mergers would:

"Enable us to more effectively strive to meet the needs of our members and their families"[1]

"Bring fresh strength to the bargaining table and also enhance the ability of the union to respond to the needs of the members in a more efficient manner"[2]

"Enable the union to deal with its employers from strength"[3]

"Strengthen our union and preserve our future"[4]

"Strengthen the collective bargaining process by eliminating wasteful competition"[5]

"[Bring about] greater efficiency and economy of management."[6]

This chapter will go beyond these generalities by identifying and measuring possible merger outcomes and relating them to premerger conditions.

Evaluating Merger Outcomes

Studies of union mergers seldom address the question of whether or not the merger produced the intended results. Most investigators seem content to explore the reasons for particular mergers or the merger forms that were adopted, rather than determining if the union leadership or membership achieved their objectives through the merger. There are some important exceptions. In their richly detailed case studies, Brooks and Gamm attempted to measure merger impact on union governance, finances, organizing, and negotiations.[7] Chitayat also briefly discussed some merger outcomes in his case studies.[8] The results of mergers were viewed on a fairly theoretical plane by Coady in his arguments concerning the role of courts and labor boards in regulating merger activity.[9] However, these investigators stopped short of any systematic analysis of the links between premerger conditions and postmerger states, or the differing impacts of amalgamations and absorptions.

My model of the union merger process proposes that many merger outcomes are shaped by the dynamics of the premerger period. As we saw in the preceding chapter, the relative strengths of the motivations and the barriers to merger determine not only if there will be a merger but also the conditions of the merger if it occurs. When the barriers created by officer and membership resistance and institutional differences are strong in relation to the degree of motivation, the merger (if there is one) will entail low degrees of organizational integration. In contrast, a powerful motivation to merge in relation to the barriers can result in high levels of integration. However, there are also some motivating factors (for example the need for protection against raids) that operate independently of the degree of postmerger integration and have a direct impact on the merger outcomes.

The evaluation of merger outcomes can be an exceptionally complex task that requires the consideration of the direct and indirect influences of the premerger state. My approach will be to evaluate the probable frequency of the outcomes and the conditions under which they may or may not occur. It is certain, however, that with enough investigation, a merger can be found which resulted in any particular outcome. The reliance on such limited evidence has been one of the major drawbacks in the use of the case study approach. I will be taking a much broader view by examining the arguments for and against the widespread appearance of outcomes while also tracing, where relevant, the interrelationships between the outcomes and the forces of the premerger state.

After a review of numerous descriptions of mergers, from brief newspaper reports to lengthy case studies, I was able to identify twelve merger outcomes. Some of these outcomes correspond to the motivating factors described in chapter 3. Logically, we would expect to be able to evaluate a merger in terms of the reasons for that merger. However, we will also see that there are merger outcomes that were not intended by the merging parties but occurred along with or after the intended outcomes (for example, enhanced organizing ability after the protection against raids). The following sections will evaluate the probability of the merger outcomes and the conditions under which they are found.

Mergers Increase Bargaining Power.
Mergers Increase Union Strike Funds and Enable Unions to
Strike More Effectively.

These two outcomes are so closely interrelated that they can be evaluated together. Because the central purpose of the North American union is to serve as a bargaining agent, one would almost automatically assume that any major structural change such as a merger would be directed at improving bargaining and striking ability.

There are various possible links between merger, bargaining power, and strike effectiveness. In his study of collective bargaining, Kochan defined bargaining power as "the ability of one party to achieve its goals when faced with opposition from some other party to the bargaining process."[10] A wide variety of economic and noneconomic forces shape bargaining power.[11] In regard to mergers, bargaining power is said to be primarily influenced through certain changes in bargaining structure and ability plus the subsequent willingness of the union to strike in order to achieve its demands. These factors can be examined individually.

There is a widespread and seldom disputed claim that mergers increase the cost of disagreement faced by the employer in negotiations. It is said that the ability to strike is enhanced when an absorbed union gains access to the strike funds of the absorbing union, or when two amalgamating unions find that their combined strike fund reaches a level at which an effective strike could be supported.[12]

Merger proponents also claim that for absorbed, absorbing, and amalgamating unions, the merger can result in the consolidation of a previously fragmented bargaining structure. This consolidation increases bargaining power because there is greater potential for a damaging strike. For example, when an employer has a multiplant operation and different plants are organized by different unions, a merger would help to combine negotiations. At first, this might be done through setting common expiration dates and coordinating negotiation proposals. In later negotiations, pressures could build for more formal centralization and the eventual goal of a single agreement negotiated for a multiplant bargaining unit. A chief advantage is that potential strikes would occur under conditions in which an employer would have little ability to continue operations or shift operations to a nonstruck plant.

Another way in which mergers are said to affect bargaining power is by increasing the expertise, experience, and resources of the bargaining team. In particular, the small absorbed union would find that after a merger, it can draw on the services of the skilled and veteran negotiators, legal counsel, and research staff of the absorbing union.

Although the link between mergers, bargaining power, and the ability to strike seems quite logical and straightforward, there is reason to believe that this is not a universal outcome of mergers. First, the impact on strike ability could be discounted for many recently merging unions that do not have the full right to strike. Strikes are largely prohibited or severely restricted among public employees. In his recent chronology, Adams listed thirty mergers between January 1979 and June 1984.[13] Eight of these were absorptions of small federal or state employee unions (often called "associations"). When they were absorbed by large public sector unions, the associations most often did not gain access to any strike fund, and when they were absorbed by a private sector union, a strike fund may have been available but their ability to strike and use it was sharply curtailed.

There is also reason to doubt the widespread impact of mergers on bargaining unit consolidation. In all likelihood, in those instances where bargaining unit fragmentation was a serious problem, unions were involved in some type of coordinated negotiations prior to the merger. If such coordination was effective, it may have paved the way for a subsequent merger, but only if additional outcomes were expected (for example, improved organizing or the achievement of economies of scale). One must ask why unions would merge to increase bargaining power and striking ability if these objectives could be more easily and quickly reached through a variety of alternative arrangements, ranging from agreements to coordinate bargaining to the more formal alliances discussed in chapter 3. Moreover, if unions could not manage to coordinate their activities effectively with such alternative arrangements, then why should one assume that they could create the mutual trust and flexibility necessary to successfully negotiate a merger?

One could also argue that in an appreciable proportion of the cases in which bargaining occurs on a highly fragmented or localized basis, a merger could do little to consolidate structures or enhance bargaining power by centralizing structures. Such a change in bargaining structures may be a radical departure from the predominant pattern in the union's industry, particularly if the industry is characterized by many small, diverse employers or by bargaining units that do not share common economic interests. Furthermore, one would naturally expect employers to strongly resist the move to consolidate bargaining structures if employers believe that this will increase the ability of the union to strike more effectively. In short, mergers may not always find their way into campaigns to centralize bargaining structures, and even when they do, they may have minimal impact.

Finally, it must be emphasized that bargaining power is shaped by a wide array of forces, ranging from macro- and microeconomic factors (such as employment and price levels, elasticity of demand for the product produced and the factors of production, and the importance of labor in the production process) to structural and organizational factors (such as the proportion of the product and labor markets which are organized by unions, and the formal and informal bargaining structures and patterns).[14] One or a combination of these factors can emerge as the main force shaping the bargaining relationship to the tactical advantage or disadvantage of the union. Under such circumstances, a merger could do little to change the balance of power between the employer and the union.

The concepts of bargaining power and the role of the strike in negotiations are exceptionally complex, and my brief discussion of these topics may have done them an injustice. However, my objective is not to fully explore these areas but rather to appraise the generalizability of two frequently proposed impacts of mergers. We can conclude that in any individual merger case, there *may* be increased bargaining power and an enhanced ability to strike, but that these are probably not outcomes which are shared by any significant number of absorbed, absorbing, or amalgamating unions. Too many other forces shape bargaining power and strike ability. It is also doubtful that many unions would go through the relatively difficult process of merger if these objectives were attainable through such alternatives as formal or informal bargaining alliances.

Union officers almost always tie their merger campaigns to greater bargaining power and the ability to strike, primarily because these outcomes are highly valued and readily supported by union members. The easiest way to sell a merger is to say that it will make the combined union more powerful in negotiations than either of its predecessors. Readers should recall that we reached a similar conclusion in chapter 3 in considering the role of the enhancement of bargaining power as a motivating force behind mergers.

Mergers Eliminate Jurisdictional Disputes in Organizing and Work Assignments.

Jurisdictional disputes occur in two forms: disagreements between unions over who should organize a group of workers, and disputes over which already organized workers should be assigned specific work by employers.

After a merger, a former interunion dispute may become an intraunion problem. Organizing rivalry can continue within a union between regional bodies or divisions and, in rare cases, between its locals. This rivalry can persist if regions, divisions, or locals are very autonomous, if organizing decisions tend to be made on their level, or if the merger (either as an amalgamation or absorption) requires only low degrees of integration. Overlapping locals or other union bodies in geographic areas could compete with each other, and organizing disputes could continue or intensify. However, few national unions could tolerate for long such internecine warfare, particularly when it reaffirms premerger identities and rivalries and threatens the stability of the merged organization.

Mergers also tend to internalize work assignment disputes. As we saw in chapter 2, mergers have historically provided a way to resolve jurisdictional disputes and have been encouraged and at times even imposed by federations for this purpose. For example, after lengthy negotiations and AFL intervention, an absorption ended the debilitating jurisdictional disputes between the Amalgamated Wood Workers and the United Brotherhood of Carpenters in 1912.[15] In 1979, the Carpenters absorbed the Wood, Wire and Metal Lathers and ended a serious jurisdictional problem.[16] This absorption was discussed in earlier chapters on the motivation to merge and the integration of union governing structures. It is worth recalling that under the merger agreement, jurisdictional disputes between lathing workers and other members of the Carpenters were to be resolved by internal union procedures previously used to handle disputes between different groups in the carpentry jurisdiction. The agreement states:

> Members of former Lathers Local Unions will have the opportunity, when employment opportunities present themselves, to work in any other branch of the Carpenters. Carpenters agree that the integrity of the lathing craft and jurisdiction will be maintained such as is presently maintained by the Carpenters for cabinet makers, millrights, dock builders and divers, etc.[17]
> . . . It is hoped that this affiliation will enable the Lathers Local Unions to grow as jurisdictional disputes are avoided and the craft of lathing strengthened.[18]

The internalization of work assignment disputes has long been a feature of mergers among craft unions. In 1915, Glocker wrote:

> To be sure, disputes do exist between American bricklayers and masons who are united in the Bricklayers' and Masons' International Union, but in places where such disputes have arisen, harmony has usually been restored by the committee on general good, which federates all local societies of the two trades throughout the community. If this committee can not settle the controversy it is referred to the international union, 'which administers justice', says an official of the society, 'and prevents another Cain and Abel episode.' Jurisdictional disputes have been serious blots in the history of many American trade unions, and an important argument in favor of trade amalgamations is the possibility that they will prevent one large class of such disputes.[19]

When jurisdictional disputes are a prime motivating force for merger, both amalgamations and absorptions are effective at reducing them. If decisions to engage in such disputes are made at the national headquarters of both merger partners, then they would be reduced soon after merger. If one or both unions has substantial local autonomy, the process may take longer. In either case, merger means that jurisdictional disputes become internal problems which are more within the control of the union's governing bodies, since now only political accommodations need be made rather than interunion agreements.

Mergers Protect against Raids.

A raid is a form of jurisdictional dispute in which one union attempts to gain the right to represent workers already represented by another union. From the perspective of the labor movement, raids are considered to be wasteful practices, a form of "organizing the organized." Raiding among affiliates has been consistently prohibited by federations, although as we saw in the historical review in chapter 2, raids against expelled unions have been supported and even actively encouraged.

Affiliates of the AFL–CIO are prohibited from raiding each other under article XX of the AFL–CIO constitution, the so-called "no-raid agreement" described in chapter 3. Consequently, unaffiliated unions which merge with or into affiliated unions find that they are immediately protected against affiliate raids. This protection is extended regardless of the degree of integration of the merging unions; even a loose affiliation will suffice.

Protection against raids is the type of merger outcome that can be immediately realized in either an absorption or amalgamation. Most often, the protection is through the coverage of the AFL–CIO no-raid agreement. In some cases, however, an unaffiliated union may enter a no-raid agreement with another union, affiliated or unaffiliated, and this arrangement will protect its absorption and amalgamation partners.

An ironic aspect of this merger outcome is that a union being raided may seek protection by joining one of its major antagonists. A "predatory" affiliated union can raid an unaffiliated one to create or intensify the motivation to merge and then turn around and offer protection against these and other raids if the unaffiliated union is willing to be absorbed. Such a strategy may have been behind many of the recent absorptions of small, unaffiliated public sector unions. In other words, the effectiveness of merger as a means to protect against raids has apparently encouraged raids as a means to intensify union's motivation to merge. A very fast way for a union to expand into a new jurisdiction is to raid a small unaffiliated union in that jurisdiction and then promise to stop if the small union agrees to be absorbed.

Mergers Enable Unions to Organize More Effectively.

When presenting a merger proposal to the membership, union officers usually claim that the merger will enable the union to organize more effectively. Although there seems to be a logical and appealing link between mergers and union growth through organizing, a closer look reveals that this outcome is far from common.

Chapter 3's discussion of motivating forces noted that merger advocates often state that a merger will result in greater financial resources for the unions (particularly the absorbed ones), allowing more funds to be devoted to hiring organizing staff, providing a legal defense to counter employer resistance during organizing, and covering such organizing expenses as the printing of leaflets and the rental of meeting halls. Moreover, for the smaller absorbed union, a merger may also provide access to skilled and experienced organizing staff, a critical resource which a smaller union might not be able to afford. Finally, absorptions and amalgamations can protect against raids, thus freeing funds and organizing staff that might otherwise be tied up in defending against raids.

Despite premerger pronouncements, in the final analysis, mergers are more closely linked to possible rather than actual organizing gains. Merger might increase organizing ability, but there must be motivation to organize before this ability can be translated into organizing activity and success. Recently, unions in general have been severely criticized for lacking both ability and motivation. One study suggested that unions are "unclear and imprecise" in determining organizing priorities and goals and seldom try to find the most effective means to utilize their organizing resources.[20] Many unions may lack interest in investing the time, energy, and resources needed to increase their size.[21] Several factors could be discouraging unions from more extensive organizing. Organizing campaigns are becoming complex and expensive as employers become more sophisticated and militant in maintaining a union-free environment.[22] Shifts in product and labor markets may pose substantial organizing barriers:

> There has been a significant decline in employment in unionized sectors (notably heavy manufacturing) and employment growth in the assumedly harder to organize sectors, i.e., white collar and professional jobs, in the Sunbelt and in the service industries. In addition, changes in the composition of the labor force, i.e., a higher proportion of females and better educated workers, have been characterized as impediments to union growth.[23]

In many cases the decision to invest in organizing has become highly politicized. Should scarce funds and personnel resources be devoted to serving the present membership (through negotiations and contract administration) or to organizing new members? Faced with this choice, elected union leaders may more frequently select the objective that satisfies the present (and voting) members.

While unions in general seem to lack the will to organize on a large scale, there is also a strong possibility that the motivation is actually decreased for absorbed and amalgamating unions. Coady has argued that:

> [M]erger . . . reduces the impetus for the resultant union to engage in organizing activities by filling the union's selfish institutional needs—survival, efficiency, power—without increasing net membership.[24]

In other words, smaller unions, or those with a declining membership, might find merger to be a substitute rather than a means for carefully planned and extensive organizing.

Past studies of union mergers have not shown any major postmerger growth for amalgamating unions such as the Bakery Workers, the Paperworkers, or most of the printing unions.[25] For absorbed unions, it is difficult to identify postmerger membership change because their membership is usually folded into that of the absorbing union.[26] In the case of absorbing unions, the evidence is mixed.

Tables 6–1 and 6–2 indicate the recent growth of four major absorbing unions, defined here as unions with more than two absorptions since 1970. We can get a broad view of the usefulness of absorption as a growth strategy for these unions by examining membership figures found in the chronologies of Janus and Adams. For our purposes, membership change was calculated as the difference between a union's membership at the time of its first absorption during the period under consideration and its membership after its last absorption. While these membership figures are certainly not precise, this method enables us to use a single uniform source of data and also excludes growth before or after merger activity. It should suffice to give us a rough approximation of aggregate growth and growth directly attributable to absorption.

The figures in tables 6–1 and 6–2 provide only partial support for the use of absorption as a major organizing and union growth strategy. AFSCME grew dramatically from 1975 to 1984 and also absorbed five unions. These mergers, particularly the absorption of the Civil Service Employees Association, accounted for about half of AFSCME's membership increase. AFSCME did exceptionally well with its absorptions but would have had an enviable growth record without them. The SEIU was also involved in several absorptions, taking in some fairly large unions, and grew by 28 percent from 1980 to 1984. However, almost all of this growth was accounted for by the absorptions, suggesting that these mergers may have become a central part of the SEIU's organizing strategy.[27] The UFCW absorbed three small unions within a fairly short period. Had it not done so, its membership would have declined. Finally, BRAC lost more than one third of its members from 1972 to 1983, although it absorbed four small unions in neighboring jurisdictions. Without these mergers BRAC's decline would have been 39 percent rather than 35 percent.

It appears that both AFSCME and SEIU have successfully used absorptions as a growth strategy. The former accelerated its dramatic growth through mergers, while the latter used absorptions to offset its inability to expand through other means. On the other hand, BRAC and UFCW both appear willing to take advantage of absorption possibilities, primarily to counter membership declines.

Absorption can be viewed as a fast, effective, and relatively inexpensive form of organizing which results in the movement of members from one union to another (similar to the results of raids) but produces no net gain in aggregate membership unless the absorption is followed by organizing campaigns among unorganized workers. It is also possible that the ability to "organize unions" through absorption may be counterproductive to the labor

Table 6–1
Growth of Major Absorbing Unions[a]

Year	Absorbing and Absorbed Unions[b]	Membership at the Time of the Absorption for the:	
		Absorbed Union	Absorbing Union
Brotherhood of Railway and			
Airline Clerks (BRAC)			
1972	United Transport Service Employees	2,000	275,000
1978	Brotherhood of Sleeping Car Porters	1,000	211,293
1980	Railway and Airline Supervisors	8,000	170,000
1983	Western Railway Supervisors Association	325	178,000
Total		(11,325)	
Amerian Federation of State, County			
and Municipal Employees (AFSCME)			
1975	State of Iowa Employees Association	2,700	648,200
1978	Civil Service Employees Association–New York State	207,000	750,000
1982	Arizona Public Employees	7,500	1,100,000
1983	Ohio Civil Service Employees	17,000	1,130,000
1984	Ohio Association of Public School Employees	25,000	1,130,000
Total		(259,200)	
Service Employees International			
Union (SEIU)			
1980	Jewelry Workers International Union	10,000	625,000
1980	Oregon State Emloyees Association	14,500	635,500
1982	National Association of Government Employees	100,000	650,000
1984	California State Employees Association	50,000	750,000
Total		(174,500)	
United Food and Commercial			
Workers (UFCW)			
1980	Barbers and Beauticians	27,000	1,300,000
1981	United Retail Workers	22,000	1,300,000
1983	Insurance Workers International Union	15,000	1,300,000
Total		(64,000)	

Source: Membership figures are derived from: Charles J. Janus, "Union Mergers in the 1970's: A Look at the Reasons and Results," *Monthly Labor Review* 101 (October 1978):18–19; Larry T. Adams, "Labor Organization Mergers, 1979–84: Adapting to Change," *Monthly Labor Review* 107 (September 1984):23–24.

[a]Unions with more than two absoprtions since 1970.

[b]The names of absorbing unions are italicized.

Table 6–2
Membership Growth in Four Unions due to Absorption

	BRAC	AFSCME	SEIU	UFCW
	1972– 1983	1975– 1984	1980– 1984	1980– 1983
Membership				
Before first absorption	275,000	648,200	625,000	1,300,000
After last absorption	178,325	1,155,000	800,000	1,315,000
Membership change	− 96,675	+ 506,800	+ 175,000	+ 15,000
Membership increase caused by absorption	11,325	259,200	174,500	64,000
Membership change excluding absorption	− 108,000	+ 247,600	+ 500	− 49,000
Change in membership	− 35.15%	+ 78.19%	+ 28.00%	+ 1.15%
Change in membership excluding absorptions	− 39.27%	+ 38.20%	+ .08%	− 3.77%

Source: Membership figures are derived from: Charles J. Janus, "Union Mergers in the 1970's: A Look at the Reasons and Results," *Monthly Labor Review* 101 (October 1978):18–19; Larry T. Adams, "Labor Organization Mergers, 1979–84: Adapting to Change," *Monthly Labor Review* 107 (September 1984):23–24.
BRAC: Brotherhood of Railway and Airline Clerks
AFSCME: American Federation of State, County and Municipal Employees
SEIU: Service Employees International Union
UFCW: United Food and Commercial Workers

movement because it may reduce the incentive to organize in the traditional sense. Brooks and Gamm believe that these mergers could be "especially attractive as an alternative to the hard, slogging job of organizing employees who are not yet in unions."[28] Accordingly, individual union growth through absorptions could actually result in a decline in aggregate union growth, although this has only been suggested and never proven.

Mergers Help Unions to Achieve Economies of Scale in Operations.

This critical merger outcome is closely tied to several others. In chapter 3, we saw that unions were frequently motivated to merge because they believed it would improve organizing and bargaining by increasing financial resources and staff expertise. Through the process of amalgamation or absorption, they could reach a size at which they would be better able to afford strike funds, specialized departments, and expert and extensive staffs.

The relationship between mergers and economies of scale may not be as clear and direct as many assume. This outcome is probably not very important to most absorbing unions because of the generally small size of the absorbed union. Tables 6–1 and 6–2 suggests two possible classes of exceptions. First, unions such as SEIU and AFSCME have managed to absorb some large unions, which may have enhanced economies of scale that were already operative. Second, some absorbing unions, such as UFCW, may have used mergers to retain rather than reach economies of scale. If growth had not occurred through absorption, they might have been forced to curtail services, close or combine departments, and lay off staff.

In the case of absorbed and amalgamating unions, economies of scale could be achieved if there were high levels of organizational integration and if transitional periods were short. On the other hand, we saw in chapter 5 that many mergers aim for low levels of integration through amalgamation into federated structures or absorption through divisional arrangements. In the latter, separate governing structures are devised for the absorbed union while in the former, additional governing or staff positions are created for the continued employment of officers. These arrangements can become permanent features of the postmerger union or can be slowly phased out over a lengthy transitional period. In either case, they are clearly the direct result of the premerger conditions. Low degrees of integration may be agreed to in merger negotiations if there is substantial membership, officer, or staff opposition to the merger because of the members' fear of submergence of interests or officers' and staff members' fear of the loss of positions. These conditions dictate that the only acceptable form for the merged organization would be one in which economies of scale may not be realized in the short run or possibly even in the long run.

Although expanded governing structures and the absence of local mergers may operate against the development of economies of scale, most mergers do combine union departments such as those for research, lobbying, organizing, and accounting. At least within these departments, if not within the union as a whole, economies of scale may be reached because of the increased size of the membership to be serviced and the greater amount of funds available.

Our conclusions about economies of scale are mixed because the conditions surrounding the merger create forces which sometimes operate against economies of scale. The agreement to merge with low integration mitigates the fullest attainment of economies of scale. Furthermore, the existence of transitional periods with expanded governing bodies and overlapping organizational structures means that we should be careful not to reach quick conclusions about the attainment of economies of scale. We may have to wait for the merger to "settle in," to reach its later or final stages before this merger outcome can be accurately appraised.

Mergers Increase Staff Expertise and Experience.

This outcome is closely related to those dealing with increased bargaining power and organizing ability as well as the achievement of economies of scale. Claims have been made that merger enables unions to enlarge and improve the quality of their staff and to train experts in such areas as negotiations, organizing, employee benefits, and union administration.[29]

The potential for a merger to increase staff expertise and experience would seem to be greatest for the absorbed union. This expansion would occur immediately after the merger if there were access to the absorbing union's staff. On the other hand, large amalgamating unions which already could afford adequate staff would probably experience little change in the quality of the staff following the merger. Smaller amalgamating unions, in contrast, might find that they were finally in the position to hire specialists, raise staff salaries, and initiate labor education programs.

Merger brings mixed results to the absorbing union. These unions would not find any widespread change in the expertise or experience of their staffs, but the addition of the absorbed union's staff might represent a valuable acquisition. When an absorbed union's officers and staff become part of the absorbing union's staff, the absorbing union can gain instant experience in negotiating and organizing in the absorbed union's jurisdiction. As a result, absorptions can be used not only for an organizing foothold in a new jurisdiction but also as a means to simultaneously acquire the staff needed to service and expand that foothold. The retention of the officers and staff of absorbed unions may be more than merely a way of overcoming resistance to merger.

Mergers Increase the Compensation of Officers and Staff.

In chapter 4 there was a discussion of officer opposition as a merger barrier. Officers' fears of the loss of power, prestige, and compensation can be reduced if positions are created for them in the postmerger governing structure. In amalgamating unions, duplicate and sometimes transitional officer positions may be created, while in absorptions the officers from absorbed unions are usually kept on the payroll as consultants. In either merger form, staff members are almost always given some guarantee of continued employment along with increased pay and benefits.[30] As one might expect, absorption has little if any effect on the compensation of the absorbing union's officers and staff because the merger usually does not bring about any appreciable change in their duties.

The increased compensation of officers and staff of absorbed and amalgamating unions has drawn particularly harsh criticism. Some observers believe that raises (and the positions that go with them) are "sweeteners" used to induce agreement in merger negotiations. Officers and staff members who negotiate their future compensation could be letting their personal interests affect a decision that should be based upon the potential gains for the membership and the union as an institution. In response to this criticism, one could argue that many amalgamating and absorbed unions were probably in financial trouble before the merger and could not afford to adequately compensate officers and staff. When these financial difficulties are resolved by merger, compensation rises to its "true" value within the healthier organization. Moreover, as I noted earlier, when officers of absorbed unions become staff members or consultants of the absorbing ones, they bring with them unique knowledge of the absorbed union's administration and political system as well as familiarity with the bargaining relationships in the industry and the potential areas for future organizing. Their knowledge and skills (which may even have been taken for granted by the absorbed union in the premerger period) become a valuable asset to the absorbing union and command generous compensation.

Mergers Result in Larger and More Powerful Governing
Bodies and Tend to Reduce Membership Participation
in Union Government.

Some critics believe that mergers counteract the democratic tendencies in unions by causing larger, more centralized governing structures and reduced membership participation. This outcome is said to occur in two ways. First, the postmerger enlargement of the union creates additional and complex layers of government.[31] Second, merger negotiations provide an opportunity for officers to rewrite the union constitution and assume powers that previously resided in the membership.

When there is a high degree of integration in either an amalgamation or absorption, more powerful and centralized governing structures tend to emerge. These can reduce membership participation because of the larger committees and meetings, the creation of additional layers of government between top officers and the membership, and the increased time and cost needed to run for higher level office. Also staff specialists, rather than member volunteers, might begin to play a greater role in decision making within the union. Coady summarized the possible antidemocratic effects of a merger:

> [M]erger tends to lead to a centralization of decision making power in the upper ranks of the union hierarchy. Worker participation in the development of the union policies which affect their day-to-day lives becomes indirect and vicarious and the relationship between their aspirations and the union's actions may become indistinct or disappear altogether. Special interest groups, and workers generally, may perceive a growing gap between their union administration and themselves.[32]

If there are low levels of organizational integration, as in the case of absorptions through affiliation or amalgamation into federated structures, governing power within the union need not become more centralized. Indeed, such low levels of integration are often negotiated by unions which fear a submergence of members' interests or a loss of officer status and power. They agree to merge only if there is extensive postmerger autonomy.

When the centralization of power does occur, it remains to be determined if it is a result of the need to govern a larger and perhaps more heterogeneous union, or if union officers have used merger negotiations to arbitrarily expand their authority. It has been suggested that a merger "may be an opportunity for retrogression from democracy under the auspices of oligarchic leaders."[33] Merger agreements (and the accompanying constitution in an amalgamation) are usually presented to the membership as a package, to be accepted or rejected in its entirety.[34] The price that the membership may have to pay for the merger could be greater power for the union's officers. The officers could be able to make changes in governing structures and practices that they might not achieve through the ordinary procedures of union government.[35] In their case studies, Brooks and Gamm found that the interval between conventions and officer elections was lengthened following the merger. Also, the merged unions' presidents tended to assume greater authority and, in some cases, local autonomy was diminished.[36]

In conclusion, the impact of a union merger on union government and membership participation depends largely on the degree of postmerger integration, the change in the size of the union, and the intent of union officers when drafting merger documents. Accordingly, generalizations should be avoided and the impact of merger should be evaluated on a case-by-case basis.

Mergers Result in Less Attention Being Paid in Bargaining to Special Groups Such as Craftspeople, Professionals, and Clerical Workers.

This outcome is closely related to the one that was just discussed. Some observers have argued that as mergers create larger unions with centralized governing structures, the needs of special groups receive less attention in negotiations. The discussion of merger barriers in chapter 4 noted that a major cause of membership opposition to merger was a fear of submergence into a larger organization. Such concerns were expressed by specialized craft groups in the earliest mergers:

> An objection to trade amalgamations is that, while related crafts have many interests in common, they have other interests which may diverge widely or may directly conflict. The difficulty of harmonizing these diverging or conflicting interests is increased when one trade outnumbers all the others added together, since the group having the majority is apt to use the amalgamation

to further its own concerns at the expense of the others. Thus, in the United Association of Journeymen Plumbers, Gas Fitters, Steam Fitters, and Steam Fitters' Helpers, the gas-fitters and steam-fitters, who are outnumbered by the plumbers, complain that often they are not given opportunity at local and national meetings to discuss matters affecting their own trades and that when given an opportunity they are outvoted by the plumbers. They declare that most of the funds are expended in behalf of the plumbers, and that most of the legislation adopted is favorable to that trade. The stone-masons make a similar complaint against the bricklayers.[37]

The common view is that minority status within a merged union leads to the representational neglect of craft, professional, and clerical workers. The basis for such conclusions can be challenged from several angles. First, special groups in the absorbing union might find little if any change in their status or representation. The absorption might have served to bring new types of employees into the union and this could increase the pressures for improved representation because of the greater diversity within the organization. Second, in either amalgamations or absorptions, there would probably be little change in the status of special groups if these mergers called for low degrees of organizational integration. Under these conditions, members who were neglected prior to merger would continue to be neglected, while if structural arrangements had been made prior to merger for protecting the interests of groups of members, these arrangements would most likely continue after the merger. Finally, and perhaps most importantly, there may be little connection between bargaining and governing structures in many unions. If bargaining was decentralized and separate agreements were negotiated for special groups, their interests could still be promoted through the determination of bargaining priorities and the ratification of proposed contracts. They might have less of a voice in running the union but would retain a great deal of control over the content of their collective agreement. Consequently, the evaluation of this merger outcome is not only dependent on the degree of integration in the postmerger state but also on the autonomy of special groups in the bargaining process.

Mergers Enable Unions to Establish and Maintain Special Departments (For Example, Departments of Research, Education, Safety and Public Relations).

My earlier discussion of economies of scale partially addressed this merger outcome. Amalgamating unions in particular may find that mergers enable them to finally reach the economies of scale needed to establish and staff specialized departments. The merged union's new size justifies the provision of new services, and its recently enlarged treasury enables it to fund and staff additional departments. Previously, such functions as legal assistance, economic research, and public relations may have been carried out by a single individual or within a single department.

Regardless of the degree of integration, absorbed unions generally find that merger has provided them with access to a variety of staff specialists and departments. An absorbed union's officers and staff can turn to the absorbing union for assistance in such areas as research in preparation for negotiations, the training of local officers, and the analysis of job safety issues. Before the merger, they may have had to neglect these areas or use the services of costly outside consultants.

Within absorbing unions, new departments are frequently created but these are usually used to satisfy the needs of the absorbed union's members and to use the skills and experience of that union's officers and staff. As we saw in chapter 5, one important way for an absorbing union to overcome officer and staff opposition in merger negotiations is to develop special departments in which their employment can be continued, often at increased compensation.

In unions resulting from amalgamations, special departments are sometimes established to overcome fears of the submergence of members' interests as well as to provide for continued employment of union staff. However, if these concerns are important and play a major role in merger negotiations, then separate governing structures, usually in the form of a federation, may be needed. The mere creation of a special department would not go far enough because it would lack a governing structure and some degree of autonomy in running its affairs.

Mergers Enable Unions to Lobby More Effectively.

American unions lobby extensively on the municipal, state, and federal levels. They attempt to influence legislators to pass laws favorable to workers or union members in general or those in specific industries or occupations. The objectives can be to protect jobs by restricting imports through quotas or tariffs, provide subsidies to American employers, expand representational rights for public sector employees, or require the provision of certain benefits by employers. Efforts can also be directed at the repeal or revision of legislation which unions believe hampers their organizing efforts, or at encouraging legislators to support bills which promote work safety, income, or job security.[38]

In many cases an absorption may lead to more effective lobbying because it provides the absorbed union with the skill and experience of the lobbyists in the absorbing union. Moreover, as union size increases through merger, either in an amalgamation or absorption, influence on legislators would also increase. Legislators would view union lobbyists as representing a larger group of voters, or a greater source of assistance or funds in future election campaigns. If the merger involved an affiliated union, the increase in size might also mean greater influence over the federation's political policies and the priorities of its lobbyists.[39]

The possibility exists that union size can also have a negative impact on lobbying. Members of a merged union, particularly an absorbed one in a highly integrated structure, could find that the lobbying voice is greater through the larger union, but that they have less influence over what is being said. If members merely become another interest or occupational group within the absorbed union, they may have to compete both for the lobbying staff's time and for a role in determining overall union policies. On the other hand, in cases of absorptions into divisional structures or through affiliational arrangements, the absorbed union is often permitted to retain its own lobbying and political staff. Under these conditions, the members of the absorbed union can find that they have control over lobbying policies as well as increased influence because they belong to a larger union.

Conclusions

In the preceding discussion, I attempted to evaluate the probabilities of various merger outcomes. Twelve outcomes were identified and discussed in regard to their prevalence and the manner in which they are affected by the forms of merger and the degree of postmerger integration. In addition to our earlier findings for each outcome, several broad conclusions can be reached:

1. *The impact of merger is not always felt equally by the involved unions.* In the case of an absorption, the benefits of merger need not be evenly felt by the absorbed and absorbing union. There might be little change in the absorbing union if there were a high degree of integration and thus no need for new union structures. The members, officers, and staff of absorbed unions would be the ones who experience the merger outcomes, particularly the protection from raids, achievement of economies of scale, more effective organizing or lobbying, and increased officer compensation. In amalgamations, the merger outcomes are more evenly shared and could often take the form of the elimination of jurisdictional disputes, more effective organizing or lobbying, increased compensation of officers, and more centralized governing structures.

2. *Merger outcomes are frequently shaped by the degree of integration of union governing structures.* Our model of the union merger process indicates that merger outcomes are shaped directly by the act of merger as well as indirectly through the degree of integration associated with the merger. The degree of integration in turn is spelled out in the compromises made in merger negotiations and is shaped by the relative strengths of the motivation to merge and the barriers to merger. Thus, the outcomes in the

postmerger state are determined to some degree by the conditions of the premerger state. For example, if low degrees of integration are specified and prolonged in the merger agreement, amalgamating unions may not fully realize economies of scale in their operations. As described in earlier chapters, this lower integration is often the result of substantial membership, officer, or staff resistance to merger, relative to the strength of the motivating forces.

This discussion also suggests that there are some merger outcomes which are the direct result of the merger and are not related to the degree of postmerger integration. Protection against raids is bestowed upon unions being absorbed into or amalgamating with affiliates, regardless of whether the merger entails high or low integration. Also, the enhancement of bargaining power and the ability to strike can occur under various degrees of integration because these two outcomes are more dependent on bargaining structure than union governing structure.

3. *Merger outcomes are not always immediately observed.* Protection against raids or increases in officer and staff compensation are outcomes that can usually be observed at the time the merger occurs. On the other hand, changes in the centralization of governing power, increased organizing ability, the reduction of jurisdictional disputes, and the achievement of economies of scale may be more accurately measured only after the merging unions go through the transitional period and settle into the final postmerger state. Changes in bargaining and striking ability may not be apparent until the merged union has gone through several rounds of negotiations or has attempted to alter bargaining structures.

4. *Merger outcomes are often interrelated and sometimes unintended.* The ability to strike and the enhancement of bargaining power are so closely linked that they were discussed together. Many other outcomes are also interrelated. For example, increased economies of scale can lead to greater staff expertise and experience, more effective lobbying and organizing, and the establishment and maintenance of special departments. The protection against raids and the reduction of jurisdictional disputes can free resources for more effective organizing.

For any given merger, several outcomes may be apparent which are linked by direct causal relationships. Moreover, one outcome may have been planned (for example, the attainment of economies of scale), while another (for example, centralized governing structures or less membership participation) may be a side effect of the degree of integration needed to achieve that outcome. It is important to recognize that not all merger outcomes may have been planned or are related to the specific factors that motivated the merger.

5. *A major problem in evaluating a merger outcome is that we often cannot say what would have happened if the merger had assumed a different form*

or degree of integration, or if there had not been a merger at all. Critics of specific mergers or merger in general seldom consider what might have happened if the unions had selected an alternative in their decision of whether or how to merge. Merging unions that fail to organize rapidly, bargain more effectively, or operate more efficiently are often criticized by their members and officers as well as by industrial relations scholars. However, a fair evaluation can only be made after consideration of what might have happened had the unions opted for a different form of merger or lesser or greater degrees of integration, or perhaps had selected an alliance as a merger alternative. Would membership and financial resources have declined even more, bargaining power eroded further, or jurisdictional disputes become more intense? In addition, critics should recognize that there are some problems, notably the impacts of technological change and employer reorganization or diversification, that lie largely outside the unions' control. Mergers cannot resolve these problems, but they may increase the unions' chances of survival in the face of such difficulties.

My objective in this chapter has been to establish a basic framework for the evaluation of merger outcomes. I have illustrated the relationship between merger outcomes and merger type and form, and the hazards of generalizing about the prevalence of the outcomes. In the appraisal of a merger, one should consider each outcome in relation to:

1. the impact of postmerger integration (and consequently premerger motivation and barriers) on the attainment of the outcome

2. the change in the outcome as the merged unions go through transitional stages

3. the causal relationships between that outcome and others

4. the link between the factors motivating merger and the outcome (whether the outcome was an objective of the merger or a side effect of other outcomes that were reached)

5. the positive or negative aspects of the outcome, relative to what might have happened had there been a merger of a different form or degree of integration, or an alliance, or no merger or alliance at all.

Notes

1. "UAW Affiliation Offers Exciting Challenges," *The Distributive Worker* (June 1979):2.

2. *Merger Agreement—International Typographical Union and the International Mailers Union* (1978), article II.

3. "Union Merger," *Labor Relations Reporter*, August 30, 1982, p. 378.

4. Charles J. Janus, "Union Mergers in the 1970's: A Look at the Reasons and Results," *Monthly Labor Review* 101 (October 1978):22.

5. "Two Leading Printing Unions Will Merge Effective July 1," *Daily Labor Report*, June 10, 1983, p. A2.

6. *Merger Agreement of the Aluminum, Brick and Clay Workers International Union and the United Glass and Ceramic Workers* (July 27, 1982), p. 2.

7. George W. Brooks and Sara Gamm, "The Causes and Effects of Union Mergers With Special Referencce to Selected Cases in the 60's and 70's," (Washington, D.C.: U.S. Department of Labor, Labor Management Services Administration, September 1976).

8. Gideon Chitayat, *Trade Union Mergers and Labor Conglomerates* (New York: Praeger, 1979).

9. Michael A. Coady, "Trade Union Mergers and Their Significance in the Canadian Labor Movement" (Toronto: unpublished LL.M. dissertation, Osgood Hall Law School, 1976).

10. Thomas A. Kochan, *Collective Bargaining and Industrial Relations* (Homewood, Ill.: Irwin, 1980), p. 310.

11. For example, see ibid., pp. 310–14.

12. Coady, *op. cit.*, pp. 103–4.

13. Larry T. Adams, "Labor Organization Mergers, 1979–84: Adapting to Change," *Monthly Labor Review* 107 (September 1984):23–24.

14. For example, see Kochan, *op. cit.*, pp. 311–16.

15. Walter Galenson, *The United Brotherhood of Carpenters: The First Hundred Years* (Cambridge, Mass.: Harvard University Press, 1983), pp. 99–107.

16. "Developments in Industrial Relations," *Monthly Labor Review* 102 (October 1979):73.

17. *Agreement of Affiliation—United Brotherhood of Carpenters and Joiners of America and the Wood, Wire and Metal Lathers International Union* (1979), article 6.

18. Ibid., article 10.

19. Theodore W. Glocker, "Amalgamation of Related Trades in American Unions," *American Economic Review* 5 (September 1915):526. Reprinted with permission.

20. James A. Craft and Marian M. Extejt, "New Strategies in Union Organizing," *Journal of Labor Research* 4 (Winter 1983):30. Also see Charles B. Craver, "The Current and Future Status of Labor Organizations," *Labor Law Journal* 36 (April 1985):215–17.

21. Joseph B. Rose and Gary N. Chaison, "The State of the Unions: United States and Canada," *Journal of Labor Research* 6 (Winter 1985):107–8.

22. Craft and Extejt, *op. cit.*, p. 30; Rose and Chaison, *op. cit.*, pp. 105–6; Jules Bernstein, "The Evolution of the Use of Management Consultants," *Labor Law Journal* (May 1985):295–96.

23. Rose and Chaison, *op. cit.*, pp. 102–3. Reprinted with permission.

24. Coady, *op. cit.*, p. 250. Reprinted with permission.

25. Chitayat, *op. cit.*, p. 137; Brooks and Gamm, *op. cit.*, p. a46; Coady, *op. cit.*, pp. 58, 350–56.

26. Gary N. Chaison, "Union Growth and Union Mergers," *Industrial Relations* 20 (Winter 1981):106.

27. The most recent sign of this strategy is the SEIU absorption through affiliation of public employee associations in Connecticut and Georgia. "Conn. and Ga. Independent Groups Affiliate with SEIU," *Government Employee Relations Report*, July 22, 1985, pp. 1042–43.

28. Brooks and Gamm, *op. cit.*, p. e61.

29. Coady, *op. cit.*, p. 69.

30. For discussions of the impact of mergers on officer salaries see Brooks and Gamm, *op. cit.*, p. a48; Coady, *op. cit.*, pp. 74–75, 104.

31. Coady, *op. cit.*, pp. 70–71.

32. Ibid., pp. 237–38. Reprinted with permission.

33. J. David Edelstein and Malcolm Warner, *Comparative Union Democracy: Organization and Opposition in British and American Unions* (New York: Halsted Press, 1976), p. 350.

34. Ibid.

35. Brooks and Gamm, *op. cit.*, p. a32.

36. Ibid., pp. b27, b53.

37. Glocker, *op. cit.*, p. 562. Reprinted with permission.

38. Charles M. Rehmus, "Labor and Politics in the 1980's," *The Annals of the American Academy of Political and Social Science* 437 (May 1984):41–42; Derek C. Bok and John T. Dunlop, *Labor and the American Community* (New York: Simon and Schuster, 1970), pp. 384–426.

39. Coady, *op. cit.*, p. 55.

7
A Comparative View of
Union Mergers

The preceding chapters developed a model of the union merger process and discussed the relationships among premerger motivations and barriers and postmerger integration and outcomes. This chapter adds a new dimension to our analysis by appraising the relevancy of the model to union mergers in two countries, Great Britain and Canada.

My review of the union merger process appears to deal with some basic forces motivating and blocking merger efforts as well as common postmerger structures. I would expect to find similar features in mergers in countries where labor union structures are comparable to those of the United States. On the other hand, I would also anticipate that mergers would be shaped to some degree by the unique characteristics of other labor movements and their broader industrial relations environments. Consequently, the model should enable us to explain general merger forms and frequency in other countries while also highlighting those merger elements that are not shared.

In order to analyze mergers from a comparative perspective, I will examine the recent merger activity in Great Britain and Canada. In both countries, the general labor movements and the specific union structures and functions are sufficiently similar to those in the United States for meaningful comparisons to be made. For each country, I will first briefly review the characteristics of their union structures and the forms and frequency of mergers. This will be followed by discussions of the forces motivating and blocking mergers, and the special features of mergers. Finally, I will examine the role that mergers may play in the recent times of stress and rapid change.

Union Mergers in Great Britain

Overview of Union Structure

In 1982 there were 11,744,000 union members in the 456 British unions. Of all these unions, 102 were affiliated with the Trades Union Congress (TUC), the British national labor federation. The TUC affiliates represented about 90 percent of the total union membership.[1]

The British unions form an exceptionally complex and diverse labor movement, particularly in comparison to that of the United States. This is primarily because British unions are older and were often formed in response to local working conditions.[2] They occur in several structural variations, including craft, industrial, white-collar, and general unions. This last type is comprised of unions that organize workers regardless of occupation or industry. In recent years, some new union forms have appeared as industrial unions began organizing white-collar workers and as craft unions merged to form multicraft unions.[3] There is also a large number of British managerial and professional unions.

If there is any one predominant characteristic of the British labor movement, it would have to be multiunionism—the presence of too many unions. Multiunionism is said to create wasteful rival organizing and the duplication of services because the workers at a plant are recruited by a different union for each occupation, or several unions compete for a given group of workers.[4] Even in those instances where there is minimal union competition or overlapping, multiunionism is still considered a negative feature of British industrial relations because many of the small unions have very narrow jurisdictions and limited growth potential. The TUC, government commissions, and even employer associations have called for structural reform entailing the reduction in the number of unions through mergers.[5] As a result of such efforts, the number of British unions fell from 1,323 in 1900 to 456 in 1982. However, new unions are constantly emerging; about 100 new unions have been formed since the early 1970s. Most are representatives of clerical, managerial, and professional employees.[6]

The gradual reduction in the number of unions through merger, and the simultaneous emergence of new unions has created a situation of both union fragmentation and concentration. On the one hand, there are numerous small unions, primarily newly formed management, professional and staff associations, as well as the long established and highly specialized craft unions.[7] In 1982, 83 percent of the unions had less than 10,000 members each and when combined represented less than 4 percent of the total British union membership.[8] At the same time, there was an exceptionally high degree of union concentration.[9] The 10 largest unions accounted for about 60 percent of the union members in Great Britain and the 25 unions with over 100,000 members each had almost 80 percent of the members.[10] Within the TUC, the 3 largest unions represented about 40 percent of the affiliated membership.[11] Several of these large unions (for example the Transport and General Workers Union and the Amalgamated Union of Engineering Workers) were formed through complex series of amalgamations or absorptions.

The potential for union rivalry that could be expected because of multiunionism has not been fully realized because British unions engage in extensive interunion cooperation. Unions operating alongside each other at the shop floor level often collaborate formally or informally in negotiations. In many industries, unions form into federations, with negotiations taking place between these federations and employer associations on the regional and national levels.[12] Interunion agreements have also reduced the potential for rival organizing. Jurisdictional disputes (called "demarcation disputes") and raiding (called "poaching") have not become predominant features of contemporary British unions.[13] Individual unions have restricted competition over members by entering into "spheres-of-influence agreements." The TUC affiliates are also bound by the Bridlington Agreement (or Principles) which blocks attempts of affiliates to poach each others members or to recruit in a jurisdiction where another affiliate customarily negotiates with employers.[14] The Bridlington Agreement has gone far to curtail rivalry, but at the same time it restricts unions seeking to expand into new jurisdictions. The result, as we will later see, is that many unions use amalgamations rather than rival organizing to increase the scope of their membership.[15]

The British union movement is under severe pressure for major structural change. Similar to their American counterparts, British unions were hard hit during the past recession. Membership fell by more than 1.5 million from 1980 to 1982, eliminating about half of the increase of the earlier decade.[16] Unionism among manual workers has sharply declined, with some unions losing up to one-third of their members during the past recession. All major unions with 100,000 or more members faced membership losses with the sole exception of a union in banking and insurance.[17] Mergers have been and will continue to be an important means for British unions to adapt to changing fortunes.

The Form and Frequency of Union Mergers

Table 7–1 shows the extensive union merger activity in Great Britain. The major merger wave from 1917 to 1922, largely a result of the favorable influence of the 1917 Trade Union (Amalgamation) Act, is discussed shortly.[18] By the end of that period the most probable merger candidates had merged, while the annual figures declined and remained relatively low with some minor fluctuations. The annual average number of mergers was about 11 from 1923 to 1931, 8 from 1932 to 1940, and 10 from 1941 to 1950.[19] The figure fell throughout the fifties and early sixties, with an average of only 4 mergers per year from 1951 to 1962. However, the impact of favorable legislation was again felt in the 1960s and there was a second major wave of mergers. There were about 11 mergers per year from 1963 to 1968, and 18 per year from 1969 to 1974. In the later 1970s, the rate began to decline again, dropping to an annual average of less than 13 from 1975 to 1979.[20]

The total number of British union mergers is high. From 1911 to 1979, there were 932 mergers.[21] The earlier mergers were primarily among smaller

Table 7–1
The Frequency of Union Mergers in Great Britain, 1911–1979

	Number of Mergers	Average Number of Mergers per Year
1911–1913	52	17.3
1914–1916	63	21.0
1917–1919	128	42.7
1920–1922	137	45.7
1923–1925	35	11.7
1926–1928	27	9.0
1929–1931	35	11.7
1932–1934	29	9.7
1935–1937	29	9.7
1938–1940	17	5.7
1941–1943	21	7.0
1944–1946	38	12.7
1947–1950	37	9.3
1951–1953	9	3.0
1954–1956	16	5.3
1957–1959	6	2.0
1960–1962	17	5.7
1963–1965	32	10.7
1966–1968	33	11.0
1969–1971	54	18.0
1972–1974	54	18.0
1975–1977	41	13.7
1978–1979	22	11.0

Source: Figures for union mergers are from R.T. Buchanan, "Merger Waves in British Unionism," *Industrial Relations Journal* 5 (Summer 1974):41; R.T. Buchanan, "Mergers in British Trade Unions, 1949–79," *Industrial Relations Journal* 12 (1981):41.

unions and those of blue-collar workers. Since the mid-1960s British mergers have increasingly involved larger unions and unions of white-collar workers.[22]

British union mergers occur in forms similar to those in the United States. In the amalgamation, each union loses its separate identity as it mergers into the new union. In the transfer of engagements, the British equivalent of the absorption, one union loses its separate identity as it transfers its obligations to another union.[23] The merger agreement is called the "instrument of amalgamation" in an amalgamation and the "instrument of transfer" in a transfer of engagements.

While the basic merger forms are similar, there are some important differences in the merger movements in Great Britain and the United States. First, British unions are more frequently engaged in composite mergers (amalgamations of three or more unions). There were only 4 composite mergers in the United States from 1890 to 1984 and the largest joined 5 unions. In contrast, composite mergers are fairly common in Great Britain and have created some of its major unions.[24] For example, in 1920 10 unions joined together to form the Amalgamated Union of Engineering Workers. The National Union of Mineworkers was formed in 1945 from 46 unions and later absorbed several other unions. In 1945, the Institute of Professional Civil Servants was created from 119 unions. The present Transport and General Workers Union, the largest British union, has been through 58 mergers and was formed in 1922 by an amalgamation of 18 unions.[25] The frequency and size of these composite mergers can be traced to the extensive British multiunionism with large numbers of unions sharing the same or neighboring jurisdictions, and the relative ease (compared to the United States) of forming complex merger arrangements because of enabling legislation. The importance of legislation will be discussed in a later section.

Mergers appear to have played much more of a central role in altering union structures in Great Britain than in the United States. As noted earlier, the TUC, government commissions, and long-time observers of the labor movement have frequently called for the rationalization or modernization of British union structures, and the main element of this structural reform has been the formation of industrial or general unions through amalgamations and transfers of engagements. Many of the largest unions were the creations of union mergers and have grown through successive mergers. As a result, one might say there is a British tradition of using mergers to resolve jurisdictional problems, reduce the diversity of union structures, and protect against the hazards of small union size. In comparison to American unions, mergers are more commonplace and are probably seen as a less radical approach by union officers and members.

Merger Motivations

There are strong similarities between the motivation to merge in Great Britain and the United States. British observers of merger activity have identified five major motivating forces: technological change, narrow or overlapping jurisdictions, economies of scale, growth and diversification, and the TUC.

Technological Change. Technological change has blurred the jurisdictional boundaries of the many highly specialized British craft unions and has led to intense rivalry, membership declines, and financial difficulties. This factor was behind mergers of unions operating in printing, construction, metal working, and textiles industries.[26]

Narrow or Overlapping Jurisdictions. There is considerable jurisdictional overlapping between the British craft, industrial, general, and white-collar unions. Mergers are frequently used to end major demarcation disputes, or to reduce the potential for such disputes by combining several neighboring unions.

This has been identified a principal reason for the mergers of the 1960s and 1970s.[27]

Economies of Scale in Union Operations. Despite the past merger waves, there remains an abundance of small unions. These organizations have recognized the need to achieve economies of scale through growth but found themselves confined to narrow jurisdictions. The increased demand by members for union services and the rising costs of these services has placed many small unions at what one British observer called "the threshold of union solvency."[28] There have been suggestions that unions with fewer than 200,000 or 250,000 members can no longer generate sufficient income to adequately serve their members.[29] Many recent union mergers, both amalgamations and transfers of engagements, involved unions with limited growth potential and a pronounced need to achieve economies of scale.[30]

Growth and Diversification. Several large British unions have used mergers for growth and diversification. The TUC Bridlington Rules make it difficult for unions to enter into organizing territories that have already been claimed. Consequently, unions rely on mergers, primarily transfers of engagement to expand the "membership market" and gain access to new areas of recruitment.[31] These mergers tend to create multi-industry conglomerate or general unions, rather than large single-industry industrial unions which are so often envisioned by the proponents of structural reform.[32]

The Role of the TUC. While the TUC has played an active and important role in British union mergers, its efforts fall short of constituting a major motivating force. The TUC proclaimed a need for mergers in reports in 1927, 1947, and 1963,[33] but confined itself to encouraging amalgamations by "stimulating and speeding up discussions."[34] In 1966, it went so far as to draw up a list of some suggested merger partners and to act as a "marriage broker" or "honest broker" in initiating merger discussions.[35] Moreover, when helping the parties to voluntarily resolve jurisdictional disputes, the TUC has encouraged closer cooperation which has occasionally led to merger.[36] The federation was also influential in the passage of the legislation facilitating mergers. Its present emphasis on mergers is said to be stronger than in the past.[37] However, like their American colleagues, TUC officials can neither force nor prevent unions from merging.[38] Indeed, in a recent survey, several affiliated unions even expressed the view that the TUC should not use the promotion of mergers as a way to create more rational union structures. It was believed that TUC assistance on mergers should be given on a pragmatic case-by-case basis "rather than as part of a program to establish some theoretically desirable framework."[39]

Merger Barriers

British unions have encountered numerous barriers in their attempts to merge. Many though not all of these barriers resemble those faced by American unions. There are four primary merger barriers: fear of submergence of interests, opposition from officers, institutional differences, and incompatible political views.

The Fear of Submergence of Interests. The membership's fear of the submergence of their interests has often derailed merger negotiations. This was found when small craft unions attempted to transfer into large general unions.[40] Membership opposition was also aroused when unions representing skilled craft workers tried to amalgamate with those representing semiskilled and unskilled workers, or when white-collar unions attempted to transfer engagements to the industrial unions in their areas.[41]

Officer Opposition. British union officers have often opposed mergers which appeared to reduce their status or eliminate their positions. This opposition has been particularly strong among branch (local) officers when national merger required mergers at their level.[42] Objections to merger have also formed from the personal animosity between the national officers of proposed merger partners.[43] Officer opposition has been behind recent unsuccessful merger negotiations of some printing, textile, and white-collar unions.[44]

Institutional Differences. Institutional differences can create a major merger barrier because of the long history, traditions, and unique characteristics of many British unions. There have been disagreements over such issues as branch autonomy in negotiations and the collection of dues,[45] the transfer of officer superannuation funds, the location of union headquarters, the employment of staff, the new union's name,[46] differences in dues and benefits, and conflicting organizing policies.[47] As one observer noted, British merger negotiations often collapse because of the "extraordinary obstacles enshrined in union rule books."[48]

Political Views. A merger barrier not generally encountered by unions in the United States but found in Great Britain is the incompatibility of the political views of union officers or the differences in union policies regarding political activity. Some British unions are and wish to remain nonpolitical while others may actively support political candidates. Observers of British industrial relations have noted that the political orientations of unions have to be similar before a merger can be successfully negotiated.[49]

Aside from this last factor, there appear to be broad similarities in the motivating forces and barriers in British union mergers and those in the United

States. The main differences between the movements in the two countries is found in the widespread use of federated structures, and the positive impact of legislation on merger activity.

Federated Structures and Divisional Arrangements

Compared to American unions, British unions have made much wider use of postmerger structures with low degrees of integration. Some British unions have devised "trade group structures," arrangements similar to the divisions within American absorbing unions. Under these structures, small unions would more readily agree to a transfer of engagements because they would feel that their interests would be considered within a trade group. Larger unions would be encouraged to merge when promised that they could form the basis of a new trade group.[50] British unions have also made extensive use of federated structures for their amalgamations. These arrangements perpetuate the identities of the amalgamating unions by creating sections with high degrees of autonomy and, in many instances, different rule books (constitutions), subscriptions (dues), and even governing systems. After merger there may be some attempt to standardize the structures and procedures of the sections, but this is usually limited in scope and carried out during a lengthy transitional period. Most federated structures are set up to provide for continued group identity and substantial autonomy and special representation.[51]

The Impact of Legislation

In the United States, the legal requirements of national union mergers generally involve questions of whether the unions' constitutions were being followed in the merger process and whether union members' representational or political rights were being protected when the merger proposal was being scrutinized and approved.[52] Although in Britain, industrial relations in general are subject to far less government regulation than in the United States,[53] there is still substantial legislation affecting union mergers.

The first legislation to designate a procedure for union mergers was the Trade Union (Amendment) Act of 1876.[54] The act required the consent of at least two-thirds of the total membership (not just those voting) of each merging union. This level of approval was exceptionally difficult for most unions to attain and, in effect, the legislation formed a significant merger barrier. This barrier was reduced with the passage of the 1917 Trade Union (Amalgamation) Act. Merging unions each needed at least a fifty-percent vote, and the votes in favor of the merger had to exceed by 20 percent the votes against the merger. Although this formula was open to conflicting interpretations, the legislation sufficiently relaxed the voting requirements and came at one of the most formative periods of British industrial relations. The 1917 act spurred the first major wave of mergers (see table 7–1), lasting for five years and averaging over forty mergers per year.

In 1940, section 6 of the Societies (Miscellaneous Provisions) Act established a procedure for the transfer of engagements. A union could transfer its obligations to another if two-thirds of the members gave their consent. There was no need for a ballot (consent could be given at a delegate conference), and consent was not required from the membership of the absorbing union. The next major legislation came in 1964, when Parliament, under pressure from the TUC, passed the Trade Union (Amalgamation) Act to replace the 1917 and 1940 acts. Under this act, amalgamating unions required the consent of a majority voting in each union. In a transfer of engagements, the majority approval need only come from the members of the union transferring its engagements. The act also established procedures for notifying members of the merger vote, conducting the vote, registering the results with the government, and handling objections.

The distinction between the processes for amalgamation and absorption has created an interesting variation. Union officers can establish a "holding union" with a skeletal rule book and a membership consisting of the executive boards of interested unions. Each of the unions can, when it feels ready, conduct a vote among its membership to transfer engagements to the new union. As a union is transferred over, its regulations, officer structures, and dues are incorporated into the rule book. As a result, unions that might not be able to meet the election requirements of amalgamations (the balloting in all participating unions) can join together over time through transfers of engagements.

The 1917 and 1964 legislation have been widely credited with increasing the frequency of mergers and forming the two merger waves seen in table 7–1.[55] The legislation does not create the motivation to merge, but it does establish a standardized, easily understood and applied way for channeling the desire to merge as well as expressions of membership opposition. Only under this framework of rules could British unions carry out such a large number of absorptions or negotiate complex amalgamations within a short period.

The Future Role of Mergers

The British labor movement is in a period of exceptional stress. As I already noted, unions recently faced major membership declines, particularly in their traditional strongholds in manufacturing. Moreover, industrywide and nationwide bargaining, long hallmarks of British industrial relations, have begun to break down and individual employers are increasingly winning important changes in work rules. Employment is growing in areas and among workers with no tradition of union membership: among women and part-time workers and in the service sectors, the smaller assembly plants, and the high tech companies.[56] The proportion of the work force in Great Britain that is organized by unions has fallen below 50 percent for the first time since 1973.[57]

The problems of the British unions are both political and economic. Under the Thatcher government there has been a major effort to weaken the influence of unions in the competitive sector of the economy, and to reduce government cooperation and consultation with the unions on the national level.[58] Legislation has been passed that introduces regulations in the election of union officers and the collection of union political contributions. One observer characterized the British unions as a "pitiful spectacle . . . in disarray, impotent and on the defense."[59] Another observer saw the unions as "more vulnerable than ever."[60] After the bitter coal miners' strike, which lasted 362 days and ended in union defeat in March 1985, many potential and present union members began to question the ability of the unions "to deliver the goods when it matters most."[61]

While there are no easy solutions to the problems of the British unions, one can expect renewed calls for the structural reform, rationalization, or modernization of British union structure. Critics inside and outside of the labor movement stress the need for large industrial unions to replace the plethora of small, highly specialized craft unions. Continuing membership declines and increased employer resistance to bargaining and organizing will force many unions to consider means to cut administrative costs and introduce economies of scale into their operations. Technological change will continue to threaten the existence of narrow craft unions.[62] Mergers will become a key element in the attempt at the restructuring and revitalization of specific unions as well as the labor movement in general. It remains to be seen however if the patterns of mergers will be based on opportunism, as some have predicted,[63] with unions going after the most ready and attractive merger partners, or if they will be planned and coordinated so as to develop a structure with one major union in each industrial category. In either case, I expect the present dilemmas faced by British unions to produce vigorous efforts to reduce multiunionism through amalgamations and transfers of engagements.

Union Mergers in Canada

Overview of Union Structure

In 1984, there were 3,651,000 union members in Canada, comprising 39.6 percent of the country's nonagricultural paid workers.[64] These members belonged to 151 national unions, 71 international unions, and 577 local independent unions.[65] The principal labor federation, the Canadian Labour Congress (CLC), had affiliates with 56 percent of the Canadian union members.

There were also several smaller federations, including one based in the Province of Québec (the Confederation of National Trade Unions), and one formed in 1982 by international building trades unions which left the CLC.[66]

The Canadian labor movement has a degree of multiunionism (usually called "fragmentation") that is comparable to that of the British labor movement. In addition, the presence of U.S.-based international unions has created a unique element in Canadian union structure. These two key characteristics of Canadian unions—fragmentation and international unionism—have strongly affected the patterns of past merger activity and the potential for future mergers.

The Extent of Union Fragmentation

The exceptional degree of union fragmentation in Canada is shown in table 7–2. In 1984 there were 222 national and international unions operating in Canada. More than half of these unions had less than five thousand members and two-thirds had less than ten thousand members.[67]

The extent of fragmentation among Canadian unions has increased as the emergence of new national unions offsets the declining number of international unions. From 1966 to 1984, the number of internationals fell by 40 (from 111 to 71) while the number of national unions increased by 96 (from 55 to 151).[68] The result is a labor movement marked by many small national unions with narrow jurisdictions. For example, in 1984, there were 23 unions in education, 27 in health care, 10 in the airline industry, and 6 for police.[69]

Several factors have contributed to the extent of fragmentation in the Canadian labor movement. First, the union structures reflect the predominance of highly decentralized bargaining structures in Canada. Negotiations are seldom conducted on an industrywide basis or across provincial boundaries;

Table 7–2
The Size of Unions in Canada, 1984

Membership	National Unions		International Unions		Total Unions[a]	
	Number	Percent	Number	Percent	Number	Percent
Less than 5,000	91	60.3	29	40.8	120	54.1
5,000–9,999	24	15.9	9	12.7	33	14.9
10,000–19,999	16	10.6	15	21.1	31	14.0
20,000–49,999	13	8.6	8	11.3	21	9.5
50,000 +	7	4.6	10	14.1	17	7.7
Total	151	100.0%	71	100.0%	222	100.2%[b]

Source: Figures are derived from Canada Department of Labour, *Directory of Labour Organizations in Canada, 1984* (Ottawa: Supply and Services Canada, 1984), p. xxx.
[a]Does not include local independent unions and directly chartered locals.
[b]Does not equal 100.0% because of rounding.

this is primarily because of the provincial rather than national scope of labor laws. It has been reported that typically there are about 10,000 collective agreements negotiated each year in Canada and about 90 percent of these are within single employer–single union bargaining structures.[70]

A second factor leading to fragmentation is the metamorphosis of government employee associations. Over the years and with the passage of protective labor legislation, government employee organizations moved from forms of consultation, to intermediate stages of negotiations in which the government retained the right to make final decisions, to collective bargaining relationships similar to those in the private sector. When reaching this last stage these associations emerged and were first categorized as labor organizations. Reflecting their earlier roles as consultative bodies, they were highly specialized in membership and confined within provincial jurisdictions.[71]

A third factor related to fragmentation is the dominating presence of international unions in Canada. It has been argued that international unions fostered fragmentation by blocking the spread of national unions while also hindering their ability to merge with each other. Later sections will examine the scope of international unionism and its past and present impact on merger activity.

International Unionism

Canada is unique in that it has a large portion of its labor force organized by U.S.-based unions. The development of the U.S. international unions began in the 1860s and 1870s as craftsworkers moved across the Canadian border but continued to be represented by the same unions. In addition, small and isolated unions in Canada found themselves strengthened by establishing ties with large U.S. unions. International unions seemed attractive to Canadian workers because they often could provide the expertise and financial resources that were unavailable in many of the Canadian national and local unions.[72]

At the turn of the century, about 95 percent of Canadian union members were in international unions. This proportion gradually declined to about 57 percent by the mid-1930s because of the emergence of new Canadian national unions in manufacturing sectors. The trend was soon reversed as international unions led the way in the rapid organization of mass production industries. However, in the 1960s, Canadian national unions made important membership gains as they organized public and professional workers.[73] As a result, the proportion of union members in internationals began a steady decline. In 1976, Canadian national unions could for the first time claim to represent a majority of union members,[74] and by 1984 they accounted for 56 percent of union members.[75]

The presence of the international unions has caused a continuing and often heated debate between those who want a purely Canadian national labor movement and those who see no conflict between international union organization and the effective pursuit of the interests of Canadian union members. Among the points of contention are whether internationals can or want to satisfy the special bargaining needs of Canadian workers, whether the political approach of the internationals is appropriate for Canada, and whether the internationals spend more or less to service their membership than they collect in dues.[76] The cases for and against unionism have been presented in several studies, so there is no need to review them here except to note the important impact of international unionism on union mergers in Canada. As we will see, one cannot analyze union merger forms, motivations, or barriers without reference to the crucial role of the international unions.

International Unionism and Union Mergers

Table 7–3 indicates the form and frequency of the union mergers in Canada for the years 1956 to 1984. Thirty-eight of the fifty-five mergers were either

Table 7–3
Union Mergers in Canada, 1956–1984

Merger Forms	*Number of Mergers*
Mergers among Canadian National Unions	
Amalgamations (national with national)	9
Absorptions (national into national)	8
Subtotal	17
Mergers among International Unions	
Amalgamations (international with international)	10
Absorptions (international into international)	21
Subtotal	31
Mergers between Canadian National Unions and International Unions	
Amalgamations (national with international)[a]	2
Absorptions (national into international)	5
(international into national)	0
Subtotal	7
Total	55

Source: Figures are derived from Gary N. Chaison, "Union Mergers and International Unionism in Canada," *Relations Industrielles—Industrial Relations* 34 (1979):775; M. Bradley Dow, "The Labour Movement and Trade Unionism: Summary Outline" in W.D. Wood and Pradeep Kumar (editors), *The Current Industrial Relations Scene in Canada, 1984* (Kingston, Ontario: Queens University Industrial Relations Center, 1984), pp. 283–85.

[a]Indicates mergers between Canadian national unions and the Canadian sections of international unions.

among international unions or between Canadian national unions and international unions. Consequently, the motivation and barriers to merge in Canada are primarily a reflection of merger activity in the United States.[77] For example, membership or officer opposition in the United States can block a merger between internationals or between an international and a Canadian national union. Jurisdictional disputes, raiding, or technological change in the United States can motivate international unions to merge their structures on both sides of the border regardless of whether these are important issues in Canada. The international labor link is so significant that reviews of Canadian merger activity tend to be mostly discussions of the activities of international unions. For example, a 1984 survey of industrial relations in Canada described eight mergers or merger attempts; seven were among international unions and one involved a national union and the semiautonomous Canadian section of an international.[78]

Aside from "importing" merger motivations and barriers from the United States, the international unions create some merger problems unique to the Canadian labor movement.[79] Mergers of international unions are negotiated at U.S. headquarters. A merger barrier arises when the Canadian members resist the merger efforts of their parent unions because they believe their interests and identity will be submerged in the new organization. Canadian members are a minority within the international unions, and while their resistance to merger may be very vocal, it is usually unsuccessful.[80] There are some instances, however, where Canadian locals may not have blocked a merger but at least have not had to participate in it. For example, the Canadian locals of the Brewery Workers were dissatisfied when their parent union was absorbed by the Teamsters. After extensive litigation, an agreement was reached between the Teamsters and the Canadian Brewery locals. The Teamsters absorbed the U.S. locals and a Québec local of the Brewery Workers, but recognized the remaining Canadian locals as a new Canadian national union.[81]

In some instances Canadian sections of internationals attempt to merge without any mergers of their parent unions. International headquarters will usually oppose the merger, considering it to be a breakaway attempt, and can effectively block it if the Canadian sections have limited autonomy. In 1975, merger negotiations were carried out between the International Rubber Workers Union and the International Chemical Workers Union. These ended in failure but soon were followed by an attempt by the director of the Canadian section of the Chemical Workers to negotiate a merger with the Rubber Workers' Canadian section. He was dismissed from his office because of these efforts but later started a new national union by combining several secessionist Chemical Worker locals.[82]

The controversy over the intentions and effectiveness of international unions has also created an important merger barrier. When a Canadian national union attempts to merge with an international union, the national union's members may resist merger because they fear that their interests will be submerged in a union with headquarters and most members and officers in the United States. For example, in 1969, the Canadian Brotherhood of Railway, Transport and General Workers called a special convention to vote on proposals to continue merger negotiations with an international, the Brotherhood of Railway, Airline and Steamship Clerks. Although promises had been made that the Canadian union would become a semi-autonomous division within the international union, the promerger motions were defeated by a hesitant membership.[83]

Unions mergers create situations which illustrate the lack of complete autonomy of Canadian sections of international unions. Case histories of mergers either blocked or forced by international unions have found their way into the critiques of international unionism.[84] International unions are simultaneously blamed for creating fragmentation and for preventing mergers from being used as an effective remedy for this fragmentation. As pressures build for increased merger activity, we can expect to see movements for greater autonomy or even the independence of Canadian sections. This will intensify an important trend which has been gaining momentum since the early 1970s.

Union Mergers and the Canadianization of the Canadian Labor Movement

The Canadianization of unions is the process through which Canadian members of international unions achieve an increasing degree of autonomy in union government and collective bargaining. The driving forces behind Canadianization include rising Canadian nationalism as well as dissatisfaction with bargaining priorities established in the United States, particularly the perceived lack of militancy and the recent concession bargaining on the part of international unions.[85] Canadianization is a trend that had been predicted by many and often considered inevitable.[86]

Although there have been several movements over the years for increased autonomy of Canadian sections of internationals as well as the creation of exclusively Canadian unions and federations, the starting point for the present Canadianization efforts may be traced to the 1970 resolution of the Canadian Labour Congress.[87] These standards of self-governance of affiliates were reaffirmed and expanded in 1974, and require:

1. Election of Canadian officers by Canadians.
2. Policies to deal with national affairs to be determined by the elected Canadian officers and/or members.
3. Canadian elected representatives to have authority to speak for the union in Canada.
4. That where an international union is affiliated to an international trade secretariat, the Canadian section of that union should be affiliated

separately to ensure a Canadian presence and voice at the international industry level.

5. That international unions take whatever action is necessary to ensure that Canadian membership will not be prevented by constitutional requirements or policy decisions from participating in the social, cultural, economic and political life of the Canadian community.[88]

There was an unsuccessful attempt at the 1970 CLC convention to add a provision demanding that Canadian sections of international unions be given a right to merge without the prior merger of their parent unions.[89] Some CLC affiliates object to the moderation of the present standards of self-governance and there is a strong possibility that there will be additional requirements in the near future.[90] Whether these include a right to merge will depend on the extent to which such freedom is voluntarily granted to Canadian sections. One recent study concluded that Canadian sections in general will be receiving greater autonomy from their parent international unions, at times to the extent that the U.S. headquarters will have no authority over the policies and actions of the Canadian sections.[91]

The increased autonomy of Canadian sections has already resulted in a few mergers. In 1980, the Canadian section of the Oil, Chemical and Atomic Workers merged with some Québec-based independent chemical unions to form the Chemical and Energy Workers Union.[92] In 1984, the Communication Workers of Canada and the Canadian section of the International Union of Electrical Workers merged to form the Communications, Electronic, Electrical, Technical and Salaried Workers of Canada.[93]

There have also been some attempts by Canadian sections to break away from their parent unions. In the 1970s, Canadian sections split off from the Communications Workers of America, The National Association of Broadcast Employees and Technicians, and the United Paperworkers International Union. The most significant breakaway occurred in the United Automobile Workers in December 1984. The Canadian section of the UAW had been developing a bargaining policy that differed significantly from that of its parent union, and emphasized direct wage increases over job security and profit sharing. It also carried out work stoppages in reaction to employer offers that were similar to those accepted in the United States. The relations between the Canadian section and the UAW headquarters deteriorated, and in 1984, the Canadian leaders asked for what has been considered by the Americans to be impossible demands, including autonomous status within the UAW, with full control of bargaining, strike authorization, and staff appointments, plus guaranteed access to the international union's strike fund. The Canadian section also asked for "the right to pursue mergers with other unions, including Canadian sections of international unions, whether or not parallel mergers are achievable in the U.S."[94] These conditions were rejected by the UAW governing board and an amicable separation was arranged.[95]

The creation of the Canadian automobile union can lead to mergers in two ways. The union's separation can encourage other Canadian sections to split off, particularly those rebuffed by their parent unions when trying to merge or when opposing mergers by the parent union. Complete autonomy may now seem a realistic goal, and threats to secede must be taken seriously by internationals. In addition, the Canadian automobile union may soon develop a broad-based merger strategy. Its officers have mentioned the possibility of using the union to build a German-style industrial union federation—the Canadian Metal Workers Federation—through mergers.[96] It may also become an attractive absorbing union; in June 1985, the Canadian Airline Employees Association agreed to merge into it and become a nation-wide local.[97] Bob White, president of the automobile union, stated: "Once we get the structure in place we'll begin to discuss mergers with other unions."[98]

The push for Canadianization will be felt through efforts to increase Canadian section autonomy, or, if these are rebuffed, to create breakaway unions. Canadianization will open up new merger possibilities as Canadian sections gain the right to merge without the permission of their parent unions. At the same time, it is possible that Canadianization will serve to perpetuate some degree of fragmentation because Canadian sections will be given the ability to choose independence as an alternative to joining the mergers negotiated by their parent unions. In either case, Canadianization will reduce the importance of international unions in motivating and blocking union mergers in Canada.

The Future Role of Mergers

The labor movement in Canada is undergoing an important transition. It has been showing signs of a vitality not apparent in either Great Britain or the United States. Membership continues to grow; the unions remain militant both in their reluctance to agree to concessions and in their willingness to strike.[99] There also appear to be relatively large numbers of unorganized workers in Canada who are willing to join unions.[100] The relations between the labor movement and the business community seem to be improving and there is a developing acceptance by employers that unions have a legitimate and positive role to play in society.[101]

A resurgence in union mergers may be an important side effect of the drift of the Canadian labor movement away from the general orientation and specific structures of the American unions. For the past one hundred years, the impetus for union mergers in Canada has been generated primarily in the United States. The fragmentation of the labor movement may have been a potent force for motivating mergers but one that could not be fully realized because of the lack of Canadian section autonomy. With the increased Canadianization of the labor movement, Canadian national unions and sections of of internationals will be able to jointly address the problems inherent in fragmentation and explore a wider variety of merger possibilities. In effect, the merger movement and the broader Canadianization movement will intensify each other and widen the gulf between the two North American labor movements.

Conclusions

The brief discussions of union mergers in Great Britain and Canada illustrate the general applicability of my model of the merger process. British unions merge for many of the same reasons as those in the United States and encounter similar barriers. Merger motivations and barriers in Canada and the United States have often been identical because international unionism meant that most mergers in Canada were planned, negotiated, and consummated south of the border. Each country, however, had a unique character to its merger activity. In Great Britain, legislation initially formed a merger barrier but later played an important role in channeling merger efforts and opposition. The British legislation built the base for the development of exceptionally complex amalgamations and transfers of engagements. In Canada, merger barriers formed around the elements of international unionism. International unions opposed the mergers negotiated independently by their Canadian sections, and Canadian sections created barriers to the mergers of international unions. While opposition from international headquarters was once an insurmountable barrier to merger efforts of Canadian sections, this is rapidly changing with the Canadianization of the labor movement.

A key characteristic of both the British and Canadian labor movements is multiunionism or union fragmentation—terms denoting that unions are too many and too small. In Great Britain this will become a pressing problem as unions react to challenges from the broader economic and political systems. In Canada, union fragmentation will be high on the agenda of problems to be addressed by unions able to finally exercise a greater degree of self-determination. In both countries, we can expect to see a new reliance on mergers to restructure and revitalize the labor movements.

Notes

1. Tony Swabe and Patricia Price, "The Forgotten Unions," *Personnel Management* (April 1984):24.

2. Ray Marshall, Vernon M. Briggs, Jr., and Allan G. King, *Labor Economics: Wages, Employment, Trade Unionism and Public Policy*, 5th ed. (Homewood, Ill.: Irwin, 1984), p. 154; John Lover, "Why Unions Won't Reform," *Management Today* (September 1980):99; Arthur Marsh, *Trade Union Handbook* (Aldershot, England:

Gower, 1984), p. 4. Marsh states: "Critics of the untidiness of British trade union structure are complaining in essence, that it was, in common with other British institutions, evolved rather than created." (p. 4).

3. John F.B. Goodman, "Great Britain: Labor Moves from Power to Constraint" in Solomon Barkin (editor), *Worker Militancy and Its Consequences*, 2d ed. (New York: Praeger, 1983), p. 58. For a brief discussion of the evolution of British union forms, see Marsh, *op. cit.*, pp. 4–6.

4. *Report of the Royal Commission on Trade Unions and Employers' Associations, 1965–1968* (Donovan Commission Report), (London: Her Majesty's Stationery Office, 1968), section 681. Also see Marsh, *op cit.*, p. 32. For a discussion of the development of multiunionism, see H.A. Clegg, *The Changing System of Industrial Relations in Great Britain* (Oxford: Blackwell, 1979), pp. 174–86.

5. Swabe and Price, *op. cit.*, p. 27; Lover, *op. cit.*, p. 98.

6. Many of these unions were actually established prior to the 1970s but chose not to register with the government. In the 1970s, legislation was passed under which unions that wanted to enjoy statutory rights had to be registered with the government as independent of employer control or domination. Swabe and Price, *op. cit.*, p. 24. Also see Marsh, *op. cit.*, p. 37.

7. Swabe and Price, *op. cit.*, pp. 24–26.

8. Ethel Lawrence (editor), *Annual Abstract of Statistics*, no. 121, (London: Her Majesty's Stationery Office, 1985), p. 134, table 6.23.

9. John P. Windmuller, "Concentration Trends in Union Structure: An International Comparison," *Industrial and Labor Relations Review* 31 (October 1981):49–50. The average size of all British unions increased from 10,000 in 1945 to 29,000 in 1981. Marsh, *op. cit.*, p. 20.

10. Goodman, *op. cit.*, p. 58.

11. Lover, *op. cit.*, p. 99.

12. For a discussion of the impact of British multiunionism on collective bargaining structures and outcomes, see Clegg, *op. cit.*, pp. 186–94.

13. Goodman, *op. cit.*, p. 79.

14. "Rule 12—Disputes between Affiliated Organizations," *Report of the 116th Annual Trades Union Congress, 1984* (London: TUC, 1984), pp. 691–92. The Bridlington Agreement originated in 1924 and was confirmed at the TUC's annual conference in Bridlington in 1939. For brief discussions of the Bridlington rules, see Cyril Grunfeld, *Modern Trade Union Law* (London: Sweet & Maxwell, 1966), pp. 223–27; Marsh, *op. cit.*, p. 19.

15. Richard Hyman, "Trade Unions: Structures, Policies and Politics" in George Sayers Bain (editor) *Industrial Relations in Britain* (Oxford: Blackwell, 1983), p. 40.

16. Goodman, *op. cit.*, p. 40.

17. Marsh, *op. cit.*, p. 3; "Chronicle," *British Journal of Industrial Relations* 22 (November 1984):410. Also see Leo Troy and Neil Sheflin, *Union Sourcebook: Membership, Structure, Finance, Directory* (West Orange, N.J.: Industrial Relations Information Services, 1985), pp. 1.1–1.2.

18. Henry Pelling, *A History of British Trade Unionism* (London: Macmillan, 1963), pp. 168–69; B.C. Roberts, *Trade Union Government and Administration in Great Britain* (London: G. Bell and Sons, Ltd., 1956), p. 10.

19. Robert T. Buchanan, "Merger Waves in British Unionism," *Industrial Relations Journal* 5 (Summer 1974):41.

20. Robert T. Buchanan, "Mergers in British Trade Unions, 1949–79," *Industrial Relations Journal* 12 (1981):41.

21. Buchanan, "Merger Waves in British Unionism," p. 41; Buchanan, "Mergers in British Trade Unions, 1949–1979," p. 41. In the same period in the United States, there were 147 mergers of national unions. It is difficult to compare the American and British merger rates because the British figures may include the activities of some organizations that could be categorized as local independent unions and that were excluded from the American tabulations. There is also greater potential for mergers in Great Britain because of the much larger number of possible merger partners.

22. Buchanan, "Mergers in British Trade Unions, 1949–1979," p. 41.

23. Jack Jones and Max Morris, *The A–Z of Trade Unionism and Industrial Relations* (London: Heineman, 1982), p. 8. For a discussion of British merger forms comparable to amalgamations and absorptions, see R. Undy, V. Ellis, W.E.J. McCarthy, and A.M. Halmos, *Change in Trade Unions* (London: Hutchison, 1981), p. 74.

24. For example, see Robert T. Buchanan, "Union Concentration and the Largest Unions," *British Journal of Industrial Relations* 19 (July 1981):233; Marsh, *op. cit.*, p. 177.

25. Roberts, *op. cit.*, p. 28; Allen Hutt, *British Trade Unionism* (London: Laurence & Wishart, 1975), pp. 91–92.

26. Robert Taylor, *The Fifth Estate: Britain's Unions in the Seventies* (London: Routledge and Kegan Paul, 1978), pp. 25–26; Buchanan, "Merger Waves in British Unionism," p. 40; Lover, *op. cit.*, p. 98; Richard Upton, "Trade Union Marriages—the Reasons and the Rites," *Personnel Management* 12 (September 1980):40; Hyman, *op. cit.*, p. 39; Undy et al., *op. cit.*, p. 190.

27. Buchanan, "Merger Waves in British Unionism," p. 39; Bernard Donoughue, Alan Oakley, and Janet Alker, "Structure and Organization of British Trade Unions," *Political and Economic Planning* 29 (1963):449.

28. Hyman, *op. cit.*, p. 38.

29. *Report of the 114th Annual Trade Union Congress, 1982* (London: TUC, 1982), p. 445; Buchanan, "Mergers in British Trade Unions, 1949–1979," p. 49; Rex Winsbury, "The Union Urge to Merge," *Management Today* (January 1969):69; V.L. Allen, *Power in Trade Unions: A Study of Their Organization in Great Britain* (London: Longmans Green, 1954), p. 21. For a discussion of the financial position of British unions, see Marsh, *op. cit.*, pp. 23–30.

30. Patrick Elias, "Trade Union Amalgamations: Patterns and Procedures," *Industrial Law Journal* 2 (September 1973):125; Hyman, *op. cit.*, p. 38; Upton, *op. cit.*, p. 41; Winsbury, *op. cit.*, p. 69; Undy et al., *op. cit.*, pp. 187, 214–15.

31. Buchanan, "Mergers in British Trade Unions, 1949–1979," p. 48; Hyman, *op. cit.*, p. 40.

32. W.E.J. McCarthy, "Introduction: Signs of Change" in W.E.J. McCarthy, (Ed.) *Industrial Relations in Britain: A Guide for Management and Unions* (London: Lyon, Grant and Green, 1969), p. 16; Hyman, *op. cit.*, p. 39; Winsbury, *op. cit.*, p. 68; Undy et al., *op. cit.*, p. 208.

33. For example, see Donoughue et al., pp. 444–47.

34. H.A. Turner, "British Trade Union Structure: A New Approach?" *British Journal of Industrial Relations* 2 (1964):169.

35. Winsbury, *op. cit.*, p. 67; Allan Flanders, *Trade Unions* (London: Hutchison University Library, 1968), p. 39; Taylor, *op. cit.*, p. 26.

36. Richard Upton, *op. cit.*, p. 39.

37. Everett M. Kassalow, *Trade Unions and Industrial Relations: An International Comparison* (New York: Random House, 1969), p. 165.

38. Upton, *op. cit.*, p. 38; Undy et al., *op. cit.*, pp. 179, 322.

39. Trades Union Congress, *The Organization, Structure and Services of the TUC* (Second TUC Consultative Document, April 1980) (London: TUC, 1981), p. 13.

40. Upton, *op. cit.*, p. 38; Undy et al., *op. cit.*, pp. 198–203.

41. This barrier blocked merger efforts of printing unions and railroad unions. Upton, *op. cit.*, p. 38; Winsbury, *op. cit.*, p. 68.

42. Upton, *op. cit.*, pp. 38–39.

43. Donoughue, et al., *op. cit.*, p. 448; Marsh, *op. cit.*, p. 22; Taylor, *op. cit.*, p. 45.

44. Buchanan, "Merger Waves in British Unionism," p. 40; L.D. Cowan, *The Clearing House Banks and Trade Unions* (London: The Institute for Banking, 1984), p. 63.

45. Undy et al., *op. cit.*, p. 181.

46. Donoughue et al., op. cit., p. 447.

47. *Idem.*

48. Taylor, *op. cit.*, p. 25.

49. Buchanan, "Mergers in British Trade Unions, 1949–1979," p. 47; Undy et al., *op. cit.*, p. 186.

50. Winsbury, *op. cit.*, p. 68; Patrick Elias, *op. cit.*, 127; Undy et al., *op. cit.*, p. 218. Major examples of the use of a trade group structure are found in the Transport and General Workers Union and the Association of Scientific, Technical and Managerial Staffs.

51. Elias, *op. cit.*, p. 130; Flanders, *op. cit.*, p. 40; Undy et al., *op. cit.*, pp. 198–203; John Hughes, "The Trade Union Response to Mergers" in J.M. Samuels (editor) *Readings in Mergers and Takeovers* (New York: St. Martin's Press, 1972), p. 153. The Amalgamated Union of Engineering Workers has a typical federated structure.

52. There are some stringent requirements for membership voting when local independent unions affiliate with national unions because this implies a change of bargaining agent. For discussions of the relevant doctrines of the U.S. National Labor Relations Board, see "Union Affiliations and Collective Bargaining," *University of Pennsylvania Law Review* 108 (December 1979):430–68; Linda Carlisle, "Notes: Union Mergers and the Amendment Certification Procedure," *Catholic University Law Review* 28 (1979):587–604; Ellen Jean Dannin, "Union Mergers and Affiliations: Discontinuing the Continuity of Representation Test," *Labor Law Journal* 32 (March 1981):170–79; "Supreme Court Will Decide Who Gets to Vote in Affiliation Elections," *Labor Law Reports*, May 17, 1985, p. 1; "Unions Must Allow Nonmembers to Vote in Merger Elections: CA-7," *Labor Law Reports* (November 1, 1985):1.

53. Marshall et al., *op. cit.*, p. 149.

54. For discussions of British legislation dealing with mergers, see Elias, *op. cit.*, pp. 127–35; Grunfeld, *op. cit.*, pp. 235–48.

55. Elias, *op. cit.*, pp. 127–30; Buchanan, "Mergers in British Trade Unions, 1949–1979," p. 41; Pelling, *op. cit.*, p. 168; D.H. Simpson, "An Analysis of the Size of Trade Unions," *British Journal of Industrial Relations* 10 (November 1972): 387–89.

56. W.E.J. McCarthy, "Address by Symposium President," paper presented at the Third Annual Oxford University/BNA Symposium on Comparative Industrial Relations, August 5, 1985. For a discussion of the declining employment in the "traditional heartland" of British trade unionism, see Marsh, *op. cit.*, pp. 11–12; "Comparative Industrial Relations: A Trans-Atlantic Dialogue," *Daily Labor Report*, September 11, 1985, pp. 5–6.

57. "Europe's Unions Are Losing Their Grip," *Business Week* (November 26, 1984):80–81, 84, 88; Marsh, *op. cit., p.* 3.

58. Robert Taylor, "Industrial Relations in Britain—A Review and Update," paper presented at the Third Annual Oxford University/BNA Symposium on Comparative Industrial Relations, August 5, 1985; Derek Robinson, "The Effects of Thatcher's Monetarism," paper presented at the Third Annual Oxford University/BNA Symposium on Comparative Industrial Relations, August 15, 1985; R.W. Apple, Jr., "British Unions Hunting For Path Back to Glory," *New York Times,* January 22, 1985, p. 4.

59. David Soskice, "Industrial Relations and the British Economy," *Industrial Relations* 23 (Fall 1984):320.

60. R.W. Apple, Jr., "At Strike's End, A Lost Cause Wins Some British Respect," *New York Times,* March 10, 1985, p. 4E. Also see James A. Perry, "British Unions Fret About Their Future," *Wall Street Journal,* March 15, 1985, p. 28.

61. Apple, *op. cit., p.* 4E.

62. Colin Hawksworth, "Industrial Relations in the 80's: Where Do the Unions Fit In?" *Personal Management* (November 1984):29.

63. Lover, *op. cit.*, p. 101; Undy et al., *op. cit.*, p. 219. For some predictions about future merger trends and possible merger partners, see Undy et al., *op. cit.*, pp. 340–44.

64. Canada Department of Labour, *Directory of Labour Organizations in Canada, 1984* (Ottawa: Supply and Services Canada, 1984),. pp. xi, xxvi–xxvii.

65. Ibid., p. xi.

66. Ibid., p. xix.

67. The term *national* is used more to distinguish between Canadian- and U.S.-based unions than to identify the scope of union organization. Many national unions have their members in a single province or region. Gary N. Chaison, "Unions: Growth, Structure and Internal Dynamics" in John Anderson and Morley Gunderson (editors), *Union–Management Relations in Canada* (Don Mills, Ontario: Addison–Wesley, 1982), p. 54; Gary N. Chaison, "Union Mergers, Union Fragmentation and International Unions in Canada" in *Current and Future Perspectives in Canadian Industrial Relations* (Québec, P.Q.: Canadian Industrial Relations Association, 1980), p. 275.

68. Canada Department of Labour, *op. cit.,* p. xi.

69. *Idem.*

70. Mark Thompson and Allen Ponak, "Industrial Relations in Canadian Public Enterprises," *International Labour Review* 12 (September–October 1984):650. For descriptions of the decentralized structure also see Chaison, "Unions: Growth, Structure and Internal Dynamics," p. 162; George Vickers Haythorne, "Canada: Industrial Relations—Internal and External Pressures" in Solomon Barkin, *op. cit.,* p. 332.

71. A discussion of the development of Canadian national unions is found in Gary N. Chaison and Joseph B. Rose, "The Structures and Growth of The Cana-

dian National Unions," *Relations Industrielles—Industrial Relations* 36 (1981):530–50.

72. Chaison, "Unions: Growth, Structure and Internal Dynamics," p. 156; Alton W.J. Craig, *The System of Industrial Relations in Canada* (Scarborough, Ontario: Prentice–Hall Canada, 1983), p. 63; John Crispo, *International Unionism: A Study in Canadian American Relations* (Toronto: McGraw–Hill, 1967), pp. 11–49.

73. The public sector, the most highly organized category of workers in Canada, has been organized almost exclusively by Canadian national unions. Joseph B. Rose, "Some Notes on the Building Trades–Canadian Labour Congress Dispute," *Industrial Relations* 22 (Winter 1983):91.

74. Chaison, "Unions: Growth, Structure and Internal Dynamics," p. 157.

75. Canada Department of Labour, *op. cit.,* p. xi.

76. For example, see Chaison, "Unions: Growth, Structure and Internal Dynamics," p. 157; Roy J. Adams, "Canadian–U.S. Labor Link Under Stress?" *Industrial Relations* 15 (October 1976):299–304; Stuart Jamieson, *Industrial Relations in Canada,* 2d ed. (Toronto: Macmillan, 1973), pp. 46–62.

77. For a discussion of the reasons for mergers in Canada, see Michael A. Coady, "Trade Union Mergers and Their Significance in the Canadian Union Movement" (Toronto: unpublished LL.M. dissertation, Osgood Hall Law School, 1976).

78. M. Bradley Dow, "The Labour Movement and Trade Unionism—Summary Outline" in W.D. Wood and Pradeep Kumar (editors), *The Current Industrial Relations Scene in Canada, 1984* (Kingston, Ontario: Queen's University Industrial Relations Centre, July 1984), pp. 238–39.

79. These mergers are discussed in Chaison, "Unions: Growth, Structure and Internal Dynamics," pp. 160–61; Chaison, "Union Mergers and International Unionism in Canada," *Relations Industrielles–Industrial Relations* 34 (1979):770–72.

80. For example, some Canadian locals of the Mine, Mill and Smelter Workers fought unsuccessfully against their union's absorption into the Steelworkers. Chaison, "Union Mergers and International Unions in Canada," p. 770.

81. Ibid., pp. 770–71.

82. Ibid., pp. 771.

83. *Idem.*

84. For example, see "Five Times Too Many Unions," *Labour Gazette,* April 1970, p. 283; Adams, *op. cit.,* p. 300; Crispo, *op. cit.,* pp. 173–76.

85. Craig, *op. cit.,* p. 102; Daniel Benedict, "The 1984 GM Agreement in Canada: Significance and Consequences," *Relations Industrielles–Industrial Relations* 41 (1985):40–42.

86. Craig, *op. cit.,* p. 102; Crispo, *op. cit.,* p. 323; Adams, *op. cit.,* p. 312; Haythorne, *op. cit.,* p. 327; Arthur M. Kruger, "The Direction of Unionism in Canada" in Richard U. Miller and Fraser Isbester, *Canadian Labour in Transition* (Scarborough, Ontario: Prentice-Hall, 1971), p. 109.

87. Rose, *op. cit.,* p. 87.

88. *Constitution of the Canadian Labour Congress,* April 1978, pp. 48–49.

89. Chaison, "Union Mergers, Fragmentation and Industrial Relations in Canada," p. 286.

90. Craig, *op. cit.,* p. 104.

91. Mark Thompson and Albert A. Blum, "International Unionism in Canada: The Move to Local Control," *Industrial Relations* 22 (Winter 1983):84–85. For a

description of an arrangement which permits a high degree of Canadian section autonomy, including the right to disaffiliate, see "Disaffiliation of UFCW's Canadian Members," *Labour Relations Reporter*, October 11, 1982, pp. 116–17.

92. Dow, *op. cit.*, p. 284.

93. Ibid., p. 239.

94. Benedict. *op. cit.*, p. 39.

95. Details on the severance of the Canadian section from the United Automobile Workers are found in "Developments in Industrial Relations," *Monthly Labor Review* 108 (February 1985):59; John Holusha, "Canadian Auto Workers Seek Greater Autonony," *New York Times*, December 2, 1984, p. 26; John Holusha, "Canadians Breaking From United Auto Workers," *New York Times*, December 12, 1984, p. A17; John Holusha, "For Disunited Auto Workers, Solidarity Stops at the Border," *New York Times*, December 16, 1984 p. E3; "Canada UAW Claims Assets Pact in Split From Union in U.S.," *Wall Street Journal*, April 1, 1985, p. 16; William Serrin, "UAW Rebel: Bob White—A 'Superstar' for Canadian Labor," *New York Times*, April 7, 1985, p. 6F; Lorne Slotnick, "UAW Chose $36 Million Deal Over Uncertain Legal Wrangle," *Toronto Globe and Mail*, April 3, 1985, p. M5. For a review of the automobile negotiations leading to the split, see Benedict, *op. cit.*, pp. 27–28. The case against the split is presented by Douglas Fraser, a past UAW president, in "Fraser's Analysis of UAW–Canada Split," *Labor Relations Reporter*, December 31, 1984, pp. 351–52.

96. Holusha, "For Disunited Auto Workers, Solidarity Stops at the Border," p. E3.

97. "Air Union Votes to Become a UAW Local," *Toronto Globe and Mail*, June 15, 1985, p. M7. Also see Serrin, *op. cit.*, p. 6F; "Canada UAW Claims Assets Pact in Split From Union in U.S.," p. 16; Lorne Slotnick, "UAW Delegates Asked to Approve Union Split," *Toronto Globe and Mail*, March 30, 1985, p. M4.

98. Serrin, *op. cit.*, p. 6F.

99. Roy J. Adams, "Industrial Relations and the Economic Crisis: Canada Moves Toward Europe" (Hamilton, Ontario: McMaster University, Faculty of Business, Working Paper Series no. 233, January 1985), p. 8; Joseph B. Rose and Gary N. Chaison, "The State of the Unions: United States and Canada," *Journal of Labor Research* 6 (Winter 1985):97–111.

100. Harvey Krahn and Graham S. Lowe, "Public Attitude Toward Unions: Some Canadian Evidence," *Journal of Labor Research* 5 (Spring 1984):149–64.

101. Adams, "Industrial Relations and the Economic Crisis: Canada Moves Toward Europe," p. 27.

8
Conclusions

The purpose of this book has been to develop a comprehensive theory of labor union mergers that is capable of explaining the forces acting for and against mergers, as well as the characteristics of, and links between the pre- and postmerger states. The introductory chapter emphasized that mergers are all too often seen as events rather than processes. By taking a broad perspective and concentrating on the process of the merger, I have been able to integrate evidence from both successful and unsuccessful merger attempts. The resulting model can be used to explain why there are mergers in some cases, while in others a merger was not even attempted, and in still others a merger was attempted but negotiations failed. In addition, we now have a way of tracing the connections between the premerger conditions and postmerger integration and outcomes.

There is certainly no need at this point to reiterate all of our earlier findings. However, the model of the merger process can be summarized in a most general sense with the following propositions:

1. Unions face two opposing forces in the premerger stage: the motivation to merge and the barriers to merger.

2. The sources of the motivating factors and barriers may vary for unions considering amalgamating, absorbing, or being absorbed.

3. Two (or more) unions will agree to merge when the strength of each union's motivating forces is sufficient to overcome the barriers that it faces. Consequently, the strengths of the motivating forces and barriers should be measured in relation to each other.

4. Union alliances can serve either as merger substitutes by satisfying the motivation to merge, or as merger preludes by reducing merger barriers.

5. The degree of integration of postmerger governing structures is determined in merger negotiations, and the compromises reached in these negotiations are shaped by the types and relative strengths of the motivating forces and barriers.

6. Some merger outcomes are determined directly and immediately by the act of merger, while others result from the degree of integration specified in the merger agreement.

The Research Approach

Although the basic merger process seems to have a straightforward and attractive logic to it, mergers can be exceptionally complex phenomena. In the development of my model of mergers, I attempted to go beyond the limited viewpoints of earlier empirical analyses and case studies. I demanded a great deal from the model. In order to reflect the reality of union mergers, rather than some abstract, unique, or simplified form of it, the model must deal with the causes of both successful and unsuccessful mergers, the merger antecedents and the merger outcomes, the role of merger alternatives, and the merger negotiation process. It must also be able to isolate fundamental merger elements that are important from both historical and comparative perspectives. My investigation was based on a belief that a meaningful and comprehensive model should do more than just describe contemporary mergers. The final test of a merger model is its ability to explain both past and present American mergers and those in other countries featuring comparable labor movements.

The research approach taken in this study has been eclectic. Short case studies and descriptive evidence from primary and secondary sources have been combined with data from surveys. Rather than selecting one predominant methodological approach and then shaping the study to the confines of that approach, I have used those methods that seem most suitable to the aspect of mergers under consideration. I tried to find a middle ground between sterile empirical analysis and overly detailed case studies. The objective was to devise an explanation that is comprehensive and generalizable, but still fully reflects the rich institutional detail and complex interactions of the union merger process.

While future studies may elaborate on or modify my model, I believe that the general approach taken in developing the model is most amenable to the nature of the union merger process in specific and to unions in general.

Union Mergers and the Problems of Contemporary Unions

Since the beginning of the 1980s, there have been numerous descriptions of the poor health of American labor unions. There seems to be a general consensus that unions are facing problems of a severity and scope seldom encountered in their long history.[1] After we outline the dimensions of these problems, we have to ask how this adversity will affect the form and frequency of mergers in the near future.

American unions are said to be in a position of general decline, and the most obvious symptom is the fall in membership. Unions lost 2.7 million members between 1980 and 1984; during that period membership as a proportion of all employees fell from 23.0 percent to 19.1 percent. Losses were particularly heavy in the goods-producing, transportation, and construction industries, the traditional strongholds of unionism.[2] Nearly every major labor organization lost members.[3] Much of the membership loss has been attributed to the employment growth in nonunion sectors and the shift toward production at facilities in relatively unorganized areas of the country. Other major contributing factors are increased employer resistance to union organizing and the failure of labor legislation to deter widespread and illegal forms of employer opposition.[4]

Faced with increased domestic nonunion competition, foreign competition, and the pressures generated by deregulation (primarily in the transportation and communication industries), many employers appear to be following union avoidance strategies. In some cases, these take the form of plant relocation or militant resistance to union organizing efforts. More often, employers have opted for "union substitution" by developing human resource policies that provide levels of wages, benefits, and working conditions comparable to those that could be achieved through collective bargaining.[5] This can greatly reduce the incentive of unorganized employees to form or join unions.

The overall effectiveness of unions as employee representatives has been challenged on several fronts. During the recent recession, widespread concession bargaining forced many unions into retreat and they are now straining to restore past cuts or freezes in pay or benefits. Concession bargaining also created tensions between union members and local and national union officers. Heated debates over whether or not to grant wage or benefit cuts have gone too far to upset internal union solidarity.[6] Furthermore, multiemployer bargaining structures, built up over the past few decades, have been splintered during the recession, and negotiations have become more closely linked to the conditions of the individual firm.[7] Unions are frequently finding that in negotiations the employer now acts and they react, a reversal of the traditional roles. These fundamental changes in bargaining occur at a time when many employers are also attempting to elicit the involvement and commitment of their workers as individuals. The introduction of employee participation programs such as quality circles, and the increased popularity of profit sharing have called into question the need for adversarial collective bargaining.[8]

Coming out of a severe recession, the American labor movement finds itself greatly weakened. Concession bargaining has continued in many cases, particularly in the form of two-tiered systems in which newly hired workers receive wages or benefits that are lower than those of workers holding jobs when the agreement was negotiated.[9] The frequency of work stoppages has fallen sharply as unions recognize the limitations of strikes against employers who can shift production to alternative nonunion operations or who face strong domestic or foreign nonunion competition. In 1984 and 1985, the number of major work stoppages was at its lowest point in the nearly forty years that such data had been collected.[10]

There have been a number of proposals to resolve the unions' dilemma and these often call for renewed membership participation, the replacement of bureaucratic and tradition-bound union officers, and the allocation of greater resources to organizing.[11] Self-appraisals have been made within the labor movement, with notable efforts by committees in the Communication Workers of America, the United Steelworkers, and the AFL–CIO.[12] It has been concluded that there must be a revitalization of the labor movement, with a greater emphasis on organizing, political action, increased membership participation, and applications of public relations techniques to improve the public image of labor unions. Many unions appear to be showing a new openness to change and a willingness to reconsider their approaches to organizing, bargaining, and administration.[13] There is also a resurgence of interest in mergers as unions search for ways to adapt and survive in a challenging environment.[14] Based on my earlier analysis in this book, predictions can be made about the shape of mergers in the next ten years.

Mergers in the Coming Decade

Increased Merger Activity among Smaller Unions

We can expect to see a flurry of smaller unions seeking absorption, prompted by the need for immediate survival. In a difficult economic environment, a smaller union faced with a declining membership and financial position can become despondent of any reversals in its conditions. Pressures build for merger as the threshold for economies of scale rises. The possibility of new organizing can be limited if jurisdictions have been narrowed by technological change. We can predict that many smaller unions, particularly those with less than twenty or thirty thousand members, will be strongly attracted to absorption as a means for continued survival, even if it entails survival as part of another union.

The general trend will be for absorptions through divisional structures. Most officers and members of smaller unions will understandably strive to retain some degree of their autonomy and identity. There may also be a few unions which find themselves at the brink of financial disaster because of precipitous membership losses. These might be found in industries that have been shaken by technological change and foreign competition, or that have seen the rapid development of nonunion sectors because of intense domestic competition and deregulation. For such unions, the motivation to merge will be so great that the officers and membership will agree to absorptions that call for nearly complete and instantaneous integration.

Mergers as Organizing and Growth Strategies

Many larger unions will be searching for new areas for organizing but may be unable or unwilling to invest the needed financial resources and personnel for large-scale campaigns. They will find it much faster and less expensive to "organize unions," building from the top down through a series of absorptions, rather than organizing individual workers. In a few cases, absorptions will be used mainly to establish footholds in new jurisdictions and obtain the services of skilled and experienced organizers. Many more large unions will come to rely heavily on absorptions to gain members because they will not have to confront employer resistance in organizing campaigns or face the costs and delays of the representation election procedures of the National Labor Relations Board.

Increased absorption activity will tend to make organizing jurisdictions irrelevant. Absorptions will often be opportunistic; who merges with whom will be determined more by whether mutually attractive merger agreements can be proposed than by whether the merger fits into some broad scheme for uniting unions in related trades or industries. Smaller unions will be more interested in the conditions offered by absorbing unions, particularly the creation of divisions, the degrees of bargaining autonomy, and the continued employment of officers and staff, rather than adherence to any plan to rationalize the structure of the labor movement.

Through series of absorptions, we may see the emergence of some new general unions which claim the right to represent all workers in all industries and some conglomerate unions representing workers in related industries. These general and conglomerate unions will probably follow the practice of their British counterparts and create semiautonomous trade and industry groups to attract merger partners. In effect, their merger objectives will become the driving force behind the development of new jurisdictions and internal structures.

The Rise of Predatory Mergers

The difficulty in recruiting new union members, the abandonment of traditional jurisdictions, and the increased reliance on absorptions for union growth may frequently result in mergers that could be considered predatory. Large affiliated unions will raid smaller nonaffiliates and then promise to end these actions if a nonaffiliate is willing to be absorbed. This is basically a carrot and stick approach, with promises of benefits to officers and members if there is a merger, and continued or intensified raiding if there is none. The smaller union may try to protect itself by entering into a merger with another affiliate under more favorable terms and lower degrees of integration than are offered by the predatory union. In other words, some vulnerable unions may have to resort to a "friendly" absorption to protect against an "unfriendly" one—a variation of a strategy used in corporate mergers. This approach may be appealing to small statewide public employee associations and local independent unions that represent workers on a single-employer, single-plant basis. Both union types are unaffiliated and therefore open to raids.

The Merger Policy of the Federation

As I emphasized earlier, mergers will not necessarily follow neat patterns by joining unions within industries or crafts, nor will they be confined entirely to AFL–CIO affiliates. We can expect that the AFL–CIO will retain its historical role of encouraging and assisting affiliate mergers; to go beyond this and force mergers would be inexcusable interference with affiliate autonomy. However, the federation will have to clearly pronounce and enforce a policy of approving mergers of affiliates.[15] The difficult question is how far the federation can or should go in discouraging affiliate mergers because the involved unions are not in the same or closely related jurisdictions. The AFL–CIO could find itself strongly promoting amalgamations that are aimed at rationalizing the structure of the labor movement in general even though these efforts may interfere with absorption plans of affiliates. There will be a need for the clarification of the federation role in mergers and this may revive the contentious issues of affiliate autonomy and jurisdiction which were discussed in the historical overview of chapter 2.

Merger Mediation and Innovation

Merger strategies will become proactive rather than reactive. Both large and small unions will no longer be able to wait for merger oportunities but will have to actively search for potential merger partners. Merger negotiations will also become more competitive and complex. Unions will frequently initiate merger discussions with more than one union at a time and may even simultaneously consider offers to amalgamate and to be absorbed. The increased frequency and complexity of merger negotiations will have two major ramifications. First, it will soon become apparent that there is a need for skilled and experienced neutrals who can mediate when there are impasses in merger negotiations. Academicians, professional mediators and arbitrators, and retired union officers will have to be recruited and then trained in regard to variations in merger proposals and the dynamics of merger negotiations.[16] A training forum and clearinghouse for such neutrals could be provided by the AFL–CIO, the Department of Labor, or a national organization of neutrals such as the American Arbitration Association. Second, we will need innovative approaches to the drafting of merger agreements and the design of post-merger structures. The challenge will be to devise structures that require low degrees of integration and overcome merger barriers, but also address the problems that motivated the parties to merge. This will call for experimentation in devising postmerger transitional arrangements that change what may be an acceptable merger into an effective one. Many of these transitional arrangements may take the form of bargaining and organizing alliances as first steps to eventual mergers, or may use affiliations or federated structures that gradually evolve into greater integration.

In this book I have proposed a model of the union merger process that enables us to examine the reasons why unions do or do not merge, the forms by which these mergers may occur, and the means for evaluating merger outcomes. Renewed interest in union mergers among students of industrial relations as well as labor leaders will be intensified as mergers increase in form and frequency and become a central part of the labor movement's reactions to its present predicament. It is hoped that this book will provide a basis for linking mergers of the past with those of the future and for enabling unions contemplating mergers to more fully appraise the possible merger forms and the potential outcomes.

Notes

1. For overviews of the challenges facing contemporary unions and the union reactions, see *Unions Today: New Tactics to Tackle Tough Times* (Washington, D.C.: Bureau of National Affairs, 1985); "American Unions," *The Economist* (March 2, 1985):31–33, 36; "2001: A Union Odyssey," *Newsweek* (August 5, 1985): 40–42; Steven Greenhouse, "Reshaping Labor to Woo the Young," *New York Times*, September 1, 1985, p. F1, F6.

2. Larry T. Adams, "Changing Employment Patterns of Organized Workers," *Monthly Labor Review* 108 (February 1985):25–31. Also see Charles B. Craver, "The Current and Future Status of Labor Organizations," *Labor Law Journal* 36 (April 1985):211–13.

3. Leo Troy and Neil Sheflin, *U.S. Union Sourcebook* (West Orange, N.J.: Industrial Relations Data Information Services, 1985), pp. 1.1–1.3.

4. For example, see Joseph B. Rose and Gary N. Chaison, "The State of the Unions: United States and Canada," *Journal of Labor Research* 6 (Winter 1985): 97–111; William Serrin, "Organized Labor is Increasingly Less So," *New York Times*, November 18, 1984, p. E3; A.H. Raskin, "Labor's Grand Illusions," *New York Times Magazine*, February 10, 1985, pp. 52–54, 67–68; Jack Barbash, "Trade Unionism from Roosevelt to Reagan," *The Annals of the American Academy of Political and Social Science* 473 (May 1984):11–32; Craver, *op. cit.*, pp. 210–25.

5. Barbash, *op. cit.*, pp. 13–16; Thomas A. Kochan and Michael J. Piore, "Will the New Industrial Relations Last? Implications for the American Labor Movement," *Annals of the American Academy of Political and Social Science* 473 (May 1984):177–89; Thomas A. Kochan, Robert B. McKersie, and Harry C. Katz, "U.S. Industrial Relations in Transition: A Summary Report" in *Proceedings of the Thirty-Seventh Annual Meeting of the Industrial Relations Research Association* (Madison, Wis.: IRRA, 1985), p. 266.

6. James A. Craft, Suhail Abboushi, and Trudy Labovitz, "Concession Bargaining and Unions: Impacts and Implications," *Journal of Labor Research* 6 (Spring 1985):167–80.

7. Kochan and Piore, *op. cit.*, pp. 184–86. For a review of the frequency and forms of concession bargaining, see Peter Capelli and Robert B. McKersie, "Labor and the Crisis in Collective Bargaining" in Thomas A. Kochan (editor), *Challenges and Choices Facing American Labor* (Cambridge, Mass.: MIT Press, 1985), pp. 227–46.

8. For example, see Thomas A. Kochan, Harry C. Katz, and Nancy R. Mower, *Worker Participation and American Unions: Threat or Opportunity?* (Kalamazoo, Mich.: W.E. Upjohn Institute, 1984); Stephen Rubenfeld, "Today's Contract Concession: Tomorrow's Impact" (Working Paper 83–6, Bureau of Business and Economic Research, School of Business and Economics, University of Minnesota at Duluth, March 1983); Kochan, McKersie, and Katz, *op. cit.*, p. 269.

9. Two-tiered wage systems are most common in nonmanufacturing industries, particularly the airline and wholesale/retail industries. "Growth of Two-Tier Wage Systems," *Labor Relations Reporter*, February 25, 1985, pp. 141–42; Agis Salpukas, "The Two–Tier Wage Impact," *New York Times*, October 30, 1985, pp. D1, D6.

10. Kenneth B. Noble, "Why Walkouts Don't Work as They Used To," *New York Times*, March 24, 1985, p. 24E; Kenneth B. Noble, "Big Strikes Found in Decline in the U.S.," *New York Times*, July 12, 1985, p. A13. Major work stoppages are those involving at least one thousand employees and lasting at least one shift.

11. Audrey Freedman, "There is No Recovery in Sight For Unions," *New York Times*, January 20, 1985, p. 2F; Steve Early, "Revival is Possible and Necessary," *New York Times*, January 20, 1985, p. 2F.

12. AFL–CIO Committee on the Evolution of Work, *The Changing Situation of Workers and Their Unions* (Washington, D.C.: AFL–CIO, 1985); United Steelworkers of America, *Forging a Future: Report of the Convention Committee on the Future Directions of the Union* (Pittsburgh: USA, 1984); Bill Keller, "A Union Copes with Deregulation," *New York Times*, November 18, 1984, p. 4F; William Serrin, "The Union Movement Looks in the Mirror," *New York Times*, February 24, 1985, IV, p. 5.

13. For example, see "Labor's Bold Pledge to Come Back Swinging," *Business Week* (March 11, 1985):96, 98.

14. William Serrin, "AFL–CIO Conceding Some of Labor's Problems, Offers Some Solutions," *New York Times*, February 27, 1985, p. A10.

15. Such as policy, including "merger guidelines," is found in AFL–CIO Committee on the Evolution of Work, *op. cit.*, pp. 33–34. Also see "Mergers as Means of Strengthening Unions," *Labor Relations Reporter*, March 4, 1985, pp. 176–77.

16. "AFL–CIO Merger Committee Report," July 13, 1981, p. 1.

Appendix:
Union Mergers in the United States
(Minimum of One-Year Duration)

1. Brotherhood of Railway Conductors (Ind.) into Order of
   Railway Conductors and Brakemen (Ind.).   1891

2. Order of Railway Telegraphers of North American (Ind.)
   merged with Brotherhood of Railway and Commercial
   Telegraphers (Ind.) to form the Order of Railroad
   Telegraphers (Ind.).   1892

3. Sailors Union of the Pacific (Ind.) merged into the National
   Seamans Union (Ind.).   1892

4. Deutsch–Americkanischen–Typographia (Ind.) merged into
   the International Typographical Union (AFL).   1894

5. Lasters Protective Union of America (Ind.) merged into
   Boot and Shoe Workers Union (AFL).   1895

6. New England Lasters Protective Union (Ind.) merged into
   Boot and Shoe Workers Union (AFL).   1895

7. Machine Woodworkers International Union of America (AFL)
   merged with International Furniture Workers Union (AFL) to
   form the Amalgamated Woodworkers International Union
   (AFL).   1896

8. United Brotherhood of Brass and Composition Metal
   Workers, Polishers and Buffers (AFL) merged with the Metal
   Polishers, Buffers, Platers and Helpers International Union

---

Affiliations:

AFL: American Federation of Labor
CIO: Congress of Industrial Organizations
AFL–CIO: American Federation of Labor–Congress of Industrial Organizations
AGE: Assembly of Government Employees
IND: Independent, unaffiliated

the Metal Polishers, Buffers, Platers and Brass Workers International Union of North America (AFL). 1896

9. Glass Workers (AFL) merged into Window Glass Cutters League of America (AFL). 1900

10. National Union of Textile Workers of America (AFL) merged with American Federation of Textile Operatives (AFL) to form the United Textile Workers of America (AFL) 1900

11. United Brotherhood of Paper Makers of America (Ind.) merged into International Brotherhood of Paper Makers (AFL). 1902

12. International Watch Case Makers (AFL) merged into Jewelry Workers International Union (AFL). 1903

13. Coremakers International Union (AFL) merged into International Molders Union (AFL). 1903

14. Amalgamated Sheet Metal Workers International Association (AFL) merged with Sheet Metal Workers National Alliance (Ind.) to form the Amalgamated Sheet Metal Workers International Alliance (AFL). 1903

15. International Union of Commercial Telegraphers (AFL) merged with Order of Commercial Telegraphers (Ind.) to form the Commercial Telegraphers' Union of North America (AFL). 1903

16. International Brotherhood of Blacksmiths (AFL) merged with the Blacksmiths and Helpers (AFL) to form the International Brotherhood of Blacksmiths and Helpers (AFL). 1903

17. Teamsters National Union of America (AFL) merged with the International Team Drivers Union (AFL) to form the International Brotherhood of Teamsters (AFL). 1903

18. United Mineral Mine Workers Progressive Union of North America (Ind.) merged into Western Federation of Miners (Ind.). 1904

19. Potters National Union of America (AFL) merged into International Union of Operative Potters (AFL). 1904

20. International Association of Allied Metal Mechanics (AFL) merged into International Association of Machinists (AFL). 1904

21. Actors International Union (Ind.) merged with the White Rats Actors Union (Ind.) to form the White Rats Actors Union of America (AFL). 1910

22. Amalgamated Woodworkers International Union (AFL) merged into United Brotherhood of Carpenters and Joiners (AFL).   1912

23. International Tin Plate Workers Protective Association (AFL) merged into Amalgamated Association of Steel and Tin Workers (AFL).   1915

24. American Brotherhood of Cement Workers (AFL) merged into International Union of Operative Plasterers (AFL).   1915

25. Lithographers International Protective and Beneficial Association (AFL) merged with International Union of Lithographic Workmen (AFL) to form the Amalgamated Lithographers of America (AFL).   1915

26. Amalgamated Glass Workers' International Association (AFL) merged into Brotherhood of Painters, Decorators and Paperhangers (AFL).   1915

27. Brotherhood of Railway Freight Handlers (AFL) merged into Brotherhood of Railway Clerks (AFL).   1915

28. Brotherhood of Railway Postal Clerks (Ind.) merged into National Federation of Post Office Clerks (AFL) to form the National Federation of Post Office Employees (AFL).   1917

29. United Brotherhood of Leather Workers on Horse Goods (AFL) merged with Travelers' Goods and Leather Novelty Workers International Union (AFL) to form the United Leather Workers International Union (AFL).   1917

30. United Brick and Clay Workers (AFL) merged with International Alliance of Brick, Tile and Terra Cotta Workers (Ind.) to form the United Brick and Clay Workers of America (AFL).   1917

31. Brotherhood of Railway Trackmen of America (Ind.) merged with Brotherhood of Maintenance of Way Employees (AFL) to form the United Brotherhood of Maintenance of Way Employees and Railway Shop Laborers (AFL).   1918

32. International Union of United Brewery and Soft Drink Workers (AFL) merged with International Union of Flour and Cereal Mill Workers (AFL) to form the International Union of United Brewery, Flour, Cereal and Soft Drink Workers (AFL).   1918

33. Shingle Weavers Union (AFL) merged into International Union of Timber Workers (AFL).   1918

34. Compressed Air and Foundation Workers (AFL) merged into Amalgamated Hod Carriers and Common Laborers (AFL).   1918

35. International Brotherhood of Tip Printers (AFL) merged into International Brotherhood of Bookbinders (AFL).   1918

36. Lithographic Press Feeders Apprentices Association (Ind.) merged into the Amalgamated Lithographers of America (AFL).   1918

37. Drop Forgers (Ind.) merged into International Brotherhood of Blacksmiths and Helpers (AFL).   1918

38. International Slate and Tile Roofers Union (AFL) merged with International Brotherhood of Composition Roofers, Damp and Waterproof Workers (AFL) to form the United Slate, Tile and Composition Roofers, Damp and Waterproof Workers Association (AFL).   1919

39. White Rat Actors Union of America (AFL) merged with Actors Equity Association (Ind.) to form the Associated Actors and Artists of America (AFL).   1919

40. Amalgamated Society of Engineers (American Branch) (Ind.) merged into International Association of Machinists (AFL).   1920

41. Hebrew Butcher Workers of America (Ind.) merged into Amalgamated Meat Cutters and Butcher Workmen (AFL).   1921

42. American Federation of Full Fashion Hosiery Workers (Ind.) merged into United Textile Workers (AFL).   1922

43. National Association of Machine Printers and Color Mixers of the United States (AFL) merged with the National Print Cutters Association (AFL) to form the United Wall Paper Craftsmen and Workers (AFL).   1923

44. International Union of Timber Workers (AFL) merged into International Shingle Weavers (AFL).   1923

45. Amalgamated Society of Carpenters and Joiners (Ind.) merged into United Brotherhood of Carpenters and Joiners (AFL).   1924

46. United Shoe Workers (Ind.) merged into Shoe Workers Protective Union (Ind.).   1924

47. International Steel and Copper Plate Engravers League (AFL) merged into International Plate Printers and Die Stampers Union (AFL).   1925

48. International Brotherhood of Steamshovel and Dredgemen (Ind.) merged into International Union of Operating Engineers (AFL).   1927

49. International Pocketbook Workers (Ind.) merged into the United Leather Workers International Union (AFL).   1928

50. International Union of Tunnel and Subway Constructors (AFL) merged into Amalgamated Hod Carriers and Common Laborers (AFL).   1929

51. Window Glass Flatteners Association of North America (AFL) merged into Window Glass Cutters League of Ameria (AFL).   1930

52. American Radio Association (Ind.) merged with Commercial Radiomen Protective Association (Ind.) to form the American Radio Telegraphists Association (Ind.).   1932

53. Associated Silk Workers of America (Ind.) merged into the United Textile Workers (AFL).   1932

54. National Shoe Workers (Ind.) merged with the Salem Shoe Workers (Ind.), the Shoe and Leather Workers Industrial Union (Ind.), and the Shoe Workers Protective Union (Ind.) to form the United Shoe and Leather Workers (Ind.).   1933

55. United Hatters of North America (AFL) merged with Cloth Hat, Cap and Millinery Workers International Union (AFL) to form United Hatters, Cap and Millinery Workers International Union (AFL).   1934

56. Journeymen Tailors Union of America (AFL) merged into Amalgamated Clothing Workers of America (AFL).   1935

57. Transport Workers Union of America (Ind.) merged into International Association of Machinists (AFL).   1936

58. Pavers, Rammermen, Flaggers, Bridge annd Stone Curb Setters (AFL) merged into International Hod Carriers, Building and Common Laborers Union of America (AFL).   1937

59. Southern Tenant Farmers Union (Ind.) merged into United Cannery, Packing and Allied Workers of America (CIO).   1937

60. Sailors Union of the Pacific (Ind.) merged into Seafarers International Union (AFL).   1938

61. Fur Workers Union (CIO) merged with National Association of Leather Workers (CIO) to form the International Fur and Leather Workers Union (CIO).   1939

62. Sheep Shearers Union (AFL) merged into Amalgamated Meat Cutters and Butcher Workmen of North America (AFL).   1942

63. Sleeping Car Conductors (Ind.) merged into Order of Railway Conductors and Brakemen (Ind.). 1942

64. National Die Casting Workers (CIO) merged into the International Union of Mine, Mill, and Smelter Workers (CIO). 1942

65. Aluminum Workers Union (CIO) merged into United Steelworkers of America (CIO). 1944

66. Air Line Communication Employees Association (Ind.) merged into American Communication Association (Ind.). 1945

67. United Financial Employees (Ind.) merged into Office Employees' International Union (AFL). 1945

68. Utility Workers Organizing Committee (CIO) merged with Brotherhood of Consolidated Edison Employees (Ind.) to form the Utility Workers Union of America (CIO). 1946

69. United Federal Workers of America (CIO) merged with State, County and Municipal Employees (CIO) to form United Public Workers of America (CIO). 1946

70. International Federation of Architects, Engineers, Chemists and Technicians (CIO) merged into United Office and Professional Workers of America (CIO). 1946

71. United Licensed Officers of U.S.A. (Ind.) merged into United Mine Workers District 50 (AFL). 1946

72. National Federation of Rural Letter Carriers (AFL) merged into National Association of Letter Carriers (AFL). 1947

73. Post Office Mechanics and Maintenance Employees (Ind.) merged with the Post Office Custodial Employees (Ind.) to form the National Association of Post Office Mechanics and Custodial Employees (Ind.). 1947

74. Telephone Workers Organizing Committee (CIO) merged into Communication Workers Organizing Committee (CIO). 1948

75. Inland Boatmen's Union (Ind.) merged into Seafarers International Union (AFL). 1948

76. Railroad Workers of America (CIO) merged into Industrial Union of Marine and Shipbuilding Workers of America (CIO). 1948

77. United Farm Equipment and Metal Workers of America (Ind.) merged into United Electrical, Radio and Machine Workers (Ind.). 1949

78. Fishermen and Allied Workers Union (Ind.) merged into International Longshoremen's and Warehousemen's Union (Ind.).   1950

79. Office and Professional Workers Union (Ind.) merged into Distributive, Processing and Office Workers of America (Ind.).   1950

80. Distributive Workers of America merged with Food, Tobacco, Agricultural and Allied Workers (Ind.) and the United Office and Professional Workers (Ind.) to form the Distributive, Processing and Office Workers Union (CIO).   1950

81. Leather Workers Union (AFL) merged into Amalgamated Meat Cutters and Butcher Workmen (AFL).   1950

82. Pacific Coast Marine Firemen, Oilers, Watertenders and Wipers Association (Ind.) merged into Seafarers International Union (AFL).   1953

83. Blacksmiths, Drop Forgers and Helpers (AFL) merged with Boilermakers, Iron Shipbuilders and Helpers (AFL) to form the International Brotherhood of Boilermakers, Iron Shipbuilders, Blacksmiths, Forgers and Helpers (AFL).   1954

84. United Railroad Workers of America (CIO) merged into Transport Workers Union of America (CIO).   1954

85. Playthings, Jewelry and Novelty International Union (CIO) merged into Retail, Wholesale, Department Store Union (CIO).   1954

86. Distributive, Processing and Office Workers Union (Ind.) merged into Retail, Wholesale, Department Store Union (CIO).   1954

87. Diamond Workers Union (AFL) merged into International Jewelry Workers Union (AFL).   1955

88. Gas, Coke and Chemical Workers Union (CIO) merged with Oil Workers International Union (CIO) to form the Oil, Chemical and Atomic Workers Union (CIO).   1955

89. The Television Authority—American Guild of Variety Artists, American Guild of Musical Artists, Actors Equity Association, and Chorus Equity (Ind.) merged with American Federation of Radio Artists (Ind.) to form American Federation of Television and Radio Artists (Ind.).   1955

90. Fur and Leather Workers Union (Ind.) merged into the Amalgamated Meat Cutters and Butcher Workmen (AFL).   1955

91. United Department Store Workers of America (CIO) merged into the Retail, Wholesale, Department Store Union (CIO).   1955

92. Government and Civic Workers Union (AFL–CIO) merged into American Federation of State, County and Municipal Employees (AFL–CIO). 1956

93. International Association of Cleaning and Dye House Workers (AFL–CIO) merged with Laundry Workers' International Union (AFL–CIO) to form Laundry, Cleaning, and Dye House Workers International Union (AFL–CIO). 1956

94. Barbers and Beauty Culturists Union of America (AFL–CIO) merged into Journeymen Barbers, Hairdressers, Cosmetologists and Proprietors International Union of America (AFL–CIO). 1956

95. International Metal Engravers and Marking Device Workers Union (AFL–CIO) merged into International Association of Machinists and Aerospace Workers (AFL–CIO). 1956

96. United Paperworkers of America (AFL–CIO) merged with International Brotherhood of Paper Makers (AFL–CIO) to form the United Papermakers and Paperworkers (AFL–CIO). 1957

97. Allied Independent Unions (Ind.) merged into International Brotherhood of Teamsters, Chauffeurs, Warehousemen and Helpers of America (Ind.). 1957

98. United Wallpaper Craftsmen and Workers of North America (AFL–CIO) merged into International Brotherhood of Pulp, Sulphite and Paper Mill Workers (AFL–CIO). 1958

99. Insurance Agents International Union (AFL–CIO) merged with Insurance Workers of America (AFL–CIO) to form Insurance Workers International Union (AFL–CIO). 1959

100. American Wire Weavers Protective Association (AFL–CIO) merged into United Papermakers and Paperworkers (AFL–CIO). 1959

101. International Brotherhood of Longshoremen (AFL–CIO) merged into International Longshoremen's Association (Ind.). 1959

102. Screen Directors Guild of America, Ind. (Ind.) merged into Radio and TV Directors Guild (AFL–CIO). 1960

103. Airline Communication Employees Association (Ind.) merged into Communications Workers of America (AFL–CIO). 1960

104. Friendly Society of Engravers and Sketchmakers (Ind.) merged into Machine Printers Beneficial Association of the United States (Ind.). 1960

105. National Agricultural Workers Union (AFL–CIO) merged into Amalgamated Meat Cutters and Butcher Workmen of North America (AFL–CIO). 1961

106. United Telephone Organizations (Ind.) merged into Communications Workers of America (AFL–CIO). 1961

107. United National Association of Post Office Craftsmen (Ind.) merged with National Federation of Post Office Clerks (AFL–CIO to form United Federation of Post Office Clerks (AFL–CIO). 1961

108. National Postal Transport Association (AFL–CIO) merged with United Federation of Post Office Clerks (AFL–CIO) to form the United Federation of Postal Clerks (AFL–CIO). 1961

109. International Glove Workers Union of America (AFL–CIO) merged into Amalgamated Clothing Workers of America (AFL–CIO). 1961

110. Laundry, Cleaning and Dye House Workers International Union (Ind.) merged into International Brotherhood of Teamsters, Chauffeurs, Warehousemen and Helpers of America (Ind.). 1962

111. International Union of Petroleum Workers (Ind.) merged into Seafarers International Union of North America (AFL–CIO). 1962

112. Association of Railway Trainmen and Locomotive Firemen (Ind.) merged with International Association of Railway Employees (Ind.) to form the Federated Council of the International Association of Railway Employees and Association of Railway Trainmen and Locomotive Firemen (Ind.). 1962

113. International Photo-Engravers Union of North America (AFL–CIO) merged with Amalgamated Lithographers of America (AFL–CIO) to form the Lithographers and Photo-Engravers International Union (AFL–CIO). 1965

114. American Federation of Hosiery Workers (AFL–CIO) merged into the Textile Workers Union of America (AFL–CIO). 1965

115. American Communications Association (Ind.) merged into the International Brotherhood of Teamsters, Chauffeurs, Warehousemen and Helpers of America (Ind.). 1966

116. International Union of Mine, Mill and Smelter Workers (Ind.) merged into United Steelworkers of America (AFL–CIO). 1967

117. Journeymen Stone Cutters Association of North America (AFL–CIO) merged into the Laborers International Union of North America (AFL–CIO). 1968

118. National Association of Post Office Mail Handlers, Watchmen, Messengers and Group Leaders (AFL–CIO) merged into the Laborers International Union of North America (AFL–CIO). 1968

119. United Packinghouse Food and Allied Workers (AFL–CIO) merged into Amalgamated Meat Cutters and Butcher Workmen of North America (AFL–CIO). 1968

120. Federal Tobacco Inspectors Mutual Association (Ind.) merged into National Federation of Federal Employees (Ind.). 1968

121. Bakery and Confectionery Workers International Union of America (Ind.) merged into International Brotherhood of Teamsters, Chauffeurs, Warehousemen and Helpers of America (Ind.). 1968

122. Switchmen's Union of North America (AFL–CIO) merged with Order of Railway Conductors and Brakemen (Ind.), Brotherhood of Locomotive Firemen and Enginemen (AFL–CIO), and Brotherhood of Railway Trainmen (AFL–CIO) to form the United Transportation Union (AFL–CIO). 1969

123. Railway Patrolmen's International Union (AFL–CIO) merged into the Brotherhood of Railway, Airline and Steamship Clerks, Freight Handlers, Express and Station Employees (AFL–CIO). 1969

124. Transportation-Communication Employees Union (AFL-CIO) merged into the Brotherhood of Railway, Airline and Steamship Clerks, Freight Handlers, Express and Station Employees (AFL–CIO). 1969

125. United Weldors International Union (Ind.) merged into the International Union of Operating Engineers (AFL–CIO). 1969

126. Railroad Yardmasters of North America (Ind.) merged into the Railroad Yardmasters of America (AFL–CIO). 1969

127. Bakery and Confectionery Workers International Union of America (Ind.) merged into the American Bakery and Confectionery Workers International Union (AFL–CIO). 1969

128. AFL Players Association (Ind.) merged with NFL Players Association (Ind.) to form the National Football League Players Association (Ind.) 1970

129. Federated Council of the International Association of Railway Employees and Association of Railway Trainmen and Locomotive Firemen (Ind.) merged into the United Transportation Union (AFL–CIO).   1970

130. Overseas Education Association (Ind.) merged into the National Education Association (Ind.).   1970

131. United Stone and Allied Product Workers of America (AFL–CIO) merged into the United Steelworkers of America (AFL–CIO).   1971

132. United Federation of Postal Clerks (AFL–CIO) merged with the National Postal Union (Ind.), National Association of Post Office and General Services Maintenance Workers (AFL–CIO), National Federation of Post Office Motor Vehicle Employees (AFL–CIO), and National Association of Special Delivery Messengers (AFL–CIO) to form the American Postal Workers Union (AFL–CIO).   1971

133. Association of Engineers and Scientists (Ind.) merged into American Federation of Government Employees (AFL–CIO).   1971

134. International Association of Masters, Mates and Pilots (AFL–CIO) merged into the International Longshoremen's Association (AFL–CIO).   1971

135. Associated Unions of America (Ind.) merged into the Office and Professional Employees International Union (AFL–CIO).   1972

136. International Brotherhood of Pulp, Sulphite and Paper Mill Workers (AFL–CIO) merged with the United Papermakers and Paperworkers (AFL–CIO) to form the United Paperworkers International Union (AFL–CIO).   1972

137. International Union of District 50, Allied and Technical Workers (Ind.) merged into the United Steelworkers of America (AFL–CIO).   1972

138. International Brotherhood of Bookbinders (AFL–CIO) merged with the Lithographers and Photoengravers International Union (AFL–CIO) to form the Graphic Arts International Union (AFL–CIO).   1972

139. United Transport Service Employees (AFL–CIO) merged into the Brotherhood of Railway, Airline and Steamship Clerks, Freight Handlers, Express and Station Employees (AFL–CIO).   1972

140. International Printing Pressmen and Assistants Union of North America (AFL–CIO) merged with the International Stereotypers', Electrotypers' and Platemakers' Union of North America (AFL–CIO) to form the International Printing and Graphic Communications Union (AFL–CIO).   1973

141. International Union of United Brewery, Flour, Cereal, Soft Drink and Distillery Workers of America (Ind.) merged into International Brotherhood of Teamsters, Chauffeurs, Warehousemen and Helpers of America (Ind.).   1973

142. Cigar Makers International Union (AFL–CIO) merged into the Retail, Wholesale, Department Store Union (AFL–CIO).   1974

143. State of Iowa Employees Association (Ind.) merged into the American Federation of State, County and Municipal Employees (AFL–CIO).   1975

144. National Customs Service Association (Ind.) merged into the National Treasury Employees Union (Ind.).   1975

145. Window Glass Cutters League of America (AFL–CIO) merged into the Glass Bottle Blowers of the United States and Canada (AFL–CIO).   1975

146. Textile Workers Union of America (AFL–CIO) merged with Amalgamated Clothing Workers of America (AFL–CIO) to form Amalgamated Clothing and Textile Workers Union (AFL–CIO).   1976

147. National Association of Air Traffic Specialists (Ind.) merged into Professional Air Traffic Controllers Association (AFL–CIO).   1976

148. International Brotherhood of Pottery and Allied Workers (AFL–CIO) merged into Seafarers International Union (AFL–CIO).   1976

149. Massachusetts State Employees Association (Ind.) merged into National Association of Government Employees (Ind.).   1977

150. Air Line Dispatchers Association (AFL–CIO) merged into Transport Workers Union of America (AFL–CIO).   1977

151. Boot and Shoe Workers' Union (AFL–CIO) merged into Retail Clerks International Union (AFL–CIO).   1977

152. Brotherhood of Sleeping Car Porters (AFL–CIO) merged into Brotherhood of Railway, Airline and Steamship Clerks, Freight Handlers, Express and Station Employees (AFL–CIO).   1977

153. Civil Service Employees Association of New York State (Ind.) merged into American Federation of State, County Municipal Employees (AFL–CIO). 1978

154. Tobacco Workers International Union (AFL–CIO) merged with Bakery and Confectionery Workers International Union of America (AFL–CIO) to form the Bakery, Confectionery and Tobacco Workers International Union (AFL–CIO). 1978

155. International Mailers Union (Ind.) merged into the International Typographical Union (AFL–CIO). 1978

156. Retail Clerks International Union (Ind.) merged with the Amalgamated Meat Cutters and Butcher Workmen of North America (AFL–CIO) to form the United Food and Commercial Workers (AFL–CIO). 1979

157. Wood, Wire and Metal Lathers International Union (AFL–CIO) merged into the United Brotherhood of Carpenters and Joiners of America (AFL–CIO). 1979

158. United Shoe Workers of America (AFL–CIO) merged into the Amalgamated Clothing and Textile Workers Union (AFL–CIO). 1979

159. Distributive Workers of America (Ind.) merged into International Union, United Automobile, Aerospace and Agricultural Implement Workers of America (AFL–CIO). 1979

160. International Jewelry Workers Union (AFL–CIO) merged into Service Employees International Union (AFL–CIO). 1980

161. Barbers and Beauticians and Allied Industries International Association (AFL–CIO) merged into United Food and Commercial Workers (AFL–CIO). 1980

162. The American Railway and Airway Supervisors Association merged into the Brotherhood of Railway, Airline and Steamship Clerks, Freight Handlers, Express and Station Employees (AFL–CIO). 1980

163. Granite Cutters International Association (AFL–CIO) merged into the Tile, Marble and Terrazo Finishers and Shopmen International Union (AFL–CIO). 1980

164. Inland Boatmen's Union of the Pacific (Ind.) merged into the International Longshoremen's and Warehousemen's Union (Ind.). 1980

165. Oregon State Employees Association (AGE) merged into the Service Employees International Union (AFL–CIO). 1980

166. American Radio Association (AFL–CIO) merged into the International Organization of Masters, Mates and Pilots (AFL–CIO).   1981

167. Aluminum Workers International Union (AFL–CIO) merged with the United Brick and Clay Workers of America (AFL–CIO) to form the Aluminum, Brick and Clay Workers International Union.   1981

168. United Retail Workers Union (Ind.) merged into the United Food and Commercial Workers (AFL–CIO).   1981

169. United Hatters, Cap and Millinery Workers International Union (AFL–CIO) merged into Amalgamated Clothing and Textile Workers Union (AFL–CIO).   1982

170. International Brotherhood of Pottery and Allied Workers (AFL–CIO) merged into the Glass Bottle Blowers of the United States and Canada (AFL–CIO).   1982

171. Aluminum, Brick and Clay Workers International Union (AFL–CIO) merged with the United Glass and Ceramic Workers (AFL–CIO) to form the Aluminum, Brick and Glass Workers International Union.   1982

172. Arizona Public Employees (AGE) merged into the American Federation of State, County and Municipal Employees (AFL–CIO).   1982

173. International Production, Service and Sales Union (Ind.) merged into the Hotel and Restaurant Employees International Union (AFL–CIO).   1982

174. National Association of Government Employees (Ind.) merged into the Service Employees International Union (AFL–CIO).   1982

175. Insurance Workers International Union (AFL–CIO) merged into the United Food and Commercial Workers (AFL–CIO).   1983

176. Graphic Arts International Union (AFL–CIO) merged with International Printing and Graphic Communications Union (AFL–CIO) to form Graphic Communications International Union (AFL–CIO).   1983

177. Ohio Civil Service Employees (AGE) merged into the American Federation of State, County and Municipal Employees (AFL–CIO).   1983

178. Western Railway Supervisors Association (Ind.) merged into the Brotherhood of Railway, Airline and Steamship Clerks, Freight Handlers, Express and Station Employees (AFL–CIO).   1983

179. National Association of Government Inspectors and Quality Assurance Personnel (Ind.) merged into the American Federation of Government Employees (AFL–CIO). 1983

180. California State Employees Association (AGE) merged into the Service Employees International Union (AFL–CIO). 1984

181. Ohio Association of Public School Employees (Ind.) merged into American Federation of State, County and Municipal Employees (AFL–CIO). 1984

182. United Cement, Lime and Gypsum Workers (AFL–CIO) merged into International Brotherhood of Boiler Makers (AFL–CIO). 1984

183. West Virginia Public Employees Association (Ind.) merged into the Communications Workers of America (AFL–CIO). 1984

Sources of Information

1890–1976: Gary M. Fink (ed.), *Labor Unions* (Westport, Conn.: Greenwood Press, 1977), pp. 457–73.

1890–1972: Microfilming Corporation of America, *American Labor Unions' Constitutions and Proceedings: A Guide to the Microform Edition, Part I, 1836–1974* (Glen Rock, N.J.: MCA, 1975), pp. 1–41.

1900–1930: American Federation of Labor, *Proceedings of the Fifty-First Annual Convention, 1931* (Washington, D.C.: AFL, 1931), pp. 36–37.

1900–1935: Leo Wolman, *Ebb and Flow in Trade Unionism* (New York: National Bureau of Economic Research, 1936), pp. 173–97.

1900–1932: Lewis L. Lorwin, *The American Federation of Labor: History, Policies, Prospects* (Washington, D.C.: The Brookings Institution, 1933), pp. 489–91.

1935–1960: Leo Troy, *Trade Union Membership, 1897–1962* (New York: National Bureau of Economic Research, 1965), pp. A1–A51.

1956–1971: Lucretia M. Dewey, "Union Merger Pace Quickens," *Monthly Labor Review* 94 (June 1971):63–70.

1971–1978: Charles J. Janus, "Union Mergers in the 1970's," *Monthly Labor Review* 101 (October 1978):13–23.

1979–June 30, 1984: Larry T. Adams, "Labor Organization Mergers, 1979–1984: Adapting to Change," *Monthly Labor Review* 107 (September 1984):21–27.

Index

About the Author

Gary N. Chaison is an associate professor of industrial relations at the Graduate School of Management, Clark University, Worcester, Massachusetts. He has also taught at the University of New Brunswick in Fredericton, New Brunswick, Canada, and the State University of New York at Buffalo. He received the BBA and MBA degrees from the Baruch College of the City University of New York and a Ph.D. in industrial relations from the State University of New York at Buffalo. His research is primarily in the areas of collective bargaining and union structure, government, and growth. His articles on union mergers have appeared in *Industrial Relations, Industrial and Labor Relations Review, the Journal of Labor Research,* and *Relations Industrielles–Industrial Relations.*